Contents

Understanding Classroom Behaviour

THIRD EDITION

Maurice Balson

arena

First published 1982 by The Australian Council for Educational Research Ltd, 19 Prospect Hill Road, Camberwell, Melbourne, Victoria 3124, Australia. Reprinted 1984, 1987, 1988. Second edition 1988. Reprinted 1991. Third edition 1992. Reprinted 1993, 1995.

This edition published by Arena
Ashgate Publishing Limited
Gower House
Croft Road
Aldershot
Hants GU11 3HR
England

Ashgate Publishing Company
Old Post Road
Brookfield
Vermont 05036
USA

British Library Cataloguing in Publication Data

Balson, Maurice
   Understanding classroom behaviour – 3rd edn
   1. Classroom management 2. Child psychology
   I.Title
   371.1'024

Library of Congress Catalog Card Number: 96-85966

ISBN 1 85742 386 0

'Bo, the Ball Player' (from *The Use of Stories for Self Understanding*) reprinted by arrangement with author M.L. Bullard and publisher Oregon Society of Individual Psychology.

Cover by Tom Kurema
Illustrations by David Pearson
Typeset by Bookset Pty Ltd
Printed by Biddles Ltd, Guildford

Preface to third edition

Since the release of the second edition of *Understanding Classroom Behaviour*, the topic of discipline has emerged as the major problem facing teachers in their classrooms. Associated with the problem of discipline, there has been the alarming increase in the incidence of teacher stress and its serious effect on withdrawals from the teaching profession due to transfer, illness, and resignation from the service.

The relationship between teacher stress and disciplinary problems has been clearly established in a survey conducted by the Applied Psychology Research Group (1989). The survey highlighted a number of factors contributing to teacher stress and concluded that the most frequently identified problem was the effect of student misbehaviour upon teachers.

At national, state, and local levels, classroom discipline has never attracted so much attention. Most Australian states have produced comprehensive reports dealing with the problem of student management while the media has had a field day reporting on the variety of problems being encountered by teachers.

The Melbourne *Age* heading (30 June, 1991), 'At last discipline gets to the top of the class' indicates the importance which teachers attach to the problem. And rightly so. The article went on to indicate that in Victorian government schools alone, 11,240 students were suspended in 1990, a doubling of the number suspended only six years ago. It is now generally accepted that, throughout Australian schools, more and more students are challenging teachers and disrupting classes.

The almost unanimous call for stricter discipline in Government schools, first documented in the 1985 Gallup Poll, remains unabated. This is not surprising given the enormous amount of negative media reporting including: 'Pupil assaults on teachers increased since the strap banned', 'Student goes berserk with hatchet after drunken binge at recess', 'Student shot in classroom' and recently 'Secondary student in NSW shoots two teachers and another student on a shooting spree on sports day'.

Calls from the lay population for a return to 'the good old days' have been supported by some teachers and theorists, the latter developing many programs which are designed to demand obedience and conformity from students. Books which have in their title, the terms 'Control' or 'Assertive' or 'Compliance' have begun to appear in response to the vacuum created by the abolition of corporal punishment and the permissiveness of the 1970s and 1980s. A never-ending series of publications on discipline has appeared, some without any theoretical orientation and presenting simply a smorgasbord of techniques, some of which, such as the use of praise and rewards as a means of promoting self-discipline, are totally contradictory.

The problems of student behaviour will continue until the basic predicament which teachers face has been recognised and addressed. Teachers share the same problem which is being experienced by parents in the raising of their children. They have been deskilled by the vast social changes which profoundly affected the traditional relationship between teachers and students and between parents and children.

The predicament has been recognised by Dreikurs (1955:1):

> Changes, so profound, so rapid, and so extensive have taken place in education that we have a veritable education revolution in these times. Few people realise as well as our teachers the reasons for the changes which all of us are experiencing in all phases of life. The teachers recognise they are due primarily to the transition from an autocratic to a democratic society.

This is the first generation of teachers with no tradition to teach children. Parents face a similar problem. Both groups find themselves with strategies of influencing children which are no longer effective. Their management techniques have been rendered invalid as society has rejected autocratic patterns of relationships and endorsed a democratic model based upon respect and equality. As Dreikurs (1955:9) observed:

> The traditional autocratic methods of raising children are no longer effective, which places the teachers of today in a dire predicament because the traditional methods, the only ones they know, no longer work and new ones are not known. This creates confusion in both children and adults.

The consequences have been devastating as evidenced by the extent to which the problem of discipline dominates schools and homes and by the tragic increase in the problem of teacher stress and burnout.

The problem has been recognised by all State Departments of Education in Australia who have commissioned major reports on student management and have implemented a wide variety of recommendations to deal with the problem of discipline. Many have been ineffective. Why? Because they failed to provide teachers with an appropriate framework to understand the nature of students and their behaviour. Further, they failed to indicate the theory upon which the recommendations were made, presenting rather, a set of procedures. Finally, their recommended strategies for influencing students were often inconsistent with the values of the school community.

The third edition of *Understanding Classroom Behaviour* remains focused on Individual Psychology, on Adlerian psychology, a framework which underpins most student management policies endorsed by the various state governments. It is also the dominant theory which supports the majority of parent education programs in Australia and is being increasingly applied in industry, business, and health organisations, and in government.

All chapters have been revised in light of policy changes in State Departments of Education, from new knowledge which has become available, from students, and from the specific comments and feedback received by the author from teachers during professional development days in schools.

A new chapter has been written which deals with the increasing problem of teacher stress. In an article published in the Melbourne *Age*, 'Teacher Stress Tops Bill for $100 million Claim', Slattery highlighted the growing problem facing teachers in Victorian government schools. The concern by government with the problem of stress, initiated a major survey in Victoria which reported:

> Between a quarter and a third of the sample were less than satisfied with their lives, and between two out of twelve and three out of twelve teachers (one fifth) felt themselves to be under some degree of strain. (Applied Psychology Research Group, 1989:18).

Another new chapter in the third edition is one on conflict resolution. There is no question that teachers frequently encounter conflict in their dealings with students, parents, colleagues, administrators, and the public. Conflict is inevitable but the way conflict is resolved today requires a totally different approach. In the past, conflicts were resolved in a simple way, a power contest which was soon won by the party with the most power. In a democratic society, victory has no duration and the defeated party seeks to retaliate. Many argue for more effective communication, more co-operation and greater levels of agreement. These have nothing to do with conflict resolution. Teachers cannot have a full-blown conflict with a principal for instance, unless both parties agree to the conflict, communicate their intention to fight, and co-operate to keep the conflict going.

It is the author's belief that all problems are social problems, that they reflect faulty relationships and that they must be resolved in the social context. For these reasons, this book aims at providing teachers with a framework which will enable them to relate more effectively with others — students, colleagues, parents, and administrators. As the improvement of the student is in direct correlation with the improvement of the teacher, the author believes that there can be no better solution to the problem of student behaviour than to improve the knowledge base and skill level of teachers. The theme of the book is expressed by Alfred Adler: 'The hope of preparing the children of tomorrow rests primarily on converting the schools and teachers of today'.

1
A New Tradition in Classroom Management

INTRODUCTION

In a major study of teacher stress (Applied Psychology Research Group, 1989) the authors indicated that 'between a quarter and a third of the teachers were less than satisfied with their lives' (p.18). In their search for the factors contributing to occupational dissatisfaction, the researchers concluded that the most frequently identified problem was the effect of student misbehaviour upon the teachers.

There is a growing perception that teachers are not adequately equipped to handle the growing incidence of disruptive student behaviour. The sheer quantitative demands made on teachers in terms of work volume have increased the pressure on teachers while qualitative demands to adapt to the increasing complexity of school requirements have seriously challenged the skills of teachers, particularly in the area of classroom management.

Concerned with the successful management of students, particularly disruptive pupils, most State educational authorities have undertaken an examination of their disciplinary procedures and have implemented a variety of management strategies. One of the clearest statements on the importance of the school discipline is that contained within the Western Australian report *Disruptive Behaviour in Schools* (Louden, 1985):

> An important priority for an educational system in the 1980s is to ensure that schools are orderly places where self-discipline and respect for others are instilled in students. It is an expectation that society has of education. The challenge facing educators in the modern age is to try to meet this expectation but also to nurture in our youngsters feelings of self-worth. This will not always be an easy task.

The South Australian *Student Behaviour Management Policy* (Education Department of South Australia, 1989) also reflects the concern with school discipline and the need for concerted action:

> The Education Department in South Australia is accountable to the community for providing a clear statement of how student behaviour is being managed effectively in government schools. Teachers and administrators need detailed guidelines to affirm their successful practices; to highlight areas that need development and the issues that need further consideration; and to provide practical and consistent direction.

The Ministry of Education in Victoria has issued a number of reports which have focused on discipline and the changing patterns of teacher–student relationships. Following a review of existing student measures, the Report of the Ministerial Review of School Discipline Procedures (1985) recommended a set of procedures designed to:

> encourage school communities — to develop discipline policies, to anticipate difficulties before they become acute, and to deal with behaviour difficulties at the school level with a minimum of formality and a maximum of co-operation and consultation between all members of the school community (p.8).

It is significant that all reports dealing with student management issued by the various State departments have recognised the major changes which have occurred in the Australian society and have recommended that similar changes be reflected in the school. It is clear that government policy guidelines are advocating, and taking firm steps in implementing, a democratic style of leadership in schools. The increase in disruptive student behaviour is a very real and serious problem whose solution is vital to the renewal of Australian education. In the United States, such behaviour has been regarded for many years by teachers, principals, parents, and students alike as the major problem in education. Noting the problem in the United States, the Phi Delta Kappa Commission on Discipline (1982:1) commented:

> In too many schools, children do not exhibit self-discipline. They violate rules and display behaviour that is not conducive to learning. Small but alarming numbers of children exhibit violent or self-destructive behaviour and vandalise school property. Such negative behaviour has generated great public concern about the school discipline problem.

There is a general agreement that classroom teachers of today face a more difficult task than did their counterparts of previous generations. The extent of their difficulty is only slowly being realised by those who have been quick to use the educational system as a scapegoat for many of the social, economic, and industrial ills of our society. It is encouraging to note in the Western Australian report the confidence expressed in the capacity of teachers to overcome difficulties associated with disruptive students. To justify this confidence, teachers will have to adopt a completely different approach in their relationships with students. It will not be sufficient to modify existing strategies. As indicated in an earlier opinion of Adler, a 'conversion' of schools and teachers is necessary, a conversion from autocratic schools to democratic schools: 'As institutions are within a democratic society, schools should ensure that their own processes are democratic' (Victorian Ministry of Education, 1985, p.12).

The problems of school discipline are related to wider societal issues and cannot be considered apart from them. Writing of the social changes, Dreikurs (1971) states:

> While the turmoil within our present society is obvious, few realise the nature of the conflict. Negroes fight for civil rights, labor and women rebel, and children and youth are involved in the warfare of generations. Each group considers its cause to be special.

Historically, teaching has been based on a tradition which emerged from an authoritarian society. In such a society, one group of individuals was regarded as being superior to another. This superior–inferior continuum applied to male–female, white–coloured, management–labour, parent–child and teacher–student relationships. Those seen to be in the superior position made all decisions on how the inferiors would behave. Teachers have traditionally made all decisions concerning student behaviour. All behavioural standards relating to students such as dress, deportment, language, manners, instructional decisions, social conduct, and interpersonal relationships were decided by teachers. A teacher's right to decide the behaviour of others was shared by parents, males, whites, and management.

The traditional control techniques used to force students to accept a teacher's decision were rewards and punishments. The use of reward carries a clear message: 'Because you have done what I wanted you to do, I will reward you'. Punishment was equally disrespectful: 'Because you have not done what I wanted you to, I will punish you'. In a society which aims to promote self-discipline, respect, and social equality, the use of rewards and punishments has no place.

In an authoritarian system, co-operation had a very specific meaning. When a fourth-grade teacher announced that she had a very co-operative class, it indicated that she had a class which did exactly as she wished. Co-operation meant simply doing what you were told. Students were co-operative largely because teachers had considerable power to enforce conformity and obedience. Student resistance found only indirect and subtle expression and failed to attract peer support. As a result, teachers were not greatly concerned with the problem of classroom management and the control techniques which had proven effective in the past were simply passed on in teacher-education courses.

In recent years, the traditional relationship between teacher and student has deteriorated and many difficult classroom situations have begun to constitute the major problem facing teachers.

The development of democratic patterns of relationships began to emerge in the 1960s. Beginning with the Black

Power movement, there was a series of similar social revolts including women's liberation, the student power movement, and the industrial power movement. All had in common a refusal by the traditionally inferior group to accept a position of inferiority. Teachers found that they could no longer dominate students while parents, males, whites, and management found a similar resistance whenever they attempted to impose their values on children, females, coloureds and labour respectively.

The democratic social system which replaced the authoritarian system is characterised by quite different values. In contrast to the traditional values and practices such as domination, competition, rewards and punishments, social inequality, pressure from above, sole responsibility, and lack of respect, the values which are acceptable in a democratic society include social equality, mutual respect, shared responsibility, co-operation, and self-discipline. The short-term consequences of these newly acquired values have been devastating for teachers who were caught between the two social systems.

The effect of the changed values was to change the pattern of teacher–student relationships. This has been the most profound change in education for generations. It is appropriate to relate problems of student behaviour to problems of teacher-student relationships. When teachers move to improve their relationships with their students, they move to reduce the incidence of problem behaviour. Rather than focus on the consequences of faulty interpersonal relationships such as aggression, rudeness, theft, truancy, lack of motivation or disobedience, teachers need to work to remedy the basic problem, the relationship between themselves and their students.

Values underlie all relationships. How a teacher treats a disruptive student will go back to a set of values. How a principal handles an angry parent, how a colleague reacts to criticism from a peer, how students treat a newly arrived ethnic student will reflect values. It is essential that teachers clarify the values of today's society and consider their relevance for schools and classrooms.

From a study of a variety of Ministerial papers, reports,

and frameworks issued by the various State educational bodies in Australia during the past five or six years, a number of values have generalised support.

They are:

1. Self-discipline

When the South Australian Ministry of Education suggested that: 'The primary responsibility for behaviour belongs to the individual', it signalled a major change in the approach to student discipline. This change was also reflected in the (Victorian) Working Party on the Abolition of Corporal Punishment (1983:7):

> In our society children are being increasingly expected to be in charge of their own behaviour. Parents and teachers share with the community at large the responsibility of assisting the development of self-discipline in children.

This position is supported by the Catholic Education Commission's 'Pastoral Care in Catholic Schools' (1988): 'An environment should be created which facilitates the development and experience of responsible self discipline'.

While accepting this challenge, many teachers are unaware of methods which promote self-discipline in students. Traditional classrooms were orderly but there was no freedom for students who did as they were told. Following the social upheavals of the 1960s and 1970s, teachers were invited to become more democratic, an invitation which was interpreted as giving students freedom but removing order. Permissiveness replaced authoritarianism. A state of anarchy resulted which produced many of the 'progressive' schools of the 1960s and 1970s, schools which gave students freedom but failed to establish any rules of order. Typical of such a school is Summerhill, a school established by A.S. Neill (1960). Summerhill is not a democratic school but a permissive school in which freedom transcends order. A democratic school is one which allows students freedom to decide but one which operates within an orderly framework. Classroom procedures which respect both freedom and order are discussed in later chapters.

When corporal punishment was abolished in most schools, many teachers felt that there was now no 'last resort' and many expressed their concern at being ill-equipped to handle disciplinary problems in their class-rooms. Many simply replaced one ineffective method with another. When corporal punishment was abolished in Victoria, the Minister of Education announced that 'Alternative forms of punishment were being considered to make sure that they were adequate'. In reality, many secondary schools simply replaced the strap with the time-out room. Some schools have developed a hierarchy of punishments ranging from a mild rebuke, to detention, to suspension, and finally expulsion. Alternatives to punishment were simply not considered.

The great variety of educational procedures which changed constantly as one ill-advised approach replaced another is testimony to the fact that the fundamental problem has not been recognised. That problem is the pattern of teacher-student relationships which is appropriate in a society which wishes to foster democratic values. Self-discipline, in a democratic school, is based on freedom and responsibility. School students must be able to assume responsibility for the choices they make. The growth of self-discipline occurs, though, when the consequences of those choices are also accepted. An autocratic school cannot teach self-discipline because students are permitted no choice. A permissive school is similarly placed because students experience no consequences. A democratic school is one which allows students freedom to decide but one which operates within an orderly framework.

2. Co-operation

As with many institutions in our society, schools have endorsed and practised the value of competition. Grading practices, streaming, prize nights, stars, stamps, scratch and sniff, house points, test construction, and school reports reflect competitive aproaches. The greatest myth in education is the myth of competition — unless students are placed in a competitive situation, they will not perform to their optimum.

A competitive system, by definition, produces winners and losers. It is from the latter group, that the majority of behavioural problems will emerge. When the harmony of a class is disturbed, it is almost certain that there is a disruption in co-operation. Students who are confident that they can meet the demands placed upon them, be they intellectual, social, physical or emotional, will not resort to difficult behaviour. It is the loss of confidence, a product of the competitive system, which creates as many problem students.

The value of co-operation has been endorsed by most State education authorities. The Victorian Working Party (1983:6) noted: 'The organization of a school should be based on a desire to achieve the co-operation of all participants in seeking a jointly determined outcome'.

Similarly, the South Australian School Management policy (1989) mandated that 'staff are committed to modelling co-operative relationships' while the School Curriculum Framework for Personal Development (1989:9) suggests that 'personal development is fostered by co-operative relationships and decision-making processes'.

Some argue against the suggestion that teachers should aim to foster co-operation in their classrooms, pointing out that we live in a competitive world and that children should be prepared for that world. Such an argument has no validity. As Dreikurs (1968:78) points out:

> The less competitive a person is, the better he can stand up to extreme competition. If he is merely content to do his job, then he is not disturbed by what his competitor may do or achieve. A competitive person can stand competition only if he succeeds.

3. Mutual respect

Closely related to the concept of self-discipline and co-operation, is the value of mutual respect. When working with difficult students, invariably will the conclusion be drawn that the individuals see themselves as being treated with lack of respect by parents, teachers or peers.

Mutual respect refers to the right of individuals to self-determination, to make decisions concerning their own values, behaviours, and attitudes and to experience the consequences of those decisions. Where no choice is given to the individual, apart from situations involving physical damage, no respect is shown; when no consequence follows a choice, again no respect is shown. While effective teachers in a democratic school enjoy their students, they also respect them by permitting them to make decisions. The Catholic Education Commission (1988) states:

> Pastoral Care incorporates and proclaims the dimensions of justice whereby the rights of all members are respected. And further states: Quality relationships require compassion, tolerance, and mutual respect for the rights of others. Justice and freedom are at the heart of any community.

Curriculum Framework (1989:9) in outlining the platform for the Personal Development Framework stresses the importance of mutual respect. 'Personal development is based on mutual respect'. Again: 'Responsible action is based on reasoning and valuing of self and others with their different backgrounds, values and beliefs'. The Victorian Ministry of Education Ministerial Paper No. 4 (1984) had this to say:

> Students, too, must see evidence of mutual respect, and they themselves must be equally respected, if their school experience is to meet their needs and aspirations. The measure of this mutual respect and trust will be reflected in the process and quality of decision-making in the school.

The implications for teachers who wish to treat students respectfully are enormous. For example, the use of reward and punishment has no place in the classroom where students are permitted to make choices. The use of compliance strategies suggests that one person has, by virtue of a superior position, the right to make others comply. Parent–teacher interviews will also include the student if respect is deemed important. School reports will be given to students not parents. The use of the word 'must' will be heard infrequently in a respectful school. And so it goes on. How can teachers relate to students in a manner which promotes mutual respect, respect for others, for property, and respect for self? Not an easy task for teachers who have been trained and are products of a social system characterised by a superior–inferior continuum.

4. Shared responsibility

The notion of shared responsibility or participatory decision-making has assumed increasing importance in Australian schools. This can be seen in a Ministerial Paper (1985) in which it is noted that those affected by decisions should be involved in those processes:

> This commitment (of the Government to democratic leadership) will mean that parents, teachers, students, principals, administrators, and others closely involved in the work of education will all have the right to participate in decision-making processes. They come together as a group charged with the collective responsibility of reaching agreement or coming to a decision on issues to be resolved.

South Australia (1989) leaves no doubt about the importance of the decision-making process:

> Participatory decision-making processes are the key to effective management of student behaviour. Involve staff, students and their families in decisions about student behaviour.

And again, from South Australia (1989):

> Schools need to develop within all students K-12 the age-appropriate skills of decision-making in a group and their skills to negotiate their environment.

Curriculum Framework (1989) suggests that the focus in personal development is on people, alone or in small groups, making responsible decisions and taking action to enhance the quality of life.

Consider the following extract which appeared under a heading entitled: 'Tale of Classroom Despair' in the Melbourne *Age*, 24 June, 1986:

> Helen was endeavouring to spend as much time as possible with James during each day. She was also endeavouring to spend time with Tim who was finding it hard to settle down after his parents' divorce. She knew she should be spending more time with Abdul, Jenny, Con, and Macey, all of whom were struggling with English as a second language. Wayne really needed her attention as he was likely to hit out at the nearest child. Amy was obviously needing her attention. Andrew really needed individual tutoring. In fact, each of the 27 children in the grade had individual needs which had to be

met. Helen knew that she could help James if she could spend more time with him — but at whose expense?

What does Helen believe about her role as a teacher? That she is personally responsible for 25 individual children and that she is the only person in the classroom who can provide the necessary help for each child. What she fails to realise is that she does not teach 25 individuals but one group of 25 of which she is the group leader. The skills to integrate a class, the use of group dynamics and the creation of an appropriate group atmosphere in which all students are willing and able to learn, to contribute, to co-operate, are imperative today. The teacher's ability to use the group is clearly the most effective remedy to the problems of teacher burn-out and stress, a condition reflecting the traditional belief that each and every child in the classroom is the teacher's sole responsibility.

5. Social equality

The most important value in today's society is that of social equality, the right of each individual to determine his or her values, ways of behaving and future activities. While teachers have a responsibility to provide guidance, stimulation, influence, direction, and motivation, they do not have the right to impose their beliefs or values on their students. For many students, the slightest attempt to enforce them into compliance is to invite immediate retaliation.

The Working Party (1983:6) clearly identified the importance of social equality:

> Schools which are best at developing social learning environment are those which accord equal status to all members of the school community and which have effective decision-making processes based on participation, rather than authoritarian models.

The term 'democracy' implies social equality and, in such a system, authoritarianism has no place. Social equality disallows the idea of one person having power over another, as there can be no dominance among equals; the autocratic tenets, force, coercion, power, and fear, no longer being appropriate, must give way to more egalitarian practices. Dreikurs (1964) states:

We no longer have the ruler, such as prevailed in the autocratic society, who was superior to and had power over the submissive. In a society of equals we can't rule over one another. Equality means that each decides for himself.

When teachers are asked the question: 'Do you have the right to make students do what you want them to do?' most respond positively. 'Of course. I am the child's teacher'. However, when asked a second question: 'Who are you totally responsible for in this world?', most respond with 'Myself'. Teachers, like parents, do not have the right to make children do what they would like them to do. While teachers and parents have the responsibility to guide, to stimulate, to motivate, to encourage, and to model appropriate behaviour, they do not have the right to impose their will on others. To do so violates the values of equality, of respect, of shared responsibility, and of self discipline. Certainly teachers are wiser, more experienced, and more knowledgeable than their students, but in terms of worth, of dignity and of the right to self-determination, students are our social equals.

A first step which teachers might take is to free themselves of the mistaken notion that they are personally responsible for controlling the behaviour of each student and accept responsibility for changing their own behaviour first. Values have become relative and the concept of social equality implies that individuals have the right to decide. Defiance, disobedience, apathy, and a lack of co-operation are typical reactions of students who refuse to accept an externally imposed set of values or rules. Dreikurs (1960) suggests that: 'It is the democratic evolution with the concomitant sense of equality which is responsible for the problems which we are facing in our schools today'.

As stated in the Preface, this is the first generation of teachers without a tradition for teaching children. While this statement may puzzle teachers, it clearly represents the basic problem underlying classroom management. Teachers, like parents, like managers, have been deskilled. The traditional pattern of teacher–student relationship which has characterised the autocratic past is of historical interest only. Patterns of relationships in schools, homes, and businesses must reflect the values of a democratic society — respect, co-operation, self-discipline, equality, and shared

Democratic	Autocratic	Laissez-faire
Mutual trust Mutual respect	Control through reward and punishment Attempt to demand respect	Students may do what they please
Choices offered wherever feasible	Demands Dominates	Anarchy
Motivation through encouragement Identification of the positive	Focus on weaknesses and mistakes	All behaviour tolerated
Freedom within limits Balance between freedom to work and responsibility to work	Limits without freedom Promotion of dependency and/or rebellion	Freedom without limits Confusion
Intrinsic motivation Teachers and students set goals together	Extrinsic motives and punishments	Motivation erratic, unpredictable
Success-oriented activities designed to build self-confidence	Activities focus primarily on producing superior products	Some activities help students make progress, others do not
Co-operation, shared responsibility	Competition	Individual rights without regard for others
Self-discipline encouraged as part of educational process	Discipline is to establish external control	No discipline is expected
Students participate in setting goals	Goals are set by teacher	No positive goals
Students contribute ideas Participation in problem solving	Teacher decides all issues	No formal decisions reached

Figure 1 Leadership styles of teachers

responsibility. At present, many teachers lack the skill, the strategies to make this change from an autocratic to a democratic pattern of leadership. The characteristics of each are contrasted by House (1991) in Figure 1.

It is the purpose of this book to provide teachers with a framework for understanding the behaviour of students and to describe the techniques for motivating them. The framework is that drawn from Individual Psychology, a psychology which embodies the democratic values of respect, co-operation, self-discipline, equality, and shared responsibility. It is an approach which the author has used for many years in the education of teachers and which, when coupled with the group-based mastery strategy (Bloom, 1976), provides the teacher at all levels with, in the view of the author, the most appropriate and effective management and instructional strategies available today. While the principles and procedures described are explained in terms of teacher-student interactions, they are also relevant to all human relationships whether in homes, industry, communities, or politics. Their validity stems from the proposition that all difficulties encountered in classrooms, homes, offices, and elsewhere are mistakes in human relationships. Problems are particularly frequent in schools because teachers are not skilled in democratic relationships and, unable to combine respect for students with respect for themselves, they violate either one or the other. The consequence is a classroom characterised by either domination or indulgence.

In 1930 Alfred Adler concluded that: 'The hope of preparing the children of tomorrow rests primarily on converting the schools and teachers of today'. It is to that purpose that the remainder of this book is directed.

Try these

(1) Read the following classroom incidents.
   Which teacher is being autocratic and which is being democratic?

Behaviour	Autocratic	Democratic
1. You will raise your hand before you speak.		
2. I do not like the way you have set out your work.		
3. I wonder if we can think of a better way of distributing books.		
4. Late again, John! Detention.		

5. John, you can make up the work you missed through being late, by working through your free-time.

6. I have decided that you will not sit together.

7. Who would like to help put the library books away?

8. I can only correct assignments which are in by Friday.

9. I will not have you speak to me that way.

10. You will all have your homework assignments done by Wednesday.

11. I am not going to keep telling you to be quiet.

12. I can go on teaching only when people are quiet.

Hint

Autocratic — pressure from outside the students.
Democratic — stimulation from within the students.

Answers

Behaviour	Autocratic	Democratic
1.	/	
2.	/	
3.		/
4.	/	
5.		/
6.	/	
7.		/
8.		/
9.	/	
10.	/	
11.	/	
12.		/

2

Psychological Framework for Understanding Student Behaviour

INTRODUCTION

It is the purpose of this chapter to provide teachers with a framework for understanding the behaviour of students. The framework is drawn from Individual Psychology and is associated with the formulations of Alfred Adler, 'one of the first humanistic psychologists' (Ellis, 1970). Individual Psychology is consistent with the values discussed in the previous chapter and has been endorsed by the various reports which have been issued by State Ministries of Education throughout Australia.

Individual Psychology makes a number of assumptions regarding behaviour, chief of which are that the basic motivation is to belong, that humans are basically social beings who can only be understood holistically, that behaviour is purposive, unified, and consistent, and that people are active decision-makers who fashion their own personalities by their subjective or phenomenological view of experience.

Many theories compete for the attention of teachers, theories which hold different views of human behaviour and models of humans. According to some, students with problems are seen as victims of organic or social deficiencies. Teachers who subscribe to this theory will search for disadvantage in individuals and locate the problem in the home, in the society, or in the school.

Freudian psychologists will reject the view that people are motivated by social factors and prefer to account for motivation in the inborn instincts of sex and aggression. The behavioural school views personality as being shaped and controlled by the environment while non-ego psychologists see individuals as being largely controlled by unconscious factors over which they have no control. Glasser and others believe that disciplinary problems arise out of need deficiencies while the Canters take the view that teachers take control of their classrooms through assertive discipline which makes no assumptions about the individuals they control.

It serves no purpose to argue the relative strengths and weaknesses of the respective positions. At this stage, no theory of human behaviour is completely adequate. Teachers are engaged in an educational enterprise and need a theory of human behaviour which offers meaningful and useful approaches in the areas of motivation, behavioural change, the social context of learning, individual responsibility for behaviour, perception, and the role of the group. The fact that Individual Psychology has been chosen reflects the author's belief that it offers a worthwhile, effective, comprehensive, and meaningful approach for teachers working with children who are the products of a new social system which has already invalidated many of the traditional approaches to managing children in educational environments.

It is interesting to note that there is currently a resurgence of interest in Individual Psychology partly because of its heavy emphasis on prevention rather than rehabilitation and partly because it is founded on a value system based upon social democracy with equality of people at the core. Individual Psychology is clearly an idea come of age and has universal support in the many fields. It has become a major intervention model for thousands of lay and professional practitioners working in teaching, counselling, industry, and parent education.

There are those who argue that teachers need only know the 'how' of discipline and decline to relate practice to any theory of human behaviour. Such a belief leaves teachers vulnerable to inconsistencies in their strategies. A recent text on classroom discipline endorses the value of self-discipline and respect, yet supports the use of reinforcement theory and contracts. The Canters assert the right of students to choose how to behave but endorses the use of time out, loss of privilege, detention, and rewards. Consistency and the ability to handle problems which have not been previously encountered, suggest the need for a sound knowledge of student behaviour. Glasser, for example, fared badly with teachers who often, unaware of the theory underlying Reality Therapy, simply adopted Glasser's ten-step approach to classroom discipline, usually beginning at Step 7, time out.

In order for a teacher to make a wise choice concerning patterns of teacher–student relationships and disciplinary strategies, a knowledge of basic psychological underpinnings is necessary. As Kindsvatter (1978:322) observed:

> A teacher who does not have a sound and defensive concept of discipline is unable to integrate cohesively its many facets, nor can he readily produce a rationale for his approach to classroom management.

The theory of Individual Psychology is derived from a sound, well-researched model, which is consistent with the democratic values and philosophy of most Australian schools. While no theory can substitute for a caring teacher, caring is not sufficient. As Walton (1974:5) points out:

> No matter how much good will or affection may be present, a better understanding of children is required. Without it, affection often yields to discouragement and even bitterness in teachers who feel unappreciated for their efforts.

Schools exist in order to facilitate learning. In the areas of cognitive, affective, and psychomotor development, the teacher's role is to promote the optimal attainment by all students of the learning goals which have been determined. To achieve this, the teacher makes certain decisions about content, resources, teaching strategies, grouping, and evaluation. Collectively these decisions constitute an instructional plan which the teacher has decided for each topic or goal and, through the implementation of such plans, most students should achieve the desired learning.

While carefully designed instructional plans are essential for effective teaching, they are insufficient in themselves. The very best teaching strategies sometimes go awry for a number of reasons. Students may not be receptive or motivated, others may disrupt the class, while unresolved problems of general classroom management create a poor environment for learning. While teachers tend to attribute their classroom difficulties to the poor attitudes of students, their lack of motivation, or their apparent inability to learn, most problems of classroom management or control stem from the teacher's lack of psychological understanding of the behaviour of students. While training courses have equipped teachers to cope with students who want to learn, they have generally been less than adequate in relation to the child who does not wish to learn, who creates problems in the classroom, and who is generally regarded as a poor or difficult student.

Many teachers have considerable difficulty in managing these 'problem' or 'difficult' children. Despite the correctives applied by the teacher, these children become no better and simply make the teacher's task more difficult. The extent of the difficulty is just being realised. A recent study of a sample of primary schools indicated that teachers were spending about 80 per cent of their time in controlling children and about 20 per cent in teaching children. A decade or so ago, these figures would have been reversed. The rapid growth of support services — psychological, counselling, remedial, and welfare — indicates that teachers are not coping adequately with behavioural problems and are relying more and more on support services to deal with children. This is an unfortunate trend as the teacher in the classroom is by far the best person to deal with all types of children. We should be encouraging and developing greater competence in teachers rather than inviting them to refer their difficulties to a variety of outside support services.

Teachers have the important task of facilitating the intellectual, social, emotional, and physical development of a considerable number of children. To discharge this responsibility successfully, it is essential that they have a sound knowledge and understanding of those principles of human behaviour which are relevant to the classroom situation.

The following principles provide a basis for teachers to understand the classroom behaviour of their students. These principles will be referred to frequently throughout this book and they provide the basic framework for the techniques, concepts, and methods suggested for classroom use.

BELONGING IS THE BASIC MOTIVATION

Throughout life, the goal of belonging is the basic expression of human nature. Whatever the evolutionary basis, all children are social beings and need to feel that they belong, that they have a place in the family, in the school, and in the community: those groups which are important to them and to which they strive to gain acceptance. The term 'belonging' is referred to by Adler as *Gemeinschaftsgefuhl* and indicates being part of, being an integral element of, and being included in one's home, school, and community. 'If one is not inside the system, one is outside, looking in — and one is alone. This is a terrible feeling, a felt loneliness, not to belong' (Manaster and Corsini, 1982:47).

Students have in common with all other individuals a need to belong, to feel significant, to count for something and to be somebody. The view of humans as social beings implies that they can be understood only in terms of their interactions with others. Through such transactions, each individual strives to satisfy the need to belong, to be a part of the larger social whole. Teachers can understand students by viewing their behaviour as their attempt to belong to the classroom group.

If a child has a conviction that he belongs and has a firm place in the class, his efforts will be to contribute to the group and to co-operate with the requirements of the situation. If he believes that he is not good enough as he is and does not belong through constructive activity, he will apply his energies towards finding a place through activities directed at obtaining only a personal benefit rather than a group benefit.

Regardless of the acceptability of the behaviour, it is always a student's best attempt to find a place for himself through whatever means are available. Thus socially acceptable behaviour or socially unacceptable behaviour both have the same purpose, to satisfy a sense of belonging. The extent to which students feel that they can belong to the classroom by constructive behaviour will determine their willingness to learn and to function co-operatively and constructively in school. It is a sense of inadequacy, of internal discouragement, and the fear of rejection which are the major factors behind learning failures and behavioural problems in the schools.

Children do not grow up in isolation but from birth onwards are involved in social interaction with others. All of life's problems are social problems which cluster around the three tasks set for every individual — work, friendship, and love. All behaviours such as language, play, interpersonal skills, emotions, and speech are social behaviours which are learnt and developed in various social situations such as the home, the school, or the community. The social environment provides the reference point for understanding behaviour, as the actions of individuals are influenced by their experiences encountered in the social environment. 'Individual Psychology regards and examines the individual as socially embedded. We refuse to recognize and examine an isolated human being' (Adler, 1956:2). Teachers can understand children by viewing them in their group situation as a child's behaviour is meaningful only when viewed within that situation. Behaviour represents the individual's way of belonging to the group.

From a very early age, children seek to find ways of behaving which will gain them recognition, a feeling of importance, and a sense of belonging to the family. Young children operate on a trial-and-error basis. In their early attempts to seek answers to the questions 'Who am I?', 'What am I?', 'Who are these people about me?', 'What can I do?',

How do I belong?', children will try various ways of behaving and observe the consequences. When children fight, mother intervenes; she is controlled. Father does not respond to crying but involves himself when a child refuses to go to bed. Each experience is evaluated by the child: 'Ah, that's how I can keep them busy with me; that's how I can feel important and be noticed; those are the things which parents like me to do or try to prevent me from doing; that's how I can belong'. This search for significance, for identification, for acceptance, and for belonging underlies all forms of behaviour and is the basis for understanding and modifying motivation both at home and in school.

Those behaviours which are effective in that they give a child a sense of belonging are continued while others which do not achieve this purpose are discontinued. It is not necessary that the behaviours be constructive or socially acceptable; they may be disruptive, unacceptable, or foolish from a teacher's viewpoint. The only criterion which determines if a particular behaviour will persist or not is whether it satisfies the child's need to belong. Whatever children do reflects their idea about how they can belong. The attitude which a child adopts is of his own creation rather than determined by the environment. While environment is a forceful influence, the decisive factor in deciding attitudes is not the influence of the environment but the attitude which the child takes towards the environment. Students do not see reality as it is, but only as they perceive it; and their perceptions are often mistaken or biased.

Behaviour always makes sense to the individual who behaves. It is the most appropriate way of behaving given an individual's view of how to belong to the group. For that reason, Individual Psychology does not attempt to modify behaviour but is interested in motivation modification. A student who believes that she belongs only if people are prepared to be involved with her may come late to class, fail to complete work, ask frequent questions or wander from her seat. All are quite appropriate ways of behaving given her faulty belief concerning her way of belonging. What needs to be changed is not her behaviour but the belief that she belongs only by keeping people busy with her. A student who is motivated by the belief that 'I belong only if I am the most powerful' will be disobedient, stubborn, and unco-operative. These behaviours are appropriate to the goal and will only change when the faulty motivation is modified.

As all behaviour has social meaning, it can be understood only in the social context — the home, the school, and the community. The importance of viewing behaviour within the social context of the class suggests that all corrective measures by teachers in relation to children must be implemented within the environment provided by the total class. A great mistake which teachers make is to deal with children in isolation, in a one-to-one situation which fails to include other members of the class. For example, if one boy is particularly difficult because he fights frequently with other students, declines or refuses to complete his work, answers back when spoken to by the teacher, or creates minor disturbances in the class, most teachers will talk to the child about his behaviour, seek assurances of future improvement, threaten or use punishment, invite the student to complete a behavioural contract, place the student in time out, give a detention, send the child to the principal's office, or seek a referral to special services. These approaches are completely ineffective as they fail to recognise that the disruptive behaviours described are meaningful only within the classroom and must be dealt with within the classroom. In almost all cases, it is the behaviour of the other children which sustains a particular child's problems and is the best resource available for helping the particular child. Therefore, to change the behaviour of one child, it is desirable to involve the total class. By observing problem children in their relationships with other members of the class, it is possible to determine the goals of their disturbing behaviour, the sources of the behaviour, and the way in which the group can be used in assisting with the particular problem. Children encourage and discourage each other far more than teachers, and the ability of the teacher to understand and utilise the dynamics of a class is essential for all corrective efforts.

Consider a typical primary school class of 30 children. Each child has a particular way of belonging. Some win recognition by doing well scholastically; others are regarded as being good at sport; some are noticed for their social skills; the role of the clown, the bully, the lazy child, the shy child, and the sullen child is well known; an increasing number of children contrive for teachers to render them special service by requiring remedial assistance; and there are those who achieve recognition by challenging the teacher through stubbornness, disobedience, and defiance. Children have learnt to pursue goals which characterise their basic patterns of activity and which are designed to secure their place within the class.

All of the above ways of belonging are effective in that they keep teachers involved in a variety of ways — praising the good student, rebuking the bully, coaxing the shy child, urging the lazy one, admiring the model child, serving the poor learner, and fighting with the disobedient child. This is a never-ending process which has little or no effect in changing children's behaviour because it is exactly what each child wants to happen and it fails to deal with the problem of faulty relationships. Behaviour is purposeful and reflects a child's belief about how to belong. Children who cannot do as well as others turn to disturbing ways of behaving; others work hard and do well in order to be better than others; some are so discouraged that they refuse to co-operate and want nothing more than to be left alone. It serves no useful purpose to deal individually with such children if their behaviour is influenced by the behaviour of others. Teachers must utilise the total group and attempt to integrate the class for common purposes, place problems in a social context, and use the group to assist with the behaviour of individuals. The procedures involved in integrating a class will be discussed in Chapter 7.

At present, corrective measures are bound to fail because they deal with symptoms and ignore the underlying motivation. The clown, the lazy one, the truant, the late-comer, the disobedient child, and the thief, all keep teachers very much involved with them. Children direct a great deal of energy towards aggravating teachers in ingenious ways. They know that they belong because teachers respond to their inadequate behaviour. A very difficult student in an Oregon school was asked whether he was good at anything. 'Yes', he said, 'I am the best at being the worst.' The 'good' student and the 'model' child, on the other hand, feel that they belong only if they are better than others. Therefore they systematically attempt to discourage other children from doing well with their schoolwork. If problem students are to improve scholastically and behaviourally, it will be necessary to change not only their goals but also the behaviour of the better students who must begin to behave less competitively and more co-operatively, to accept some responsibility for the adverse effects which their behaviour has had on others, and to learn that they belong irrespective of their achievement. Until each child is sure of his or her place in the group through constructive activity, it is impossible for the class to function co-operatively and harmoniously.

Many teachers will find this concept difficult to accept as, in the past, they have assumed that they were single-handedly responsible for the behaviour of each child in the class and rewarded or punished according to needs of the situation. They failed to recognise the influence which children have on each other and the purposeful nature of the behaviour. How many times do we observe teachers correcting, praising, or admonishing individual students, sending children to the principal, having a quiet talk to difficult children at recess time, or sending children to special service staff? These are ineffective approaches as they fail to recognise the social significance of all behaviour, the purposeful nature of behaviour, and the role of the peers in influencing, contributing to, or correcting inadequate social behaviour or school performance. Before teachers can presume to influence students, they must first establish the premises upon which their action will be based. The recognition of the social nature of individuals, the social significance of behaviour, and the power of the group to influence individual members must form part of any corrective strategy.

ALL BEHAVIOUR IS PURPOSEFUL

Rather than attempting to isolate the causes of behaviour, Individual Psychology attempts to understand the individual by determining the goal towards which behaviour is directed. 'Ask not whence but whither', advised Adler. While the effects of the past and the importance of the present are not denied, the force of the future is impelling. We are not pushed by forces from the past or present but pulled by our future intentions.

Teachers who view student behaviour as movements towards a goal will recognise that behaviours which were not understood by them in the past will become meaningful and appropriate in terms of the purpose of the particular behaviours.

> The direction in which a person moves, the goals which he has set for himself, present the only access to an understanding of the total personality. Behaviour is movement toward a goal which the person pursues, and it implies action for a specific purpose. It is impossible to understand a person correctly unless one recognizes the purpose of his behaviour (Dreikurs, 1977:176).

Our concept of humans is that they are social beings whose primary motivation is to belong. All actions of children are purposeful and consistent with their efforts towards social integration. The force behind every human action is its goal. A knowledge of the goal towards which behaviour is directed is essential if teachers are to understand children's behaviour. When teachers complain that they do not understand particular children, what they are saying is that they are not aware of the purpose or the goal of the child's behaviour. Knowing the goal, the child's behaviour would appear logical, consistent, and by far the best way of belonging in view of the child's faulty psychological interpretation of how to belong.

No individual acts are random. Behind all the behaviour there is a clear purpose or goal, a phenomenon which prompted Allport (1950:169) to write: 'Goal striving is the essence of personality'. Observe any individual and it is clear that he moves of his own accord and is directed towards goals perceived as important to him. 'All his actions, emotions, qualities, and characteristics serve the same purpose. They show him trying to adapt to his environment' (Dreikurs, 1953:13). Teachers cannot understand student behaviour unless they are aware of the goals towards which the behaviour is directed. A student who misbehaves simply has wrong ideas about how to belong.

A teacher who understands behaviour will always ask 'for

what purpose' rather than 'why'. Once aware of the purpose behind students' behaviour, teachers will realise that their efforts to change behaviour will invariably have the opposite effect. For example, a child who provokes other children into fighting in the classroom will successfully involve the teacher who will stop the fight, adjudicate the dispute, and punish the offender. For a child whose typical way of behaving is: 'I can prove my importance by doing whatever I like', the teacher's intervention is exactly what he wants. The child fights to show you that he can do anything he wishes; whatever you feel like doing is exactly what the child wants you to do. Similarly a child who clowns will not cease clowning simply because she is punished. She knows she belongs as long as she can keep you busy with her. Your attention, whether a rebuke or a punishment, is exactly what the child wants: 'Stop everything and look at me' is the purpose of such behaviour. To understand behaviour one must see it in terms of its purpose and realise that children attempt to find a place for themselves by whatever behaviours are available and are not concerned whether these are socially useful or socially useless.

As all human behaviour has a purpose, the key to understanding and changing a child's behaviour is to identify the purpose and then act in such a way that the behaviour does not achieve its intended goal. At present, many teachers experience difficulty in coping with disturbing behaviour in the classroom because they are unaware of children's motivation or goal. As a result, they usually do exactly what children want them to do and strengthen the unsatisfactory behaviour which the intervention was designed to modify. The ineffectiveness of many corrective procedures used by teachers is the result of their concentration on the behaviour itself rather than on the purpose of the behaviour.

Teachers rebuke the late-comers, praise the model child, punish the bully, admonish the talker, fight with the rebel, moralise with the cheat, flatter the vain child, correct the deficient, and urge the lazy. With what effect? Almost none because the intervention is the purpose of the behaviour. Children's behaviour must be viewed in terms of the counterpart played by teachers. Action and reaction are completely logical on both sides and equally faulty in a psychological sense. A teacher's intervention, far from weakening unsatis-factory behaviour, has the opposite effect. Dreikurs has stated the position cogently: 'What we do to correct children is why they are misbehaving'.

Consider a boy whom you would regard as lazy. He is slow to open up his book and the last to begin his work; his assignments or projects are usually incomplete and submit-ted late. He does not clear up after art and craft periods and does not put his mathematics materials away when he has finished with them. When volunteers are called for, he rarely responds and his attitude is one of doing as little as possible to get by. His teacher urges, coaxes, reminds, threatens, cajoles, punishes and criticises, but all to no avail. The child is described as 'unmotivated' and that description is used as an explanation of his behaviour. Why doesn't John complete his problems? Is he not interested in mathematics? The purpose of his behaviour is clear — to put the teacher into his service. Whom do you spend your time with each day? The lazy child who has learnt that laziness achieves the purpose of involving the teacher by obtaining special atten-tion and assistance. Through his behaviour, the student communicates this message: 'I know I belong as long as you are prepared to be kept busy with me'.

Reflect on the children who constantly disrupt your les-sons, who are argumentative, stubborn, defiant, and disobedient. Such children threaten the teacher's authority and make themselves a powerful force within the class. These individuals are threatened, argued with, fought with, punished, sent to the principal, and occasionally expelled. None of these procedures has any effect in changing the child's behaviour; on the contrary, they strengthen the child's belief that power is important and that those who have the power win. It is then a matter of becoming more skilled in how you use your power, a lesson which juvenile delinquents have learnt very well. If teachers were aware of the child's purpose, to prove that he is the most powerful member of the group, they would not fight with the child. Power is important only when it is contested and a teacher who refuses to fight has won. Trying to make the child conform will result in certain defeat. Can you make anybody do anything? No! By accepting responsibility for their own behaviour, rather than the behaviour of students, teachers will have taken the first step to improve relationships.

Not only are behaviours designed to achieve a purpose but emotions are also employed by students for the same reason. The function of emotions has not been understood by teachers who have assumed that emotions themselves are a driving force and are instrumental in many acts of misbehaviour. The assumption is often made that students behave badly because they are emotionally upset. On the contrary, they become emotionally upset in order to misbehave.

In terms of functions, individuals are thinking, feeling, and acting people. The relationship between these three functions is that thinking or cognition furnishes the direction for behaviour and feeling or emotion is the fuel which triggers the individual into action and subsequent behaviour. We are not controlled by, or victims of, our emotions but we generate them to achieve the purpose decided by the intellect. Typical purposes of emotions are to gain control, to seek special service, to frighten, to get even, to gain attention, or to force compliance.

Consider the function achieved by various emotions. A student who believes that 'I belong as long as I can keep people busy with me' will display shyness, sadness, fear or boredom. Teachers must recognise the purpose of these emotions and render them ineffective by refusing to give special service. Crying is an attempt by the child to regain control; depression is a silent temper tantrum; apathy is an expression of passive power by students who are fully motivated to defeat teachers; sadness is designed to evoke pity; ambivalence is self-deception; anger is an attempt to control others, and guilt feelings attempt to prove good intentions without any intention to change. Thus, emotions are not the driving force behind behaviour but are the fuel which enables us to move towards our goals. We think, then feel, then act — an order which places thinking in the driver's seat. Rather than attempting to modify emotions, which are always appropriate to the goal sought, teachers should aim to modify the faulty cognition which generates the emotion necessary to action.

While all social and emotional behaviour is clearly

designed to achieve particular purposes, it is important to view unsatisfactory intellectual behaviour within the same framework. The large number of school failures, the low level of numeracy and literacy, and the lack of interest and motivation for school work in many students are a cause of concern to many people. Efforts to overcome the problem of learning deficiency are evidenced by the provision of remedial services, the growth of psychological and counselling services, courses in diagnostic testing and prescription, reduction in staff–student ratios, withdrawal facilities, and the like. These approaches fail to recognise that all behaviour is purposeful and that the majority of children who do poorly at school choose to do poorly. This is a rather startling statement, for it suggests that the rapid growth in remedial provisions is misguided. It is essential to realise that 'whatever a child is doing depends on his decisions and not on his abilities. Thus, deficient behaviour may not result from real deficiencies, but from wrong decisions' (Dreikurs, 1971:6). Consider a typical case:

John is in second grade and has a sister, Sally, in fourth grade. Sally reads very well and her reading ability is a source of parental pride, attracting frequent praise and admiration. John knows that at any time he will not be able to read as well as his sister and, therefore, makes a decision not to learn to read well. John is aware that this decision will gain him far more attention from others than will be obtained by his more capable sister. John begins to fall behind in his reading and his lack of progress is detected by his teacher. Each reading period, after the other students are given their reading assignments, the teacher approaches John and says: 'I see that you are having difficulty with your reading. Let me help you'. This is exactly what John wants, special service from the teacher. He is unlikely to improve as this would result in a loss of this special attention which he receives.

Parents will now be brought into the scene as John's reading fails to improve. John's teacher will seek an interview with his parents and seek their co-operation by hearing John read for ten minutes each night after dinner. Note that it is always reading or mathematics which children choose not to learn; parents are rarely asked to help with art, music, nature study, or science. Children know what subjects worry teachers and parents. So every night, there is John with a captive parent. What do the other members of the family receive? Nothing. John receives far more attention through his inadequate behaviour than do others with their more competent behaviour.

John will not improve despite the efforts of his teacher and his parents. Special assistance will now be sought in the form of a remedial teacher, a psychologist, or a special educator. They will use the usual diagnostic tests to detect weaknesses such as reversals, substitutions, in inability to blend sounds. Prescriptive programs will be written for John and implemented by his teacher. The futility of such approaches is obvious as it treats symptoms rather than the basic problem. We do not rub measles spots off to cure measles yet we think that by correcting deficiencies we will improve John's reading. The cause of the problem, the decision made by John not to read well, remains intact and teachers and parents wonder why his reading does not improve in view of all the special assistance which he receives.

Despite the endeavours of reading experts, teachers, and parents, many children fail to read adequately. Such children are finally labelled and this label excuses an inability to motivate them effectively. Just look at the variety of labels which are available to excuse poor teaching. We can say John is suffering from peripheral and central nervous disorders, sensory deprivation and handicaps, neurophrenia, dyslexia, aphasias, disgraphias, intrasensory and intersensory disabilities, deficiency in auditory perception and disorders of auditory comprehension, problems of visual imagery and special visual distortions. He may be disadvantaged, deprived, or be suffering from cultural or perceptual deprivation and a dysfunction of the brain. He may even be a perceptual cripple. Our failure to recognise that all behaviour is purposeful leads us to adopt many ineffective strategies in teaching. Children's unsatisfactory behaviour, intellectual, social, and emotional, will change only when we are aware of its purpose and act to modify the motivation rather than the behaviour. Rarely are problems limited to the academic sphere. Students are whole beings who cannot be understood by some partial characteristic. The whole is greater than the sum of the parts. A holistic study of problem students will generally indicate the mistakes which teachers and parents are making, the source of a student's discouragement, and the ways in which the student might be helped. Consider one final example:

> A 12-year-old boy who attended a special school was affected with convulsions and each day engaged in bodily seizures and muscular spasms. He had been doing this regularly for about nine years and was treated medicinally. His convulsions were preceded by other erratic behaviour such as throwing papers into the air. The teacher was advised to withdraw her 12 students from the room immediately the boy gave indications of an impending convulsion. For three days this procedure was repeated — papers thrown, children removed, and the convulsion. On the fourth day there was no convulsion nor has there been any since. Why? The audience has been removed and there is no point convulsing unless you have an audience.

LIFE STYLE IS UNIQUE AND UNIFIED

Students have their own particular way of behaving which distinguishes them from one another. They have a particular view of themselves and of their relationship to the environment. This typical way of behaving, this cognitive map which we all have, may be referred to as personality or, as Adler described it, 'style of life'. It is the guiding theme in one's life and gives unity and stability to behaviour. To understand students, teachers must be aware of their life style, the concept which accounts for the uniqueness of each individual student.

So important is an understanding of life style, that Dreikurs (1954:9) has written:

> It is impossible to understand any adult without information about his first four to six years of life, which are the formative years. In this period, every person develops concepts about himself and about life which are maintained throughout life, although the person remains completely unaware of the premises he had developed for himself and upon which he acts.

Adler (1930:23) described the unity and pervasiveness of a child's life style when he wrote:

> The psychic life of a child is a wonderful thing, and it fascinates at every point where one touches it. Perhaps the

most remarkable fact of all is the way in which one must unroll the whole scroll of the child's life in order to under- stand a single event. Every act seems to express the whole of a child's life and personality, and is thus unintelligible without a knowledge of this invisible background. To this phenomenon we give the name, unity of personality.

The major implication of this description of life style is that teachers cannot understand why children choose par- ticular forms of behaviour such as truancy, bullying, lying, learning difficulties, and clowning unless they understand the total child, as these behaviours are expressions of par- ticular life styles. An error made by advocates of behavioural modification is to attempt to modify behaviour rather than understand and help the child change a faulty life style which is reflected in inadequate behaviours. This holistic view of individuals is a basic premise of Individual Psy- chology and stands in contrast to the reductionist or atomis- tic approach of other psychologies.

'Like a flower which comes from a single fertilized cell, we are a unity; we are not an assemblage of parts like a machine' (Manaster and Corsini, 1982:32). The word 'Individ- ual' in Individual Psychology comes from the Latin term *individuum* which means indivisible. This holistic approach suggests that it is neither efficient nor necessary to fragment behaviour in order to understand it. The whole individual reveals himself through movements. It is the total individual who uses mind and body and it is impossible to understand people by examining the characteristics of their parts, their physical, chemical, biological, physiological, intellectual, and psychological mechanisms. A holistic approach will attempt to modify motivation while a behavioural approach seeks to modify behaviour.

It is important to relate life style to the problem of self- determination. Many teachers have not thought through the question of self-determination and often rely on causation. Teachers have expressed the following beliefs to me:

'You should know that this is the highest percentage of single parents in the Dandenongs.'
'Well you should see the homes they come from; then you would see why they are incorrigible.'
'She comes from a single-parent family.'

'The town has one of the highest incidence of unemployment.'
'Don't expect much of the students; this is a low-level hous-
ing area.'
'Well you should know that he has a profound hearing loss'
(after a child has smashed the afternoon-tea set).

These statements expressed the belief in causation and
are totally inappropriate because they suggest that correction is outside a teachers' influence. In all of the above
examples, it is not that the children coming from the various
environments cannot behave responsibly; rather they
choose to behave badly in their pursuit of goals. Always ask
this question when given difficult students: 'Could they
behave responsibly if their lives depended on it?'. Invariably
the answer is positive. Students are responsible for their
behaviour and should not be excused for behaving irresponsibly through reference to environmental or hereditary
influences.

The formation of life style begins from birth as young
children seek to understand the world and their relationship
to it. The child learns to interact with people, particularly
those in the family, and comes to conclusions about how to
live effectively within the family. The various social interactions and the child's evaluation of these experiences provide
the child with an opportunity to establish guiding principles
which will govern or guide the child's characteristic patterns
of behaviour through life and which will result in the establishment of a specific style of life. Once formed, a child's
response to each new situation is decided by the particular
life style which the child has adopted, and any attempt to
change this life style will be met with the strongest opposition. Dreikurs (1953:43-44) has described the development
of life style as follows:

> A child's life plan does not grow out of a certain peculiarity
> nor out of isolated experiences, but out of the constant
> repetition of the difficulties, real or imagined, which he
> encounters. Each individual will find out special ways and
> means which appear to be serviceable for his special plan.
> Out of the individual's special life plan develops the life style
> which characterises him and everything he does.

It is impossible to predict what type of life style an
individual will adopt because behaviour is not influenced by

the particular hereditary or environmental forces but by the individual's interpretation of them. Different individuals respond in different ways to similar experiences and influences. This is the basis of individual uniqueness, for each person decides what to perceive and how to interpret the perception. An individual does not merely react to the environment but is active in interpreting it. Man acts according to his own self-determination. This spells the end of an exclusively causalistic orientation. An individual's perception and interpretation of an event influence behaviour more than the reality of the event. An individual does not merely react to the environment but is active in interpreting it. This ability to interpret and assign personalised meaning to events has been described by Adler (1957:49):

> A perception is never to be compared with a photographic image because something of the peculiar and individual quality of the person who perceives it is inextricably bound up with it.

Consequently an individual's life style and characteristic behaviour are the result of his creative power to interpret experiences. The ability of the individual to direct forces around and within him, to interact actively, is described by Adler (1930:5):

> Every individual represents both a unity of personality and the individual fashioning of that unity. The individual is thus both the picture and the artist. He is the artist of his own personality.

The individuality of people is the result of this creative process. As Dreikurs (1977:175) observes:

> We have evidence that neither heredity nor environment determines the child's personality nor 'causes' his development, because it is the child himself who determines hereditary and environmental influences.

Life style is the result of a child's interpretation of the inner and outer environment during the early years of life. This private logic which individuals develop becomes a reality and is used to justify mistaken behaviour. The need for a teacher to understand a child's 'private view' of the environment is essential as all behaviour will reflect this private logic and will be unintelligible without this knowledge. Frequently teachers observe students behaving in what is considered to be an inappropriate manner. From the student's viewpoint it is not inappropriate, as the behaviour is consistent with their view of life and themselves which they formulated during childhood. Children always make the best choices of which they are capable in view of their perception of the various situations. They have learnt to justify and to be logically correct about their inadequate behaviour. The target of a teacher's attention should not be the behaviour but the faulty assumptions and mistaken views which the student holds concerning the ways in which group belonging is possible. While those assumptions and beliefs are faulty, they constitute the reality which determines the goals towards which the student's behaviour is directed.

By the time children are about five or six years old, they begin to integrate their subjective impressions of group living into typical ways of behaving, their life styles, their plan of living which guides subsequent behaviour. Having formulated a life style, children no longer grope on the basis of trial and error but act in accordance with a set of stable concepts. They view each event from their own personal bias or prejudice and their interpretation is always in accord with the direction established by the life style. Children will always view their behaviour as being logical for they adjust their perception to their own private logic and this enables them to act logically though others may view their behaviour quite differently.

In our society, certain life styles are common. Among those which teachers would identify are:

I belong if I am the smartest one.
I belong if I am the funniest one.
I belong if I am the most powerful one.
I belong if I am the most hopeless one.
I belong if I am in control.
I belong if people are prepared to serve me.
I belong if I can obtain approval.
I belong if I am superior.

Think of the children in classrooms who fit the above life styles — the bully, the clown, the cruel child, the boss, the remedial child, and the shy child. What is the disobedient child saying to you? 'I belong as long as I am the most powerful. You can't make me do anything'. All of the above types of belonging result from faulty interpretations made during each childhood and will tend to persist because children initiate those experiences which they desire or anticipate, exclude experiences which would be inconsistent with their life style, and correctly judge which consequences of their behaviour achieved the goals sought after.

Life style and the long-range goals which support a particular life style remain remarkably consistent. Life style remains relatively stable because, in accepting his basic beliefs and life patterns as truth, the individual interprets new life events in line with his prior convictions rather than altering his convictions in the face of the new experiences (Ferguson, 1984:14). Changes which do occur in the short-range goals are designed to achieve the more permanent life goals. For example, a student whose life style reflects a belief that 'I must be the best' may be a top student in primary school. However, when unable to achieve that goal in secondary school, he may turn to other ways of expressing his long-range goals such as being the best at being funny, the best at being powerful, or the best at being the worst. Although these behaviours differ widely, they reflect a stable life style which believes that belonging depends on being the best.

Biased apperception, the ability to be logically correct about mistaken behaviour, is a reason why teachers find it difficult to change the behaviour of children. 'The individual', wrote Adler (Dreikurs, 1953:45), 'sees all his problems from a perspective which is his own creation'. Again:

> The private logic which each person evolves appears to justify his mistaken behaviour, and prevents him from seeing that most of the difficulties and disappointments in his life are the logical consequences of mistakes in his life plan (Dreikurs, 1953:45).

Many of these perceptions are based on faulty assumptions which are no longer relevant or applicable yet they guide behaviour more strongly than any other factor. For example, a boy may see his parents' delight with the reading skill of his older sister and conclude that he will never read as well as she does. Another boy sees the additional responsibility and privileges given to his older brother and concludes that he has been unfairly treated. Children who have been 'spoilt' may think that people are there to do their bidding and they need not submit to the rules which apply to all other individuals in society. These mistaken views are the reality on which faulty life styles are based and, once established, children always behave logically because their behaviour is in accordance with their life style. Adler (1931:61–2) gives the following example of the logic behind children's behaviour. A boy at school, the laziest in the class, was asked by his teacher, 'Why do you get on so badly with your work?'. He answered, 'If I am the laziest boy here, you will always be occupied with me. You never pay attention to the good boys who never disturb the class and do their work properly'. So long as it was his aim to attract notice and to rule over his teacher, he had found the best way of doing it. A child's actions and attitudes are expressions of life style and, to understand any particular behaviour, teachers need to study the total child, to look below the surface for the guiding influence on a child's behaviour, that is, life style.

Individual Psychology believes that the most important factor influencing life style is the child's ordinal position, the socio-psychological configuration of a family group. Dreikurs (1953:41) is of the opinion that the only fundamental law governing the development of a child's character is that 'he trains those qualities by which he hopes to achieve significance or even a degree of power and superiority in the family constellation'. Adler (1927:147) agrees and notes:

> Before we judge a human being, we must know the situation
> in which he grew up. An important moment is the position
> which a child occupied in his family constellation.

Children do not grow up in isolation but as a part of a family group. The family includes not only the parent or parents but other siblings and it is the latter which exert the greatest influence on a child. Children in the same family each have a different environment because of their ordinal position. The second child is born into a different psychological situation from the first and each subsequent child has a unique situation. It is not the actual birth order which is important but rather the psychological interpretation of the position. If the eldest is scholarly, co-operative, and tidy, it is likely that the second will be unscholarly, unco-operative, and untidy. However, if the first child chooses not to be scholarly, co-operative, or tidy, it is likely that the second will adopt these characteristics. Birth order is not a determinant of behaviour but is a major influence on the types of behaviour which children adopt.

In the life style of every child there is the imprint of his or her position in the family. The first-born child is in the unique position of being, for a year or two, the only child. During that time the child is the sole object of parental attention, suffers from parental inexperience, and is subjected to more pressure, closer scrutiny, and higher expectations than any other member of the family. The position does have some rewards as the child establishes a 'kingdom' with a range of persons serving him — mother, father, uncles, aunts, and grandparents.

This rather attractive situation is rudely shattered by the arrival of the second child, an event for which the first cannot be adequately prepared. Clearly he is 'dethroned' and will strive to regain his 'rightful' place. Depending partly on the age gap and sex of the other child, the first-born is likely to conclude that he belongs only when he is the first or the best. From then on there will be no mistakes in his behaviour, no doubts or uncertainties. The first-born will engage only in those activities where he can be the first or the best. He will enter school and attempt to be the best student. If he is unable to be the best at school work, he may be the funniest child in the class, the clown. Failing this, he can be the most powerful or vicious child in the class, the bully. If this position is denied, perhaps by another more powerful child, he may be a most hopeless student, the best at being the worst. Usually ambitious, first-born children are frequently high achievers, more conservative, and fond of authority. It is not difficulty to see why. There was a time in the past when they were unchallenged.

The second-born child will almost invariably be what the first child is not. As the second child searches for behaviours which will provide her with a place within the family, she will become aware that there is someone ahead of her who is older, larger, and more capable and has already successfully staked his claim in certain areas. Whatever those areas are, the second will be careful to avoid them as there is no point in competing with a more able person when there are so many other avenues available which will achieve the same purpose of belonging.

Not wishing to compete with the older child in his areas, the second child will frequently adopt the behavioural patterns diametrically opposite to the first child. An indication of their extreme difference can be judged by the often repeated remark made by parents concerning their second child. 'Helen is just so different from John. I swear that we brought the wrong child home from hospital.' Extreme differences in personality are usually found between the first two children, as competition leads to the development of opposite character traits, interests, temperaments, and abilities. Where one succeeds, the other gives up. Feeling unfairly treated because she does not have the privileges of the first, squeezed out by the arrival of a third child, the second has the most uncomfortable position in the family and will frequently be the most difficult child to manage.

Competition is strongest between the first and second child as the second seeks to overtake and supplant the pacemaker in terms of parental attention while the oldest, believing that he must maintain his superiority, acts to prevent the younger from competing successfully in areas where the first is achieving well. For instance, when the second child brings her work home from kindergarten, the following conversation is quite typical:

Younger child:	Do you like my paper mask?
Mother:	Yes, dear, it looks very realistic.
Older child:	It is all out of shape, the eyes are too small and the mouth too large.

What the older child is actually saying is, 'It is not as good as I can do and don't you ever forget it'. While competition is not limited to the first two children, it is most intense between them.

A recent study on reading problems in primary school children indicated that when a first-born child in a particular family was classified by the school as a 'poor reader', then, without exception, the second-born in the family was classified by the school as a 'good reader'. When the second-born was referred to as a 'poor reader', the first-born child was regarded by the school as a 'good reader'. It is quite incredible how often the second-born child displays those characteristics lacking in the first. Even in twins, the characteristics of first-born and second-born quickly emerge.

Youngest children quickly learn that they are surrounded by more able people, people who are prepared to do things for them, to make decisions for them, and to take responsibility for them. As a result they may decide to retain this dependent role and place people in their service. Being last-born has its advantages. The last-born is never displaced by other children and the parents are generally better established economically. Further, the last born has fewer parental pressures and does not suffer from parental inexperience. Look at the baby book for the first-born 'where every step, every landmark, every tooth, every stage of development is lovingly recorded, often documented with pictures and drawings' (Dreikurs and Grey, 1968:11). The last child is lucky if his name is ever recorded in the book. Photographs abound of the first child but are virtually non-existent for the youngest. Pressure is off last-born children, as more experienced and older parents do not demonstrate their fierce concern for their development and are more inclined to let the children be themselves. While these children tend to have a problem in developing independence, of breaking away from their baby image, they benefit frequently by having relaxed and pleasing personalities.

Only children have a difficult position as the advantage gained in having no other child to displace them is more than offset by the fact that they live much of their lives in an adult world and their childhood is spent with people who are always more proficient. Their orientation is to adults and their choice is to join them or to be served by them. Depending on the particular decision made, only children will tend to become precocious or 'hopelessly baby', behaviours which will not gain them acceptance by peers. It is important that the only child be brought into contact with other children at an early age through play groups, pre-school, and home visits by other children. This will help them develop the social skills of relating to other children, skills which will not be acquired in the adult world.

While the effect of a child's ordinal position in the family is naturally influenced by the size of the family, the ages and sex of the children, and parental reaction to children and to each other, teachers are urged to consider the effects which children have on each other and how often these effects reflect ordinal position. Ordinal position is dynamically significant but does not predict a certain personality type. Children use their position in the family to develop particular character traits and an observant teacher will see that differences in abilities, interests, and temperament will invariably reflect competition between children. The strongest influence on the behaviour of each child is exerted by the major competitor in the family, the child who is most different. If you greet your new student, Jim, with the following remark: 'I see that you are Sandra's brother. I taught Sandra last year and she was very good at mathematics', do you think that Jim is going to excel at mathematics? It is most unlikely.

> As each member strives for his own place within the group, the competing opponents watch each other carefully to see ways and means by which the opponent succeeds or fails. Where one succeeds, the other gives up; where one shows weakness or deficiencies the other steps in (Pepper, n.d.).

It is, however, the adult reaction rather than the ordinal position which is critical. Teachers or parents are not the cause of the problem of peer competition; they simply make it possible usually by encouraging strong competition. If teachers or parents were to promote co-operation the behaviour of children would change. In many ways, a class is like a large family. Each child has a special way of belonging which is strongly influenced by the behaviour of others in the class. Certain students are determined to belong by being the cleverest; others excel at gaining attention through minor mischief; power is the motive of others while some want nothing more than to be left alone. If the children do not believe that they belong to the class through co-operative behaviour, they will strive competitively, at each other's expense, to try to find a place. They will believe they have to fight for a place and will push one another down in competitive striving. The glory of one will be the defeat of the other one, in a see-saw pattern that finds no winners (Ferguson, 1984:18). If the clown finds that there is another who is funnier than he, with whom he cannot compete, he will cease clowning and adopt another method of gaining attention. The bully or boss will not remain in that area if a stronger or more powerful child enters the scene. The over-ambitious student gives up if a more talented student begins to overshadow her. Each student needs to belong to the class and his or her way of behaving is designed to achieve a particular purpose which is consistent with the student's life style. As long as behaviour achieves its purpose, it will persist. To provide an opportunity for all students to belong to the class through co-operative and constructive activity is a major challenge facing teachers today.

ORIGINS OF MISBEHAVIOUR

Students are not born with behaviour problems; they become behavioural problems in the course of their psychological and social development. Being children in an adult world, helplessness is imprinted but should diminish gradually as children begin to find their place in the family or the school through contributing, co-operating, participating and being valued. If they do not gain a sense of belonging through the above means, then they begin to strive for prestige, special status, and superiority in order to overcome feelings of inadequacy and inferiority. Maladjustment or misbehaviour is the individual's misdirected goal of achieving an apparent superiority in order to overcome feelings of inferiority. In this sense every misbehaving student is a discouraged student, an individual who feels less than others, an individual with a felt discrepancy between 'what he thinks he is' and 'what he thinks he should be'. In their efforts to find a place in the class group, children meet with many difficulties. Their initial attempts at achieving, learning, contributing, and co-operating are often discouraged by teachers and by other children. Consequently they begin to lose faith in their ability to cope with the demands which school places upon them. This loss of confidence in one's ability is the antecedent of

Discouraging parent–child discouragement	Probable results of the relationships
Overprotection	Child does not learn to take responsibility
Overindulgence	Child becomes a 'getter', irresponsible
Rejection	Child is discouraged about her worth
Authoritarian methods	Child depends on a power, tries to defeat it
Excessive standards	Child is discouraged about her ability
Pitying	Child feels sorry for herself
Inconsistent discipline	Lack of trust, believes life is arbitrary
Lack of harmony	Becomes a 'fighter' or seeks excitement
Hopelessness	Develops feelings of hopelessness
Disparagement	Child becomes a cynical pessimist
Denial of feelings	Learns to 'cover up' or avoid feelings
Competitiveness	Becomes anxious, strives to be 'best', or if this seems impossible, becomes the 'best worst'

Figure 2   Sources of discouragement and probable results (Adapted from Dewey, 1978)

behavioural and learning difficulties. A summary of potential sources of discouragement and their likely effect on children is presented in Figure 2.

Parents are the initial source of a child's discouragement. They refuse to accept children as they are but conditionally on being better. A small child may offer to run an errand, open a can, light a fire, pour the milk, or set the table. Such offers will often be refused on the grounds that the child is 'too small', 'too slow', or 'too young'. Tasks which are completed imperfectly are corrected by parents; offers of co-operation are declined; and children are denied an opportunity to discover their own strengths and abilities. Indirectly children are being constantly reminded that, as they are now, they are not much good. Their usefulness or worth will come when they are older, bigger, stronger, faster, or more skilful. Acceptance is made conditional upon their being better. When initial attempts to belong to a family through contribution and co-operation are turned into a sequence of discouraging experiences, children begin to lose their confidence and their feeling of belonging is impaired. They begin to regard themselves as less than others and doubt their capacity to belong usefully.

Children know that they are smaller, less competent, and slower than adults but it is the interpretation of their experiences in relation to adults and other children which is important. If their efforts to learn, belong, co-operate, and participate at home or at school are rejected or discouraged on the above grounds, children begin to feel that they are not good enough, that they cannot belong through useful or constructive behaviours. Consequently their development of social interest, and a capacity to co-operate with others, is inhibited. Feelings of inferiority begin to make their appearance in the form of inadequate and unacceptable behaviour. Belonging now depends on setting up against others and being better than others, all to overcome the imagined superiority of others. As soon as a child establishes a feeling of inferiority, the development of social interest is impaired. 'One cannot develop a feeling of belonging if one considers oneself looked down upon' (Dreikurs, 1953:21).

Teachers often impress pupils with their own efficiency, knowledge, strength, ability, and speed. A child might struggle for ten minutes with an unsolved problem which the teacher solves in seconds. A poorly drawn house which required considerable time and effort by a child is 'corrected' by the teacher with a few deft strokes. The task of reading aloud to the class is removed from the hesitant reader and undertaken by the teacher. We must consider the number of times when we discourage children by impressing them with our own efficiency and their inefficiency.

The school is a learning environment in which children must acquire a large number of skills. While teachers carefully attempt to transmit knowledge and skills, many of them refuse to accept a child's current level of performance as they feel that such acceptance will remove the incentive for the child to improve. 'That's a very good painting, John, but if only you had ...' or 'You read that very well but next time try to ...' or 'You kicked very accurately Tim but your handball ...'. From a child's point of view, nothing is ever good enough because it could always be better. As a result many children give up because they can never be as good as others want them to be. Teachers fail to convey to children that they are acceptable as they are and they begin to lose confidence in themselves. Teachers hesitate to accept children unconditionally out of a fear that they will not improve or develop unless teachers constantly point out their deficiencies. This is an extremely negative and discouraging expectation which leads to discouraged teachers and discouraged children each fortifying the other's sense of inadequacy.

Apart from the teacher, there are other influences which contribute to feelings of inferiority in children. Other students who are already more proficient in performing various skills are used as standards of comparison. This practice is reflected in grading schemes which use norm-referenced approaches to assessment. A student's performance is judged against the achievement of other students and the award of grades such as A, B, or C indicates relative rankings of performance. Competition is inevitable in such a situation and many children will be reminded day after day that, as they are, they are not adequate because other children are always better. For many children, school becomes a confirmation of their private evaluation, an assessment in which they view themselves as inadequate and inferior. One of the saddest statistics in education is the finding (Bloom, 1979:1) that the correlations between measures of school achievement of Year 3 and Year 11 are about +0.85, which demonstrates that, over this eight-year period, the relative rankings of students in a class or school remain almost perfectly fixed. The best remain the best while the worst remain the worst.

Peers are also a source of discouragement. Children who believe that they belong only if they are the best students will set out to systematically discourage others. On receiving their test papers back, with 10 out of 10, these children will ask others what they received. 'Three out of ten — you are dumb.' If a child is told often enough that he is dumb, he begins to believe it and drop out of the academic race. This, unfortunately, is our educational system in which children are encouraged to excel. How many children can excel? We pay a high price for excellence in this country for many children give up because they cannot meet the standards of excellence set by teachers and parents. The few that attain excellence do so by systematically destroying and discouraging the large majority of students. In a selective educational system, this practice is quite acceptable. In a democratic society where each child must be given equal opportunity for quality education, the competitive classroom has no place.

From these various sources of discouragement — grading practices, competitive classrooms, streaming, emphasis upon deficiencies, criticism, and comparisons with others, children develop a sense of inferiority which results in their avoiding social responsibilities, concealing their imagined deficiencies, avoiding possible failures, and attempting to obtain superiority over others. They turn from what Adler has called the 'useful' side to the 'useless' side.* Fearing defeat on the useful side, children's basic urge to participate, to co-operate, to meet the various problems associated with the demands of the school, the home, and the community now becomes side-tracked and their goal becomes that of self-enhancement, self-centredness, self-boundedness, and they seek personal superiority over others. Feelings of inferiority impel individuals to strive for significance on the useless side and lead them to seek individual compensation or to withdraw.

> Maladjustment is characterised by increased inferiority feelings, underdeveloped social interest, and an exaggerated unco-operative goal of personal superiority. Accordingly, problems are solved in a self-centred 'private sense' rather than a task-centred 'common sense' fashion (Ansbacher and Ansbacher, 1956:2).

All disturbing or unacceptable behaviour in the classroom can be traced to a loss of self-confidence, to a sense of inferiority resulting from discouragement. Failure is not the cause of inferiority but a consequence of such a feeling. The only reason children need to disturb is because they fear defeat on the useful side. They believe that they are unable to meet societal demands in relation to life's three tasks — school, friendship, and relationship to the opposite sex. As a result of the many discouraging experiences, children lose confidence in themselves and turn to disturbing ways of behaving in their attempt to salvage some

---

* 'Useless' side of life refers to behaviours which demonstrate no interest, respect, or concern for others, are socially unacceptable, reveal a lack of co-operation, and are directed towards personal superiority and power over others. 'Useful' side of life indicates behaviour which reflects co-operation, concern, and respect for others, confidence in one's ability to cope with life's problems, and a feeling of belonging.

semblance of worth and significance. The cumulative effects of discouraging experiences finally become too much for individuals. They no longer hope for significance through contributing constructively but now misbehave and defy teachers and others in the belief that this will gain them social status.

> Discouragement is the final outcome of a process of testing and trying, of groping and hoping; it is the stage that is reached after one has hoped against hope, tried without expectation of success, and finally given up in despair (Dinkmeyer and Dreikurs, 1963:35).

If teachers would set out to provide each child with a set of encouraging and successful experiences, refrain from criticism and other mistake-centred approaches, and focus on students' abilities and strengths rather than on disabilities and weaknesses, they would greatly assist their students in developing healthy personalities, in achieving high levels of school performance, and in developing social interest on which success and happiness in life depend. At the same time, they would make their own profession more rewarding and less difficult. Helping persons redirect their goals and beliefs towards removal of inferiority feeling, and towards increased feelings of belonging is the aim of all Adlerian education.

Try these

(1) Which teacher creates a feeling of inferiority in Mark who has received 75 per cent on a mathematics test?
  A   Mark, I know you can do better than this. You obtained 90 per cent last term.
  B   Mark, I see that you are continuing to work well in mathematics.

( )

(2) Robert does not open his reading book until you have told him two or three times and have threatened punishment. What is his likely life style?
  A   I know I belong when I am the most powerful one.
  B   I know I belong when I am taken care of by others.

( )

(3) Which teacher knows about the purpose of behaviour?
A   Jenny will not clear up after art work; she is so lazy.
B   Jenny is lazy so that she has me to help her clean up her art materials.

( )

(4) What principle is the teacher violating when she confronts a third grade child at recess time: 'Andrew, you know that it is wrong to steal money from other children's lockers'.
A   The basic motivation is to belong.
B   Life style is patterned and unified.
C   Deal with behaviour in the total group.
D   Minimise mistakes and deficiencies.

( )

(5) I recently encountered the following family constellation:
John age 8, Year 3; doing very poorly in school, does not play sport and has few friends; kept in Year 1 for two years.
Jenny age 7, Year 3; doing extremely well in all school subjects; wins 'Little Aths' events and is very popular; is now in John's class. Reminds John of how well she is doing.
Ann age 5, Year 1; very attractive and liked by all. Very passive and doesn't help at home.
Questions:
(a) How does Ann feel that she belongs to the family?
(b) What is Jenny's life style?
(c) What is the major source of discouragement for John?
(d) How effective would a daily withdrawal program in reading and mathematics be for John?

(6) On a recent high school visit, a teacher discussed a difficult student with me. I asked her what she thought was the problem. She replied: 'Single-parent family, you know'. What false assumption has the teacher made regarding human behaviour?

Answers

(1) A
(2) A
(3) B
(4) C

(5) (a) I belong as a long as I can attract.
   (b) I belong as long as I am No.1.
   (c) Jenny and a competitive home environment.
   (d) Useless because it tackles the wrong problem. Before John can begin to improve there must be a change in Jenny's behaviour as she is the major source of his discouragement.

(6) She assumes that behaviour is caused, that students are victims, and that they are not self-determining. It is evident that excellent students and well-behaved students come from both single-parent families and from traditional families.

3

The Goals of Classroom Misbehaviour

INTRODUCTION

Approaches to the management of difficult or disruptive students have typically sought to determine the 'causes' behind the problem. This causalistic–deterministic approach is an obstacle to understanding students because it directs teachers' attention away from seeking effective strategies and locates the behavioural problems in areas which are outside the influence of teachers, such as the effect of sidedness and its confusion, leading to the concepts of dyslexia, cerebral dysfunction and minimal brain damage.

As indicated in Chapter 2, students' behaviour is viewed as purposive. Rather than ask 'Why?', the teacher asks 'For what purpose?': 'The force behind all behaviour is its goal.' When teachers can accept this premise and recognise the purpose of a student's behaviour, they can begin to help students. At present, teachers try to correct deficiencies rather than change goals. As Dreikurs (1971:12) writes:

> What can one really do if a child is lazy, passive–aggressive, daydreaming, irresponsible, hyperactive? These are labels which merely describe what the child does, but not why he is

doing it ... The locked door opens as soon as the teacher realises the mistaken goal, for then he can help him discover better alternatives.

As discussed earlier, students are social beings who need to belong to the classroom. Those who choose to disrupt the class, who violate order, and who refuse to co-operate have chosen faulty ways of belonging. Although the behaviour is inappropriate from a teacher's viewpoint, it reflects the conviction of the student that it is the best and only possible way of behaving in order to gain a sense of belonging. Teachers who understand a student's 'private logic' can facilitate change; teachers who ask a student 'why' he misbehaves, will run into a dead-end and no corrective effort is possible.

Life style, the cognitive map for each individual, provides the behavioural theme for dealing with teachers, parents, peers, and others. The goals which children pursue reflect their life style, their way of viewing themselves, and their relationship to the environment. Although many of these life styles are based on faulty interpretation of early experiences, they are the realities which teachers must understand. A student's behaviour, when studied closely, will always reveal a purpose; without knowledge of this purpose, behaviour will appear illogical and inexplicable. When teachers recognise behaviour as purposeful, new and practical avenues to an understanding of students are opened. A teacher who fails to be aware of a disturbing student's goal will not only fail to counteract it but will actually worsen the situation by his or her reaction.

Although a knowledge of a child's purpose is essential to any corrective approach, most schools of psychology fail to appreciate this view. Some systems of psychology, especially those that view individuals as objects, tend to understand the individual in terms of the past. Students are seen as 'conditioned' by past experience, a deterministic point of view found in the behavioural psychologies. Others adopt a developmental approach which attempts to explain why a child is behaving in a particular way, an explanation which does not assist the teacher by providing means for influencing the behaviour. Equally ineffective is the school of psychology which focuses on how a child feels in relation to a particular experience. The relationship between emotion and purposeful behaviour is overlooked by this school. Another common approach used, particularly in special education, is the attempt to describe or label the child as hyperactive, dyslexic, or disadvantaged.

People are not influenced by what they are or how they developed that way but by what they aim to achieve, their intention or their goal. Of the three influences, the past, the present and the future, only one can be changed. Children cannot change what they are, or how they developed that way, or how they feel about it. However they can all change their goals or purposes because these are in the future not the past. Individuals are not driven through life by the past but impelled to go forward into the future in pursuit of goals which they have subjectively determined. The major influence on behaviour is not the push of the past but the pull of the future. Students have the power to change in any direction for they all move of their own accord.

From a student's point of view, it is quite refreshing and helpful for teachers to talk to them about the purposes of their behaviour. They think: 'Here at last is somebody who understands me'. Children are not aware of the purpose of their actions and are, therefore, unable to change. Dreikurs (1953:50) made this point when he wrote:

> Everyone has very little idea of how his mind works. He does not know that all his actions betray a bias although this may be plain to the onlooker. We are thus brought face to face with a remarkable fact — that it is possible for an individual to have 'unconscious' tendencies, inclinations, and motives.

Problem students would prefer to behave appropriately but do not know how to stop being difficult. They are not aware of their goal. There is never any point in a teacher saying to a student: 'Why do you annoy me so often?'. Children are unaware of their purposes and can change their behaviour only when they become aware of their purposes. For example, a teacher who says to a student: 'John, I am not going to speak to you again about coming late' will find no improvement in the child's punctuality. A teacher who says: 'John, would I be right in thinking the reason why you come late is to keep me busy with you?' will note an improvement

The effects of the family constellation, methods of training, and the family atmosphere created by the parents will interact to provide a set of experiences which will result in a unique life style for each individual.

in punctuality as the late-coming attracts no further attention and the student becomes aware of the purpose of this behaviour. 'Tell me what I am. So what! Tell me how I got that way. So what! Tell me what my purposes are. Ah! There is the possibility of change.' For instance: 'You are a thief'. 'You were taught to steal by your parents.' 'Would I be right in thinking that you steal because you feel people don't like you?'

Teachers make a great mistake when they concentrate on student behaviour rather than on the purpose of student behaviour. When asked what types of problems they experience in classrooms, teachers will indicate a variety of student behaviours such as disobedience, stealing, stubbornness, cheating, clowning, and so on. To concentrate on them is futile. Students who engage in these behaviours are cautioned, rebuked, punished, and advised to mend their ways. By attempting to suppress these behaviours, teachers are responding exactly as the students would want them to respond. The inappropriate ways of behaving will continue because they are effective in achieving their purpose. It is only when teachers are aware of the purpose of such behaviour that they will be in a position to cope with it constructively.

A student who feels that his importance or belonging lies in being the most powerful member of the class will seek to challenge the teacher at every conceivable opportunity. The student will be defiant, disobedient, argumentative, stubborn, and unco-operative. Such a student will not respond to requests to do or stop doing anything. If teachers understood the purpose or the intention behind these forms of behaviour and refused to fight or become involved in the power struggle, there would be little point in the student continuing to behave in these ways. It takes two to fight and a student who cannot involve a teacher in a power contest has lost. Consequently, behaviours such as defiance, stubbornness, and disobedience are likely to change, particularly when a teacher, having declined to be drawn into battle, begins to apply corrective methods. These will be discussed later in this book. All unacceptable behaviour in a classroom is directed towards the teacher; when teachers change their response or reaction to these behaviours, the behaviour of students will change as their goals or purposes are no longer obtained. Whether it changes for the better or for the worse depends on how effective the teacher is in using the encouragement process, in employing other students to assist particular students, and in overcoming the student's feelings of inferiority which lie behind the misbehaviour.

WHAT ARE THE GOALS OF STUDENT MISBEHAVIOUR?

Within the framework of the life style which expressed the long-range goals in life, for example, 'I belong as long as I am in control', there are short-term goals which provide teachers with an understanding of the psychological motivation of students.

All unsatisfactory behaviour in the classroom or school, whether social, intellectual, or emotional, is directed towards one of four possible goals which have been identified by Dreikurs (1968): (i) attracting attention; (ii) demonstrating power; (iii) seeking revenge; (iv) escaping by withdrawal. As these goals are not immediately apparent, teachers fortify and strengthen unacceptable behaviour and mistaken goals by reacting to them. It is impossible to counteract mistaken goals unless teachers are aware of them and have the ability to modify their students' motivation.

The four goals and some examples of the behaviour which reflects the goals are presented in Figure 3. Behaviours which are classified under attention, power, or revenge may be either 'attacking' where a student actively pursues a goal, or they may be 'defending' in which case the student passively achieves the desired result. For example, a student whose goal is power may carry out forbidden acts or refuse to do what he is told; the former attacks in the pursuit of power while the latter defends. The goal of withdrawal is limited to 'defending' behaviours.

ATTENTION SEEKING

Attention seeking is by far the most common form of misbehaviour, particularly with primary school children. As used in this book, 'misbehaviour' refers to departure from commonly accepted standards for classroom behaviour in the social, intellectual, and emotional areas. It is in fact a violation of order and a refusal to co-operate.

Attention seeking would account for the majority of problem behaviour in any primary school and, while not as serious as the other three goals, it involves teachers in an inordinate amount of time. In a recent visit to a Year 6

Types of classroom behaviour		
Student's goal	Attacking behaviour	Defending behaviour
Attention seeking	The clown The nuisance The smart alec The show off Obtrusive Instability Walking question mark Unpredictable Bright sayings	Lazy Anxious Speech problems Bashful or shy Untidy Self-indulgent Excessively pleasant Frivolous Lack of stamina and fearfulness
Power	Argues Rebels Defiant Contradicts Bully Temper tantrums Untruthful Disobedient (carries out forbidden acts)	Unco-operative Dawdles Stubborn Disobedient (won't do what he's told) Forgetful
Revenge	Stealing Vicious Destructive Cruel Delinquent behaviour Violent Bullying	Sullen Moody Morose Passive hatred Refuses to participate Negativism
Escape by withdrawal		Stupid Idle Incapable 'Hopeless' Juvenile ways Won't mix Fantasy activities Solitary activities

Figure 3 Classification of behaviours with undesirable goals

classroom, the author observed that in a 30-minute period, 16 of the 20 students were able to involve the teacher unnecessarily in a wide range of minor attention-getting behaviours. While the range of attention-seeking behaviours is remarkably wide, as seen by the examples presented in Figure 4, the response of teachers to these behaviours is uniform, predictable, and ineffective.

Student's goal: Attention seeking			
Attacking behaviour		Defending behaviour	
Student's strategy	How teacher feels and reacts	Student's strategy	How teacher feels and reacts

Is a nuisance
The show off
The clown
The smart alec
Walking
  question mark
Mischief maker
Pushing,
  obtrusive
Late-comer
Instability
Embarrassing
  behaviour
Pencil tapper
The talker
	Annoyed and
	  irritated
	'For goodness
	  sake, stop it'
	Feeling of relief
	  when the
	  annoying
	  behaviour
	  ceases
		Lazy
		Wants help
		Bashful, shy
		Fearful
		Too tired
		Untidiness
		Self-indulgent
		Vain
		Cute
		Speech
		  impediment
		Anxious
		Frivolous
			'I must do
			  something'
			Sense of
			  responsibility
			Urges or coaxes
			  into action
			Feeling of
			  encouragement
			  when student
			  responds

Figure 4 Types of behaviour classified as attention seeking and teacher's feelings and reactions to them

Attention seeking: Attacking behaviour

One form of attention-seeking behaviour is that in which a student actively provokes or annoys a teacher in a way that cannot be ignored. While these behaviours may irritate teachers, they are very effective in achieving their purpose. Just think of the number of times teachers have to rebuke, admonish, caution, prevent, remind, correct, or punish students and you will realise how clever children are in achieving their purpose. Strangely, teachers are seldom aware of the game being played by students and fail to see that all of the annoying and irritating behaviour of students is for the teacher's benefit. In summary, many students misbehave in order to gain the teacher's attention and whatever the teacher feels like doing is exactly what the child wants the teacher to do.

Stand back and observe how skilfully students are able to involve and control teachers almost all day long. When teachers consider the purpose behind attacking behaviours, they will find that they are the unwitting target of children's mistaken belief that they belong only as long as teachers are prepared to pay attention to them. They act in such a way as to say: 'Stop whatever you are doing and pay attention to me. I am nothing unless I can keep you involved with me'.

A teacher began a chalkboard demonstration on the method of calculating the area of a triangle. John came in late during the demonstration and was rebuked. He sat down very noisily and dropped his books to the floor, actions which prompted further admonitions. John found it necessary in the next ten minutes to tap loudly with his foot, hum a small tune, talk to his neighbour and ask two irrelevant questions. The teacher finally became exasperated and ordered John from the room. As he left, John knocked a chair over and slammed the door, each time giving the teacher a cheeky look.

Such scenes are not uncommon in classrooms as attention-seeking behaviour of students continues to prove successful. Teachers who are not aware of the purpose of the child's behaviour will concentrate on eliminating the undesirable or unwanted behaviour through the use of punishment. Their intervention is exactly what the children want and the behaviours will persist because they achieve their purpose of attracting attention. What attention-seeking children dread is to be ignored. But are they ever ignored?

Attention seeking: Defending behaviour

While some students actively disturb for the purpose of gaining attention, there are others who achieve a similar purpose by remaining passive, by involving the teacher unnecessarily, or by pleasantly defending against the demands of the classroom. These students achieve a sense of belonging by inducing the teachers to give them special service.

If teachers were asked to list those behaviours which worry them most in their students, those belonging to the defending attention-seeking category would appear infrequently. These children do not disturb the classroom nor do they make a teacher's task more difficult. In fact, children who are cute, vain, charming, or excessively pleasant and polite are frequently admired and approved by teachers. Likewise the model child, the extremely conscientious student, the frequent questioner, and the especially good reliable, industrious, and co-operative students are very much in favour with teachers.

In assessing whether behaviour should be regarded as being of a problem nature, the criterion used is self-centredness or self-enhancement. No one else benefits from the behaviour of the maladjusted individual whose triumphs have only a personal meaning. Self-centredness is not the normal condition of humans but is a sign of maladjustment. Children will seek to find their place in the class through co-operation and useful contribution but, when discouraged, begin to think that they cannot succeed through co-operative activity. Consequently they engage in a variety of compensatory behaviours in their attempt to gain a sense of belonging and importance. They now strive for goals which have purely a personal, private, or self-centred advantage. No longer is the child interested in co-operating with others in meeting the demands of the new situation, but only in moving ahead of other children, in self-enhancement and self-elevation. Most misbehaviour in classrooms reflects students' mistaken beliefs that these behaviours will place them above other children, will gain them special significance, and will afford them particular recognition. Discouragement has created such a deep sense of inferiority and one cannot develop a feeling of belonging or a willingness to co-operate if one feels inferior to others.

Consider the model child in this light. A teacher asks the Year 1 children to take a sheet of paper and rule a line in red, 15 centimetres from the top and 10 centimetres from the bottom. What does the model child do? Exactly what is requested. The other children will complete the task with considerable errors in their measurements. How does the teacher feel about the model pupil? 'Why can't the rest of you do it as well as Sandra?' This is Sandra's moment of glory. Who benefits from her behaviour? She does. Why is she so perfect? Because she wants to be better than all of the other children. Her goal is clearly self-elevation. What would happen if the teacher did not commend Sandra for her excellent work? She would cease to be a model child and would turn to more disturbing ways of gaining attention. If Sandra were co-operating because she wanted to co-operate, the withdrawal of praise or special recognition would have no effect on her behaviour. While the model child is not a problem to the teacher, time will prove to be the enemy of such children who must later enter more competitive fields where they cannot shine or excel. In these situations model children simply give up because they cannot be the best.

To differentiate between behaviour which has attention seeking as its goal from behaviour which stems from a genuine desire to contribute and co-operate, a teacher should ask the question: 'Would this behaviour continue if I were to ignore it?'. Attention-seeking behaviour will cease because it no longer works. A child who is cute, charming, especially industrious, or excessively pleasant or conscientious will cease these behaviours if teachers fail to respond to them and may become annoying, fretful, and anxious when special recognition is withdrawn. The fact that these children are completely dependent on others and doubt their ability to contribute co-operatively to the class goes unnoticed. They defend against the reality of inadequacy by invoking others into their service. 'Only if I gain attention am I of value.' Would children be so cute if they did not receive special recognition? Would excessive diligence persist if it was not recognised by the teacher? Children who engage in defending behaviour are more discouraged than those who engage in attacking behaviour but, unfortunately, many of them will remain discouraged because nobody bothers to redirect them. They are just too pleasant, too good, and too conforming. Given constant approval, praise, and reassurance, they will remain that way. Their lack of social interest and willingness to co-operate become apparent only under circumstances where their behaviours do not achieve the intended outcome.

There are some types of defending behaviours which are more annoying to teachers. Laziness, fearfulness, untidiness, frivolity, instability, learning deficiencies, anxiety, or tearfulness are irritating behaviours yet they invariably have the effect of having teachers render undue service to children. A child who will not complete assignments, fails to put materials away, refuses to stay on task, is always slow in starting work or leaving the class, consistently learns poorly or leaves things at home, makes a heavy and unfair demand on a teachers' time and energy. Children are slow, lazy, or careless for the purpose of winning special service and the teacher's response to these behaviours has the effect of strengthening them. By identifying the purpose of these behaviours and refusing to respond to them, teachers can begin to assist students to develop more adequate and co-operative methods of coping with their problems while, at the same time, freeing themselves of the constant and unreasonable demands which students make upon teachers.

Teachers aim to develop responsibility in children. No other objective would have such universal support. Yet, by involving themselves in areas which are the students' responsibility, teachers act to teach children to be irresponsible. For instance, lateness often goes without a consequence and teachers explain the work missed to the student. Life consists of choices, decisions, and consequences; if teachers llow students to choose their behaviours but ensure that they experience the consequences of their decisions, students will begin to behave responsibily.

Before leaving the topic of attention-seeking behaviour, check to see that you are able to classify the following types of misbehaviour and that you can recognise the nature of attention seeking in a classroom situation.

Try these

(1) Match the form of attention seeking with the classroom behaviour.

Form of attention seeking   *Classroom behaviour*

A Attacking behaviour
1. John asks a string of questions and rarely waits for an answer before asking the next question.

B Defending behaviour
2. Janet never seems to know what is expected of her and rarely finishes her work.

3. Much to the delight of his peers, Tim pulls faces, contorts his mouth, and crosses his eyes.

4. When asked a question, Margaret colours slightly, drops her eyes, and fails to respond.

(2) The second-grade teacher was correcting her students' spelling tests. Sally, who was painting at the easel, came to the teacher and asked how to make purple. The teacher told her and pointed out the two colours which should be mixed. 'I want you to help me', said Sally.

'In a little while', said the teacher, 'I want to finish correcting the tests'. Sally went slowly back to her painting but was back again in a few minutes and said, 'I don't think that I know how to mix the colours. Will you show me?' 'Not yet Sally, I am too busy', said the teacher absently. Silence for a few minutes. 'Can I paint something else now?' 'Yes', said the teacher. 'But I don't know what to paint', said Sally. 'You think of something', said the teacher. Sally made a few half-hearted attempts before the teacher came over and suggested they paint a horse. Sally began to paint the outline, which the teacher had drawn. Presently she was back at the teacher's desk with a complaint about the paint being too thick. The teacher again helped her. After a short time, Sally came up to the teacher and said, 'I like painting'. The teacher put her work down and told Sally how well she was painting.

1. What was the goal of Sally's behaviour?
2. What is Sally saying through her behaviour?
3. How do you distinguish between a genuine request for assistance and attention-seeking behaviour?

Answers

(1) 1 A; 2 B; 3 A; 4 B
(2) 1. Attention seeking.
   2. 'I am nothing unless I can keep you involved with me. I belong only by receiving special service.'
   3. Sally is unreasonable in her request. She knows that the teacher should be left alone for a short time to finish her corrections but that is the time she makes her heaviest demands for attention. Genuine requests for assistance are made less frequently and at more appropriate times.

POWER

Many problems of discipline in schools are related to the goal of power. The struggle for power has grown out of all proportion and teachers are being drawn into conflicts with their pupils from which they cannot escape. Many classrooms are full of acts of retaliation as teachers strive to maintain their traditional dominance or authority over students who, in turn, refuse to be dominated or suppressed. Certainly the most common purpose of those behaviours of adolescents which are disturbing for teachers have as their goal the demonstration of power. A state of open conflict exists in some schools as both teachers and students are locked into battle, each intent on achieving a victory over the other. The need to understand behaviour which has power as its goal has never been greater. There is, as Dreikurs (1968:5) pointed out, 'a war on in our schools'.

Student's goal: Power

Attacking behaviour		Defending behaviour	
Student's strategy	How teacher feels and reacts	Student's strategy	How teacher feels and reacts
Rebelliousness Argues Defiance Plays truant Contradicts Disobeys (carries out forbidden acts) Temper tantrums Bullies Bosses	Feels threatened Feels angry Feels authority is being challenged Wants to get on top 'If you think I'm going to stand for this, you're mistaken' 'I'll teach you to defy me' 'You won't get away with this' Feels victorious when behaviour is quelled	Stubborness Unco- operativeness Forgetfulness Disobedience (refuses to do what he is told) Frequent sickness Weaknesses Apathy	Feels exasperated Feels irritated Feels challenged Feels frustrated 'You won't get out of it this way' 'You'll fall into line or else' Feels victorious when student falls into line

Figure 5   Types of behaviour classified as power and teacher's feelings and reactions to them

Behaviours which demonstrate power are disobedience, stubbornness, dawdling, temper tantrums, defiance, apathy, and argumentativeness. As with attention seeking, power-goal behaviours may be either attacking or defending. Examples of the behaviours, together with a teacher's typical reaction or feeling about them, are presented in Figure 5.

Consider a student who refuses to begin or complete work, forgets to bring books to class, will not clean up after science practical work or home economics, contradicts and continues with acts which are forbidden by the teacher or the school. What the student is saying through his behaviour is: 'I can prove my importance by refusing to do what you want' (defending) or 'I can prove my importance by doing whatever I like' (attacking). Children who hold a life style in which they feel they belong only by being the most powerful are obliged to challenge others, to prove that nobody can make them do anything or stop them from doing what they like. Whether they do this through attacking behaviour (You cannot stop me) or through defending behaviour (You cannot make me) students are generally able to involve teachers in a contest and, regardless of the outcome, subsequently strengthen their mistaken belief that power is important.

Students who engage in power struggles upset teachers because the latter feel that their authority is being threatened and challenged. In the traditional authoritarian classroom, teachers were absolute decision-makers who had the right to tell students exactly what to do and how to do it. That dominance has gone today and teachers who attempt to impose their will on students will find increasing resistance and even outright rebellion. It is the authoritarian demand of teachers which many students are fighting today in our schools. When a teacher demands: 'You will speak only when I have given you permission to speak', it is inevitable that some students will accept this challenge and respond, 'I will speak whenever I want to speak'. Tell students what they must do and invariably some will be obliged to do the opposite.

Without realising it, many teachers have become more interested in maintaining control than in educating their students. They may rationalise their demands that students sit quietly, complete homework, arrive on time, submit work, wear uniforms and the like on the grounds that they know what is best for the students. In reality, many are simply attempting to dominate their students with the unspoken demand: 'You will do what I tell you to do'. It is this dominance which many youngsters are fighting today. It is the same dominance which produced such violent reactions from labour, blacks, women, and students over the past decade.

Consider this typical classroom situation. A teacher has completed a short discussion with a class and sets the students a task to be completed. He announces, 'Now you all know what to do. I want nobody out of their seats until the work is finished. Now start'. Within two minutes, a student from the back stands up, wanders down to the front of the room looking for a bin in which to deposit a piece of paper, giving the teacher a sideways glance every now and then. 'Didn't you hear what I just said?' explodes the teacher. The child gives a slight nod and continues with his search for the bin. This is the attacking-power child who says through his behaviour: 'I can prove my importance by refusing to do what you want'. Seeing his authority threatened, the teacher enters the power contest, a contest which he cannot win. What is he to do now? How can he extricate himself from the struggle without loss of dignity or face?

Regardless of the outcome of a power contest, a student has won whenever teachers allow themselves to be drawn into battle. Power is important only when it is contested and a student who is unable to involve a teacher in a struggle has lost. It takes two to fight; there can be no victor in an empty field. For example, a teacher may ask several children to read a verse of their own creation. Jane reads first and Tim follows but when Michael's turn comes, he bluntly says: 'No'. Recognising the purpose of the behaviour, a wise teacher might say: 'If Michael doesn't feel like reading perhaps Sandra will'. Teachers cannot make students read and their attempt to do so would invite a power contest. What can you do if you enter the fight and demand that Michael reads? He still refuses and is now given the choice of reading or leaving the room? He accepts neither. Now what can the teacher do? Drag him out? The point is this. Whenever teachers find themselves being caught up in a power contest or feel that their authority is being threatened, they should refuse to become involved, remain friendly, or leave the scene of the conflict. By doing so, they defuse the situation and, in a sense, win because the student was not able to involve them in a power struggle.

If teachers enter a contest and make a student conform to their demands, what have they taught the child? Those who have the power win, and next time the student will be more skilful in how he uses power. The child's mistaken belief about the importance of power is confirmed and victory for him is only a matter of time. His faulty life style, 'I belong only if I am the most powerful', will be strengthened and behaviours such as disobedience, hostility, and stubbornness will increase in frequency and intensity.

The use of power by many students has become widespread in recent years. Conflict which has always existed in the past is now plainly visible as the authority or dominance of teachers over students has lessened with the advent of more democratic relationships. It is an interesting observation that the matters over which teachers and students fight are never the real issues. For example, students may provoke teachers into power contests through failure to return books to the library, lateness, speaking rudely, lying, not completing their work, or arguing. These are the issues which provoke teachers who will generally emphasise the importance of homework, the lack of consideration when library books are not returned, the courtesy involved in punctuality, forms of address, and the like. These are not the real issues. The game which students are playing is this: 'Who wins and who loses'. They are not concerned about the virtues of completing homework, returning books, speaking acceptably, and so on. Students enter these fields in order to win and win they will until teachers recognise the purpose of such behaviours and refuse to fight with students over them.

Consider the following incident which occurred in a large high school earlier this year. A group of Year 12 students approached the principal on the first day of the school year and said: 'Here, sir, is a list of teachers whom we are prepared to be taught by this year'. This is an obvious display of power. The students, however, did not reckon with a very wise principal who replied: 'Thank you, boys. Leave the list and call back tomorrow and I will give you a list of students whom we will be prepared to teach'. The students said nothing, took their list, and left quietly. The principal recognised that the real issue was power, refused to fight, and defused the issue. A less enlightened principal would have taken exception to the students' demand and entered a contest which could not be won. And so it is with students who argue every point, contradict frequently, and continue to flout school rules. The student who argues consistently is really not interested in arriving at the truth; he wants to involve the teacher in argument and see who wins or who loses. Rational explanation by the teacher misses the point as the purpose of the student is to force the teacher to become impatient, to lose his temper, or to admit defeat. We cannot overpower power-drunk students and it is better to disengage from them at the beginning of a conflict rather than attempt to defeat them.

Many teachers complain today that their students are apathetic. This is particularly so in secondary schools. 'They just don't care.' 'They are not motivated.' 'They have no interest in school work.' 'You just can't make them do anything.' Teachers must recognise that the goal of apathy is passive power, a subtle form of resistance by which students say to teachers: 'I will do just so much for you and no more. If you want to make me do more, have a try'. Teachers cannot resist this challenge because they have a strong sense of responsibility. Teachers must recognise that apathetic students are fully motivated to defeat teachers and not fall into the trap set. Students who resort to apathy feel that they have no real influence on their school or their classes. 'This is your school not ours' is the message they convey to teachers. Consequently, they refuse to contribute fully and will do just so much to get by. If teachers refused to engage the apathetic student in a display of power and involved them in meaningful decision making, their apathy would not be the concern which it is today.

If teachers are to assist students, they must stop fighting with them. One of the most important lessons which a teacher must learn is to side-step the struggle for power. Whenever they feel personally challenged, frustrated by a student's behaviour, or provoked by a particular incident, they must refuse to become involved and withdraw from the situation. Do not be drawn into a power contest but look for methods of dealing with the incident which take into account the needs of the situation rather than your own personal desire. Teachers should not hesitate to admit to students that they cannot make them do anything. That is the truth of the situation and it is very disarming for power-conscious students to be told that nobody can make them do anything. Their primary motivating factor is to seek personal victories, to put teachers down, and to control others. Suddenly there are no opponents. Take the sail out of their wind. Teachers can invite co-operation, establish equality, state what they intend to do, and look to encourage the problem student. However, in the final analysis, it is only the individual who can decide what he or she will or will not do.

Try these

Match the behaviour with the form of power goal.

Form of power goal	Behaviour
A Attacking behaviour	1. 'I wish you would stop contradicting everything I say.'
B Defending behaviour	2. 'I am not going to tell you again. Open that book and begin your work.'
	3. 'If you continue to fight with other students, it will be a trip to the principal's office.'
	4. 'That is the third time this term you have left your books at home.'

Answers

1 A; 2 B; 3 A; 4 B

REVENGE

Some children who feel that they are unfairly treated by teachers and schools will pursue a goal to get even, to seek revenge against teachers, students, schools, and society itself. These children may engage in attacking behaviours such as stealing, violence, brutality, destruction, cruelty, and various forms of delinquency. Or, passively, students may exhibit defending behaviours such as being sullen, morose, or moody or exhibit attitudes which you interpret as indicating violence and hatred. The range of behaviours characterising revenge together with teacher's feelings and reactions to them are presented in Figure 6.

Dreikurs (1968:29) writes of the child whose goal is revenge:

> The mutual antagonism may become so strong that each party has only one desire: retaliation, to revenge his own feeling of being hurt. The child no longer hopes merely for attention or even power; feeling ostracised and disliked, he can see his place in the group only by his success in making himself hated.

Student's goal: Revenge			
Attacking behaviour		*Defending behaviour*	
Student's strategy	How teacher feels and reacts	Student's strategy	How teacher feels and reacts
Viciousness 'Tough guy' Cruelty Brutality Stealing Destruction Vandalism	Feels badly upset Feels deeply hurt Feels measure of trepidation 'What will he do next?' 'What have I done to deserve this?' 'How could he do this to me?' 'What an ungrateful person!' 'Must be punished' Feeling of immense relief and hope at any sign of improvement	Sullenness Moodiness Moroseness Refuses to participate	Feeling of injustice Feels that child is ungrateful 'Well, two can play this game' 'This won't get you anywhere' 'It's not my job to placate or appease you' 'You can make the first move' Feeling of self-justification if child displays acceptable behaviour

Figure 6 Types of behaviour classified as revenge and teacher's feelings and reactions to them

Students who have revenge as their goal are so discouraged that they have given up hope of belonging through constructive and co-operative activities, have been unsuccessful in gaining attention or in demonstrating power, and now feel that the only way of attaining a social position is by being disliked. Not only do they seek to dominate but they seek vengeance in the process. They provoke hostility in order to be recognised. In schools, they will steal from lockers, damage library books, set upon younger children, physically attack others, engage in illicit sexual activity, take drugs, remain sullen, moody, or morose, and destroy property. In the community, these individuals will vandalise trains, physically assault people, burn down schools, send threatening letters, make threatening phone calls, light bush-fires, steal cars, and destroy property. In doing so, they gain some satisfaction in getting even with those people and that society which deny them a place. They see themselves

Revenge

These children may engage in attacking behaviours such as stealing, violence, brutality, destruction, cruelty, and various forms of delinquency.

as worthless, unfairly treated, pushed around, and disliked; consequently they behave accordingly.

Indeed, they attempt little else but revengeful behaviours and generate in others considerable resentfulness, hostility, dislike, hurt, and a desire to punish.

The principal objective in helping students whose goal is revenge is to convince them that they can be liked and accepted by the other students in their class. Yet everything they do tends to influence others to dislike them more. They are destructive, cruel, violent, and threatening; they know how to hurt and do it often. When their offences are detected, they are punished and told what despicable people they are. A student who badly beats a smaller child will be punished and told what a horrible person he is; an adolescent who tears the pages out of the library books will be punished and rebuked for his loutish behaviour; a child who steals money from lockers will be punished and reminded of his moral violation. All of these corrective measures are ineffective. The effect of punishment is to invite the student to retaliate and to seek further revenge. The result of being told that one is vicious, contemptible, worthless, and the like is to confirm the faulty self-image which the student already holds about himself and to increase the likelihood that revengeful behaviour will continue. The circle is now complete, a self-fulfilling prophesy. We communicate to children that they are disliked, unacceptable, and rejected and they behave logically; they seek to get even by hurting others as they themselves have been hurt. These children are fighting with society, with schools, and with the members of both.

Students whose goal is revenge are the most disturbing group for teachers to manage. Many schools now choose not to assist these individuals but rather expel or exclude them from school for acts of vandalism, defiance, or delinquency. Society is given the rather unenviable task of attempting to rehabilitate these young people whose only goal is to hurt and to get even with that society which they see as denying them a place. Teachers must recognise the purpose of revengeful behaviour, sense the deep discouragement, futility, and sense of worthlessness which characterise these individuals, and realise that it is always the inability of young people to gain a sense of achievement and self-worth in our schools which is the major contributor to resultant vicious and violent behaviour.

Many school programs must stand condemned when we consider that many adolescents find their only significance in behaviours which are unacceptable to society. Their membership of peer groups which offer exciting activities involving alcohol, sex, fast cars, drugs, and vandalism is more satisfying than school membership and activities. This situation is aggravated today by the many thousands of unemployed youths who feel that they are not wanted by schools, by society, by the economy, or by their homes. They are frequently abused in the media and referred to as 'dole bludgers'. As a result, they strike out and seek revenge against a community and its members who deny them a place. The riots in 1990 in the western suburbs of Sydney provide an example of such behaviour. We as teachers must look for ways of providing successful, meaningful, and rewarding school experiences which counter the students' utter lack of faith in their own ability and their resultant negative self-concept and sense of worthlessness.

We should recognise that 'anything is possible' in dealing with difficult students. The position taken is that students are responsible for their own behaviour and are not the victims of heredity, emotions, upbringing, schooling or environment. They are self-responsible, self-determining and can improve their situation at any time by making better decisions about their lives. To the question of: 'Could this student behave well if his or her life depended on it'?, the answer is clearly 'Yes'. To take the pessimistic view that certain students are 'victims' is to render teachers powerless to influence them.

Try these

(1) I recently spoke to a group of youth leaders. One leader who was a policeman cited a youth who had been convicted 15 times for car stealing. 'What he needs are stiffer penalties', he maintained. Do you think that stiffer penalties would have the desired effect? Why do you think the youth continues to steal cars?

(2) A student in Year 7 at school steals money from the

lockers. His form teacher has spoken to him about it and he has had two visits to the principal's office. He has now been referred to the psychologists at the special services division. Why do you think the child steals? What error is being made in his treatment?

(3) Students who vandalise school property, terrorise younger pupils, and steal others' possessions are punished and told what worthless people they are. What is the likely effect of such treatment?

Answers to (1), (2), (3)

Children who engage in revengeful behaviour feel unfairly treated and they seek to get even with those whom they blame for their difficulty. They want to hurt as they themselves have been hurt. They see themselves as disliked, unacceptable, and ostracised.

Punishment has the effect of inviting retaliation by them and of confirming their belief that they are bad and unacceptable. Calling them names such as 'louts', 'contemptible', and 'vicious' has the same negative effect of confirming their faulty view of themselves.

Revenge must be dealt with in the group situation where members of the group who are being hurt by the revengeful child must attempt to convince the individual that he is acceptable to the group. If a child begins to believe that his assessment of others is wrong, that others do not dislike him, then there is no point in continuing to get even with them.

ESCAPE BY WITHDRAWAL

The fourth classification of behaviour having an undesirable goal is that in which students seek to withdraw in order to safeguard prestige by an assumed or real deficiency.

These behaviours are characterised by a lack of activity, by a submissive or inert attitude, and can be identified by a feeling of hopelessness by a teacher. Collectively the behaviours are classified as 'escape by withdrawal' and their range, together with a teacher's feelings and reactions to them, are presented in Figure 7. Unlike the other three goals — attention, power, and revenge — there can be no attacking

Student's goal: Escape by withdrawal	
Defending behaviour	
Student's strategy	How teacher feels and reacts
Stupidity	Feeling of inferiority
Idleness	Feeling of helplessness
Indolence	Feeling of despair
Incapability	'I just don't know what more I can do.'
Inferiority	'I am at my wits' end.'
Won't mix	'I give up.'
Solitary activities	'What can I do with her?'
Fantasy activities	Instances of improved behaviour are seized
Babyish ways	upon hopefully. (Perhaps he's a late
'Hopelessness'	developer.)
'Helplessness'	Expects nothing of students

Figure 7 Types of behaviour classified as escape by withdrawal and teacher's feelings and reactions to them

forms of this goal as the students' purpose is to be left alone and have nothing asked or expected of them.

Students who are deeply discouraged no longer hope for any success or recognition in school and cease to make any effort. They appear stupid and inept and generally withdraw from all activity. Their sole purpose is to avoid any further hurt, humiliation, or frustration and this is achieved by impressing teachers with their stupidity, their hopelessness, or their incompetence. These students seek excuses, hide behind displays of inadequacy, and impress teachers with their lack of ability so that their real or imagined deficiency will not be so obvious. What they say through their inadequacy is: 'For goodness' sake leave me alone and don't ask me to do anything else or you will see how stupid I really am'. A teacher who, after observing that no improvement has taken place in a student's reading despite an intense effort by the teachers, throws her hands in the air and declares, 'John, you are hopeless', has been a target of a child's escape by withdrawal behaviour.

The worst effect which withdrawal by students has on teachers is to discourage them also. Discouraged students know how to discourage others and the reciprocal discouragement which results ensures that neither teachers nor students are able to break the self-fulfilling prophecy of negative expectation.

... When asked by the teacher 8×6 he fails to respond and puts on an expression which says : 'I cannot do mathematics.'

Withdrawal behaviours are usually very effective. There are many pupils for whom teachers hold very low expectations. These pupils impress teachers with their apparent low levels of ability and, from then on, little is expected of them. Once a child has convinced the mathematics teacher that he or she is hopeless in that subject, what is going to be expected of that child? As nothing will be expected, nothing will be demanded. The unsoundness of this negative expectation has been adequately discussed by Bloom (1976) who has demonstrated clearly 'what any child can learn all can learn'. If we identify a child's source of discouragement and remove it, the child will learn. However, if we accept the invalid assumption that children differ in learning capacity, we deny successful learning experiences to many thousands of students. Teachers should approach their classes with the expectation that all children are going to learn the curricular objectives which have been predetermined. The evidence supporting children's ability to do so, when provided with optimal learning conditions, continues to accumulate while contrary evidence is rare. The techniques of achieving mastery learning by all students are discussed in Chapter 8.

Withdrawal behaviour may be complete or partial. It is more common for a student to display partial withdrawal in certain subjects though functioning well in others. For instance, a student may do very well in English, mathematics, reading, and science yet perform poorly in art and music. Most teachers would conclude that the student has little interest or ability in these subjects and, in view of the high performance in the other subjects, will excuse the poor attainment in music and art. In fact, the child's poor performance is not a consequence of limited ability or lack of interest but reflects a wrong interpretation of early experiences and a resultant belief that there is no personal gain to be achieved in these subjects. A child whose life style is that she must be the best will not participate in musical activities if she observes that there are other children in the class who, as a result of private tutoring, are already more competent in music. Whenever the teacher announces that the class will have a music period, this particular child will show no interest in participating because she knows she cannot be the best. The interpretation of lack of interest, while understandable, is faulty. The student will only be interested and participate when she can be the best. Over-ambition often results in children giving up in despair.

You have seen an animal use a 'play dead' reflex; touch a spider and it will curl up as though dead. Children have a similar reflex which may be referred to as a 'play stupid' reflex. Whenever they are asked to do something which they feel is too difficult for them and which might make them look foolish, they put on their play stupid reflex which excuses their inability to cope. A child keeps the scores very accurately when taken to a football match and can quickly convert 8 goals 11 behinds into 59 points. However, when asked by the teacher, '8 times 6', he fails to respond and puts on an expression which says: 'I cannot do mathematics'. By playing stupid, the child lowers the teachers' expectation of him and escapes responsibility for making progress in mathematics. Of course, playing stupid is not confined to children. What would you do if your car broke down this evening? Try to fix it or put on a display of inadequacy?

Refuse to accept children's displays of inability or inadequacy. Teachers scold, criticise, and humiliate such children but unwittingly fall for their means of evasion and, in the end, relieve the children of their responsibility. Criticism and ridicule contribute to the problem as they heighten children's negative evaluation of themselves. Students who despair of success, either wholly or partially, are discouraged children who have lost faith in their ability; they need encouragement and a display of confidence and faith in their ability, a recognition of their efforts, and acknowledgement of their achievement rather than constant reminders of their general inadequacy. All children can learn and learn well. When children are not learning, determine the sources of their discouragement, remove them, and the children will begin to make progress. 'Withdrawal' children are discouraged, not stupid. They have been told so often that they are hopeless that they have come to believe it and act accordingly. They need positive reassurance by teachers of their worth and ability so that they can begin to function usefully, constructively, and co-operatively.

Try these

(1) Match the student's goal with the student's feeling.

Student's goal	Student's feeling	
A Attention seeking	1. 'That will teach you a lesson.'	( )
B Power	2. 'It's no use. I just can't do maths.'	( )

C   Revenge   3. 'You can't make me do
                        anything.'   ( )
D   Escape by   4. 'I matter only if I can keep you
    withdrawal   busy with me.'   ( )

(2) Which goal?
   A   Attention   1. Clown   ( )   6. Thief   ( )
       seeking
   B   Power   2. Bully   ( )   7. Charmer ( )
   C   Revenge   3. Lazy   ( )   8. Disobedient
                                                        ( )
   D   Escape by   4. Morose   ( )   9. Stupid   ( )
       withdrawal
                    5. Model   ( ) 10. Vandal   ( )

(3) Attacking or defending?
   A   Attacking   1. Bullying
       behaviour
   B   Defending   2. Argumentative
       behaviour   3. Clinging vine
                    4. Show off
                    5. Anxious
                    6. Cruel

(4) Decide which goal the following students are pursuing.
   A   Attention seeking
   B   Power
   C   Revenge
   D   Escape by withdrawal
   1. Jane, a first grade pupil, has not completed a single
      worksheet in three weeks. When you urge her to make
      progress, she looks blank and does nothing.
   2. You are supervising a Year 6 mathematics test. David
      is copying answers from John's paper. You catch his
      eye but he continues to copy.
   3. Alan, a Year 11 student, initiated a fight with a much
      smaller Year 8 student. He soundly beat the other
      child and was quite aggressive when punished by the
      principal.

4. Two boys are talking in the back of the room during a film. You call their names, they stop but continue after several minutes.

Answers

(1) C 1; D 2; B 3; A 4
(2) 1 A; 2 B; 3 A; 4 C; 5 A; 6 C; 7 A; 8 B; 9 D; 10 C
(3) 1 A; 2 A; 3 B; 4 A; 5 B; 6 A
(4) 1 D; 2 B; 3 C; 4 A

4

How Teachers Can Identify the Goals of Student Misbehaviour

INTRODUCTION

All teachers can acquire the knowledge and sensitivity to understand the behaviour of students. Without such an understanding, teachers cannot take effective action. Would you believe? The behaviour of students is their answer to your behaviour. What teachers do about misbehaviour, is what keeps students misbehaving. Therefore, inadequate forms of classroom behaviour will persist because of the teachers' highly detrimental role in evoking and maintaining such behaviours.

All misbehaviour reflects children's decisions about how they can most effectively belong to the group. Students who are confident in their ability to find a place — to belong through constructive activity — will tend not to be a problem. Such individuals have developed feelings of equality and worth and are interested in co-operating with others and in participating usefully within the group. They face each school demand, be it intellectual, social, physical, or emotional, with confidence in their ability to cope with the demand. There is no need for them to misbehave because they know that they can function constructively and co-operatively in the class.

In contrast, there are discouraged children who feel that they cannot cope with the various school demands and decide to adopt unacceptable ways of behaving which they believe will gain them status and a sense of group belonging. Even the most vicious student or the most hopeless student can still be the 'best' in those particular areas. The sources of discouragement are varied and include methods of training (spoiling, overprotection, indulgence, or rejection), fault finding, comparisons with other children, overambitious or perfectionistic parents or teachers, ordinal position, conditional acceptance, grading practices, and the use of rewards and punishments. As a result, many students are deprived of an opportunity to experience their own strengths and abilities and are presented with a whole sequence of discouraging experiences. As belonging is the basic motivation for all individuals, problem students believe that by adopting unacceptable ways of behaving they will gain a place within the group and salvage a sense of importance and respect.

The previous chapter classified the range of unacceptable classroom behaviours:

1. Attention seeking: 'I want special recognition and service.'
2. Power: 'You must do what I want.'
3. Revenge: 'I will get even.'
4. Escape by withdrawal: 'I am hopeless; leave me alone.'

The extent to which these goals are sought and successfully achieved in a typical classroom is quite staggering. Students know exactly how to act in order to provoke a reaction from each particular teacher. Almost every classroom situation is seized upon by the various goal-seekers in pursuit of the above goals. A teacher, for example, might ask students to summarise a chapter on rainfall and allocate 15 minutes for the task. The attention seekers will not begin until they receive special service in the form of additional explanations or they may begin very quickly and complete the task in a manner which will evoke a favourable comparison by the teacher. The power-directed individuals will not begin the task despite several reminders from the teacher, because they are seeking to demonstrate that nobody can make them do anything; or they may spend a few minutes on the task in a gesture of passive power. The withdrawal child will judge the task as being too difficult and unemotionally accept the teacher's offer of assistance, rebuke, detention, or display of despair.

It is important to note that the same behaviour may have quite different goals. For example, a Year 1 teacher may ask the children to form a circle for the purpose of playing a game. One particular girl makes no attempt to join the group but stands some distance from it. What is her goal? If the teacher goes over to her, takes her hand which is willingly offered, and leads the girl to join the others, the goal is attention. She wanted to put the teacher into her service and receive special recognition. If the child's goal was power, her hand would not be offered and she would refuse to accompany the teacher. Revenge would result in a more violent form of reaction by the child such as a sharp kick to the teacher's ankle or a display of violent passivity. A student who seeks to escape by withdrawal will not offer her hand and will unwillingly accompany the teacher. The child has withdrawn co-operation and wants nothing more than to be left alone. Behaviour *per se* gives no indication as to the child's purpose. Verification is necessary before appropriate corrective action may be undertaken.

The above example demonstrates that the same behaviour may have quite different goals. A child who steals from other pupils may do so in order to gain attention, demonstrate power, or seek revenge. A poor reader either looks for constant help, demonstrates power through refusing to read, punishes teachers and parents by non-reading, or displays inability to learn. As each goal requires a different response from the teacher, how are the purposes identified? There are two basic ways to determine which of the four mistaken goals is being pursued by a misbehaving child.

HOW DO TEACHERS FEEL ABOUT THE MISBEHAVIOUR?

The most reliable method of diagnosing a student's goal is unfortunately one of the most distressing aspects of the teacher–student interaction (Dreikurs, 1959:88). If teachers wish to know the purpose of a student's misbehaviour, they must observe their own spontaneous and impulsive reaction to the student's misbehaviour. Whatever teachers feel like doing is precisely what the students want them to do. Students act because they know how teachers will react. By being aware of the reaction of a particular teacher to certain behaviours, students are able to control that teacher in numerous ways. For instance, a student who seeks attention may come to class late, clown, ask incessant questions, fail to return materials, or fail to be ready to leave on time. Some teachers become impatient and annoyed by these behaviours and respond by giving the student the attention he or she so desperately needs. Consequently the teacher's action serves to strengthen the various attention-seeking behaviours of students. Other teachers who do not react to these forms of behaviour will find that they are not troubled with these particular disturbances.

Students misbehave in a classroom for the teacher's benefit. Teachers are the target for disruptive behaviour and their corrective measures are invariably in line with the expectations of students who misbehave. A visit to a typical classroom will confirm the consequences for a teacher who, unaware of the goals of misbehaviour, consistently acts in a manner which is in line with the purpose of the provocation. How does a teacher feel when a student arrives late, leaves books at home, taps loudly with a ruler, fails to begin work, or moves noisily around the room? By causing the teacher to feel annoyed, students can expect a particular reaction by the teacher; this reaction is the purpose of the behaviour in the first instance. Teachers who feel themselves becoming impatient and annoyed by students' behaviour can be reasonably certain that the goal of the student is that of seeking attention.

If a teacher feels provoked, angered, threatened, or personally challenged by the behaviour of a student and resolves to impose his or her will upon the student, then the teacher is involved with an individual whose goal is power. Students who believe that they belong only by being the most powerful are obliged to challenge the teacher's authority and will aim to defeat teachers by refusing to do what they want or engaging in behaviours which are forbidden to them. They argue, contradict, dawdle, or are disobedient, defiant, and stubborn. A student who talks back or is rude to a teacher aims to provoke and involve the teacher in a power contest. Regardless of the outcome of a dispute, the student has won whenever he successfully manipulates a teacher into a display of power; a teacher who is prepared to fight acts in accordance with the student's expectations.

The goal of revenge can also be identified by the feelings of the teacher. Students who operate on this goal feel disliked, rejected, worthless, powerless, and unable to belong usefully to the class. Consequently they seek to revenge, to hurt, to get even and to punish others as they themselves feel they have been treated. Their behaviours include stealing, vandalism, abuse, and violence — behaviours which upset and frighten teachers. When a teacher feels deeply hurt by the behaviour of a student and wonders how a student could be so vicious or vindictive, then the teacher is feeling exactly as the student wanted. While an act of defiance may involve elements of both power and revenge, it is the personal nature of the hurt which distinguishes revenge.

The incidence of learning difficulties and the growth of remedial services in this country indicate the effectiveness of the fourth goal, escape by withdrawal. When teachers are inclined to throw up their arms in a gesture of despair, the instigators of their discouragement are students who are using the escape-by-withdrawal goal. Convinced of their inadequacy and devoid of confidence in their own ability, some students have given up trying and use inability or disability as a means of excusing themselves of any further responsibility. How do teachers feel about a pupil who still cannot differentiate between 'd' and 'b' even though the pupil has been taught the difference over and over? 'Hopeless. I give up.' It is the purpose of such behaviour to convince the teacher that the child is incapable of learning so that the teacher will expect nothing of the student. When teachers feel that they have tried everything but nothing works for a particular student, escape by withdrawal is likely.

By analysing their own feelings in relation to the unacceptable behaviour of students, teachers have a reliable guide for determining the purpose of the misbehaviour. Recognising that a pupil's behaviour is always directed towards them, teachers can identify the goal by noting how they feel about the behaviour. In summary:

if a teacher feels minor annoyance, the purpose is attention seeking;

if a teacher feels personally challenged, the purpose is power;

if a teacher feels deeply hurt, the purpose is revenge;

if a teacher feels like giving up, the purpose is escape by withdrawal.

HOW DO STUDENTS REACT TO A TEACHER'S CORRECTION?

Once a teacher has formulated a tentative impression of a student's goal by employing the above procedure, it is possible to confirm this assessment by observing how a student reacts when the teacher corrects, reprimands, or responds to the misbehaviour.

Students who seek attention by clowning, talking, asking frequent questions, misusing equipment, making loud noises, coming late to class, or failing to finish assignments are inviting you to give them special service. What they are saying through their behaviour is: 'Stop whatever you are doing and pay attention to me. I only count when I am being noticed'. Teachers naturally feel annoyed by these tactics and respond to restore order. The clown, for instance, will be tolerated for just so long before the teacher becomes exasperated and resorts to correction in the form of punishment or some aversive measure. This is exactly what the clown wants, to be the centre of attention. Having achieved this goal, the student will now temporarily desist from further attention-seeking behaviours. A little later on, there will be something else which will invite the teacher's rebuke, reprimand, threat, or punishment. Attention seeking has an insatiable appetite. However, at the time when a particular attention-seeking act is responded to by the teacher, the behaviour will temporarily stop.

While an attention-seeking student will temporarily desist from annoying behaviour, a student whose goal is power will

... This is exactly what the clown wants, to be the centre of attention.

react quite differently. Students who involve teachers in power contests aim to win; they will persist with the unacceptable behaviour which is designed to demonstrate that teachers cannot make them do anything or prevent them from doing as they wish. Through their behaviour, these students are saying: 'I count only when I am dominating and in control of others'. A student who refuses to commence work will view the teacher's reminder as a signal to defeat the teacher. There will be no attempt to commence, an action which is in direct defiance of the teacher's instruction. A second reminder, threat, or coercion from the teacher will meet with an equal determination by the student. And so the battle continues, with each party determined to impose his will on the other. No final victory by the teacher is possible as any 'success' merely serves to stimulate the pupil to be more skilful in the use of power.

Attention-seeking behaviour will stop on receipt of a teacher's recognition while power will continue. A student who talks loudly to his neighbour while the teacher is describing a particular event to the class may be engaging in either attention seeking or power. If the teacher stops the presentation, rebukes the student for rudeness, and observes that the student now remains silent, the goal is attention. If, however, the teacher observes that the student continues to speak with his neighbour, perhaps in an even louder voice, the goal is power. To defeat the teacher, to confirm a life style of belonging by being the most powerful, is the purpose of the latter student's behaviour.

On those occasions when revengeful behaviour is encountered, teachers will find that their efforts to correct the student will meet with more violent and vicious responses for the individual who will often become abusive when reprimanded. Students whose goal is revenge are saying through their behaviour, 'I count if I can hurt others as I have been hurt'. By punishing students for revengeful acts such as stealing, vandalism, or violence, teachers provide students with further grounds for wanting to get even. Further, the name calling that is usually associated with revengeful behaviour serves to confirm students' faulty evaluation of themselves. Never regard a student as 'bad', 'vicious', or 'cruel'; avoid retaliation; maintain order with a minimum of restraint; and attempt to communicate to the student that, while the behaviour is unacceptable, the student is completely acceptable. Any attempt to punish the student who is bent on revenge will only escalate the situation.

Students whose goal is to escape by withdrawal want only one thing, to be left alone. These students believe they can do nothing right and are so convinced of their inadequacy that they hope for no success and seek none. A teacher's rebuke, punishment, threat, or despair in relation to their lack of endeavour will be met with a martyr-like disposition. These students believe they can do nothing useful and are beyond caring. Therefore the teacher's response to their inactivity is of no consequence to them. Convinced that they cannot cope with the demands made upon them by school, these students interpret the teacher's disapproval and despair as a confirmation of their hopelessness.

Two methods of determining a student's goal have been suggested. First, how does a teacher feel about the misbehaviour? Secondly, how does the student react to the teacher's correction? In summary:

Student's goal	How teacher feels	How student reacts
Attention seeking	Annoyed	Temporarily stops
Power	Personally challenged	Continues to disturb
Revenge	Deeply hurt	Becomes more violent
Escape by withdrawal	'Hopeless'	Uninterested

HAVING IDENTIFIED THE GOAL, WHAT NOW?

Teachers will not find it difficult to determine the goals of classroom misbehaviour. Their own feelings and the reaction of students are two reliable procedures. For example, a student fails to clear up the home economics bench. How does the teacher feel? She is angry. What does she do? She keeps at the student until it is done. How does the student respond? She makes only half-hearted efforts after each fresh demand by the teacher. What is the goal? Power (defending).

One of the most important principles in helping teachers deal with misbehaving students is: 'If you want to change the behaviour of another person, change your own behaviour first'. This is one of the strongest statements in the whole approach of Individual Psychology. Dreikurs (1972:205) referred to this principle when he wrote:

If, as you feel weak and hopeless when you are confronted

with somebody who doesn't behave properly, you stop thinking about what he should do, and begin to think about that you could do, the doors open wide. You suddenly become aware of the power which you never dreamt you had. Then you can use encouragement, logical consequences, persuasion, all these ways for helping him to change — merely by changing yourself.

Teachers invariably try to make students change their behaviour. The following are typical remarks heard in any classroom: 'Why don't you stop that talking?' 'Don't you know what to do, John?' 'Who gave you permission to leave your seat?' 'Where have you been?' 'I am not going to speak to you again, Jones'. 'Any more of that and you are out, Smith'. Teachers must recognise that these types of behaviours arc directed at them and whatever they feel like doing is always what the students want them to do. This process of 'act–react' goes on in all classrooms and will continue until teachers are prepared to change their own behaviour so as to render the misbehaviour ineffective.

To break this cycle, teachers must learn to go against their first impulse. The first impulse is always wrong because it is precisely what the pupil wants to the teacher to do and fulfils the expectations of the pupil who behaves inappropriately. Dreikurs (1959, 1968) has consistently emphasised that, before teachers can begin to help students, they must stop behaving inappropriately. As Sweeney (1975:27) writes: 'Behavioural research on conditioning affirms the Adlerian notion that what most adults do impulsively when they respond to misbehaviour is incorrect'. Teachers must learn to 'catch themselves' and not act impulsively.

If the goal of attention seeking has been identified, the teacher should act in such a way that the student does not receive attention for the particular behaviour. For instance, students who arrive late for class are ignored but required to make up the lost time in their own time. The child who seeks special service by laziness is by-passed by the teacher. Students who dawdle or are slow find they miss out, a consequence which concerns nobody but themselves. Pupils who are nuisances, show offs, pests, or tattlers are ignored or are given attention in a manner which is not desired. The child who steals, finds that the teacher is not personally hurt by this behaviour, but requires the student to make retribution. The power seeker finds that he has no opponent. The temper tantrum attracts no audience, while shyness, dependency, cuteness, timidity, and functional learning problems are behaviours which are no longer effective as teachers withhold special service.

Consider the following incident which recently occurred in a secondary school. A young teacher had completed a lesson and was leaving the room. A student sitting near the door said to the teacher; 'What you are teaching is a lot of ——. And you are a great ——.' The teacher naturally became very upset at this obscenity. What mistake had he made? He let himself get hurt by a student whose goal was revenge. What should he have done? He could have changed his own behaviour by refusing to be hurt and by saying to the student: 'I am sorry that you did not like this lesson'. From such a reaction, the student would learn that the teacher cannot be hurt and would stop his offensive language; all because the teacher was able to change his own behaviour.

Teachers need constantly to remind themselves that they are the targets of disturbing classroom behaviour and that their reactions tend to sustain and strengthen undesirable behaviour. Before teachers can begin to assist individual children, they must stop following their first impulse; that is, they must stop giving undue attention, fighting, retaliating, or accepting students' displays of inability. That is the first and necessary step in any corrective program. Students who consistently disrupt, fail to learn, invite attention, rebel, or violate order are discouraged individuals who feel that they cannot find a place in the class through constructive and co-operative behaviours and consequently turn to more destructive and inadequate behaviour in their attempt to find a sense of significance. There are a number of processes designed to help pupils to develop more adequate ways of behaving but, before these approaches can be used, teachers must stop responding to unacceptable behaviours. As a first step, teachers should train themselves to go against their first impulse and, consequently, break the detrimental cycle whereby a student acts and a teacher reacts.

Try these

(1) How does a teacher feel about a student's misbehaviour? Match the feeling with the probable goal.

Goal	Teacher's feeling
A Attention seeking	1. 'You are driving me crazy with your constant talk.'
B Power	2. 'I give up with you, Charles.'
C Revenge .	3. 'You are not going to get away with that, young lady.'
D Escape by withdrawal	4. 'How could you do that to me, John?'

(2) During a science lesson, Helen is having difficulty in adjusting a microscope. You have previously seen Helen competently adjust the same instrument. You go over and offer assistance with the task. Match her most likely reaction with the appropriate goal.

Goal	Reaction
A Attention seeking	1. She accepts your offer without comment or interest.
B Power	2. She turns her back to the teacher and continues adjusting.
C Revenge	3. She knocks the microscope over, damaging a lens.
D Escape by withdrawal	4. She beams and willingly accepts your offer.

(3) Which teacher is aware of the principle: 'Go against your first impulse'? John, a Year 4 child, arrives late for class. He has been late three times this week.

Teacher A: 'Well John, what is your excuse this time?'.
Teacher B: 'You can stay in at recess and make up the lost time'.
Teacher C: Ignores his late-coming and continues with the lesson.

(4) The class has been asked to spend the period completing a work sheet which the English teacher has prepared. Michelle spends most of her time reading a novel and, at the end of the period, hands in an incomplete work sheet. Her teacher feels personally challenged. As a first step, she should:

A Ask Michelle when she intends to complete the work sheet.

B Say to Michelle, 'Well I can't make you do anything'.

C Refuse to accept the work sheet and require Michelle to stay and complete it.

D Make an exhibition of Michelle and give her a detention.

Answers

(1) 1 A; 2 D; 3 B; 4 C

(2) 1 D; 2 B; 3 C; 4 A

(3) Teacher C

(4) B (Principle: You cannot help a student until you have stopped fighting)

5

Encouragement: The Subtle Giant

INTRODUCTION

The importance of encouragement cannot be over-emphasised. So central is the concept in the classroom that Adler (1930:84) wrote of it:

> An educator's most important task, one might almost say his holy duty, is to see that no child is discouraged at school, and that a child who enters school already discouraged regains his self-confidence through his school and his teacher.

Courage forms the foundation upon which children construct their personality and it is clearly the most valuable gift which teachers may offer students. It is the 'subtle giant' (Popkin, 1983) which is always available to teachers and so desperately needed by students. 'A child needs encouragement like a plant needs water' (Dreikurs and Cassel, 1972).

Almost without exception, every misbehaving student is a discouraged student. Students who have confidence in their ability to cope with the various demands placed upon them will create neither learning nor behavioural problems. In contrast, there is a high probability that students who are experiencing problems in functioning, learning, or relating to others are discouraged individuals who have lost confidence in their ability to meet the demands which the school makes upon them.

The key to improving relationships with students and in promoting their learning and development is the use of procedures which have the effect of encouraging students and restoring or maintaining faith in themselves. Regardless of the rationale behind a technique, the sincerity of a teacher who employs it, or the effectiveness of its implementation, the ultimate validity of the technique can only be judged by the degree to which it encourages or discourages students.

Behind all forms of classroom problems, whether social, intellectual or emotional, are discouraged students who feel that they are unable to cope with the demands which schools place upon them. Many of them have lost faith in their ability to meet the challenges ahead and, in their attempt to belong, have turned to inappropriate behaviours, the goals of which have been described as attention seeking, power, revenge, and escape by withdrawal. No students would turn to unacceptable behaviour if they were not discouraged in their belief that belonging to the group, the class, the home, or the community was possible through constructive and co-operative behaviour. Although this factor was first recognised in the treatment of neurotic patients, it has ceased to be restricted to psychiatric treatment and has become a major premise in education. Commenting on the relationship between discouragement and failure, Dinkmeyer and Dreikurs (1963:42) wrote:

> It is incontestable that discouragement is a basic factor in all deviations, deficiencies, and failure with the exception of brain damage and mental deficiency. No one fails, with all the consequent suffering and deprivation, unless he has first lost confidence in his ability to succeed with socially accepted means. Wrong doing takes so much persistence, endurance, and self-sacrifice, that no one would choose it unless he felt he had no alternative.

Discouragement is based on the belief that one is not adequate to meet life challenges. It is in this basic loss of confidence, that all inadequate behaviours have their origin. All inadequate behaviours have their origin in a basic loss of confidence. Children turn to disturbing ways of belonging which will gain them recognition because they are denied successful learning experiences in schools and in homes.

They begin to regard themselves as incompetent, inadequate, and worthless. These students gain status, special glory, and recognition by striving to excel through attention, power, revenge, or escape behaviours. By doing so:

> ... they can be something special, be admired by peers, feel important, and gain status, merely by defeating the adults and violating their commands. The switch to socially unacceptable behaviour is the most frequent consequence of discouragement (Dinkmeyer and Dreikurs, 1963:42).

It is particularly important that teachers view students' misbehaviour as a product of discouragement rather than as the behaviour expected of a lazy child, an aggressive student, a vicious person, a hopeless pupil, or a stubborn child. The purposeful nature of these forms of behaviour has been described earlier and the futility of trying to 'correct' them should now be apparent. The growing level of defeatism and discouragement in many teachers reflects a loss of confidence in their traditional methods of classroom teaching and management. The rapid growth in courses and textbooks devoted to classroom management reflects this growing uncertainty. The use of encouragement techniques should end this two-way cycle whereby discouraged students lead to discouraged teachers. Effectively applied, encouragement procedures may 'actually revolutionise educational procedures in our families and our schools' (Dinkmeyer and Dreikurs, 1963:3). By identifying and removing the sources of students' discouragement, teachers may stimulate students into more effective and personally satisfying forms of behaviour.

WHAT ARE THE SOURCES OF DISCOURAGEMENT IN SCHOOLS?

Mistake-centred approaches

Our present methods of educating children constitute a series of discouraging experiences for many of them. Although encouragement is of paramount importance, tragically, many of our teaching devices are actually discouraging to the child (Nickelly, 1971:200). Yet, curiously enough, it is the concerned, well-intentioned, and conscientious teacher who is frequently the major offender in discouraging students. Almost without exception, teachers are sincere in their endeavours to assist students with their learning. Yet their attempts to do so frequently have the opposite effects.

How do teachers help students who are having difficulty with their cognitive or psychomotor learning? Consider a typical learning task faced in primary school mathematics. The teacher has introduced the topic of linear equations and has worked several examples on the board. The students are now asked to solve the six problems which are presented on a work-sheet which has been distributed. During her supervision, the teacher points out the errors which students have made or their inappropriate work habits. This is a typical reaction as teachers feel that no improvement will occur unless the nature of the errors or deficiencies is indicated to pupils. This approach is one of the greatest obstacles to student learning. It reflects a belief that children will not improve unless their mistakes, slowness, untidiness, or shortcomings are pointed out to them for correction. It forces teachers to act unnecessarily and undermines the self-confidence and self-respect of students. Our focus on mistakes indicates that teachers have very little confidence in a child's ability and willingness to improve without their intervention. Consider the following practices which are typical of classrooms. When children speak incorrectly, they are corrected; when they spell poorly, they are corrected; when they sit poorly, walk poorly, read poorly, or write poorly, the inevitable correction will follow. This focus on mistakes is calamitous. As Popkin (1983:41) suggests:

> If someone who is big and important to you spends a lot of time telling you the things you do wrong, you come to believe that there's more wrong with you than right. It gets harder to do things right because you are paying so much attention to your mistakes and blunders.

When teachers are asked why they constantly correct children they will reply that their intention is to help students. This attitude, while understandable, constitutes one of the most serious barriers to student progress. It is an attitude which communicates a complete lack of faith in a child's ability and willingness to acquire more adequate ways of behaving. What the teacher says through his or her behaviour is this: 'You will continue to make mistakes or behave inappropriately unless I point out the errors of your ways'. This approach which is aimed at detecting weaknesses and then providing remediation has been generally accepted, particularly in special, compensatory, or remedial education. There is no surer way of destroying a child's confidence than to focus consistently on his or her deficiencies. The faulty pattern of behaviour or performance becomes more firmly established and further discouragement is inevitable. Anticipation is, after all, the strongest of all motivations. We bring to reality those things which we anticipate.

There is nothing wrong in making a mistake. In almost all cases, a mistake represents a lack of skill. Children read, write, spell, or speak poorly because they lack skill. Skill comes with practice and children will practise those activities which they feel confident of being able to learn. However, if their imperfect performance is constantly subjected to criticism, no matter how well-intentioned, children begin to lose confidence in their ability and doubt whether they will ever be able to cope with the demands made upon them. The number of students who drop mathematics at the first available opportunity is ample testimony to the effect of aversive experiences. Problem behaviour in the mathematics class is a product of poor teaching and has nothing to do with the mathematical ability of students.

A fault-finding attitude has no place in a school. Teachers must communicate to children that they have faith in their ability and desire to achieve, so that students may have faith in themselves. Avoid discouraging approaches which emphasise mistakes and deficiencies and shift to an attitude which reflects faith and acceptance, acknowledges achievement, and recognises either a task performed or improvement or effort and one which builds on strengths and assets. Far too many classrooms are mistake-centred in which students are made to feel inferior or incompetent because nothing they do ever comes up to the teacher's standard or expectation. Teachers are concerned that their students should learn well, but by pointing out student mistakes, they steer a course which is self-defeating. Remember that to be human is to be imperfect.

During her supervision, the teacher points out the errors which students have made or their inappropriate work habits.

Conditional acceptance

Discouragement results not only from a concentration on mistakes or deficiencies but also from a refusal to accept children as they are and only conditionally upon their being better. As Dreikurs (1971:75) observes:

One of the most frequent and deadly means of discouraging a child is pointing out to him how much better he could be. Instead of spurring him onto greater efforts, it usually stops him from even trying. Has he not been told that he is not good enough as he is? This is the worst thing one can tell a person.

Teachers constantly impress on students, directly or indirectly, that their current levels of achievement are not adequate because they could be improved. 'Come on Alice, you can do better than that.' Is there anybody who can't do better? While this evaluation is true, it is not the way to promote an improvement in student achievement. As Soltz (1967:201) observes:

> She (the teacher) must also *accept the child as he (the pupil) is now* — not as she expects him to be later. 'As you are right now, you are fine. Now let us learn and grow together'.

Consider the effects on the students of the following incidents:

- A pupil takes a drawing to the teacher for comment. The teacher responds: 'You have drawn the house very well but what a pity you didn't use more colour'.
- 'Yes, you can have the part in the play but you will need to attend practice more regularly than you do now.'
- 'You seem to have solved the problem correctly but I don't care for the method which you used.'
- 'The puppet you made is very lifelike. Let me fix its arms and then you will have a puppet you can feel proud of.'
- 'You served very well today but your backhand really let you down.'
- 'No John, that book is far too hard for you. Put it back and choose an easier one.'
- 'Well, yes, you have put the books on the correct shelves but you took far too long.'
- 'No Jane, you are too young to try that. When you are a bigger girl you might attempt it.'

There is only one way in which such comments may be interpreted by students. 'As I am now I am not much good but when I am older, wiser, faster, bigger, or smarter, I may be acceptable.' A child does not feel encouraged if a teacher gives with one hand and takes away with the other. 'Complimenting a child with "but" kills any encouraging words' (Dreikurs, 1971:76). Teachers much accept children and their performance as they are now and not conditionally upon their improving in the future.

The frequency with which teachers discourage students through their refusal to accept current levels of performance is high. No matter what a student does, there is always somebody who is more able, competent, skilful, efficient, or knowledgeable who will impress the child with his or her imperfections. An incorrectly performed mathematical problem which required almost a period's work by a student will be corrected by the teacher in seconds. A poorly-drawn horse which pleased a child will be reshaped by a teacher with a few strokes. A plasticine representation of a family which showed patient care and considerable effort will be rejected because of the faulty proportions between adults and children. By refusing to accept performance as it is now, rather than what it might have been, teachers cause children to give up by destroying their confidence. How can you improve when you have lost faith in your ability to improve? Instead of motivating students to improved performance, conditional acceptance actually stops them from trying because they feel that they cannot meet the standards of others.

Competition

Competition within a classroom is another potential source of discouragement which may lead to students losing faith in their ability. The practice of competition damages far more children than it assists; for every child who seems to progress under the stimulus of winning, hundreds give up and feel discouraged and defeated because they sense that they are nothing unless they are on top (Soltz, 1967:200).

Teachers often highlight differences between students' performance or achievement by praising successful individuals and criticising unsuccessful ones and, by their comparison, fostering competition between students. Grading, grouping, and assessment practices also promote a competitive climate while school reports which rank students foster the fiction that one has a place and value only when one is superior to others.

In Chapter 2, the importance of belonging was stressed. In a co-operative classroom, students, through learning and achievement, develop an awareness of their own strengths and the capacity to cope with school demands. They demonstrate a willingness to co-operate with others in meeting the needs of each situation and their behaviour reflects concern for the well-being of their peers. In a competitive classroom, students are not provided with a sense of worth but are measured against the performance of other students. Being unsure of their position, each student attempts to find a place by being better than others in acceptable or non-acceptable ways. A competitive spirit which parents and teachers instil in students — a spirit reinforced by grading practices — fosters the idea that one must excel and be better than others. 'A competitive society reveres those who succeed in their self-elevation, and fills its mental hospitals and jails with those who gave up' (Dreikurs, 1968:41). Many students live in dread that they cannot be as good as others want them to be while others give up because they cannot meet the demands of others. However, they still must belong, and do so by pursuing the goals referred to earlier, those of attention, power, revenge, or inadequacy.

Grading practices where a student's achievement is ranked against other students represent one of the most obvious sources of discouragement. Based on a system of reward and punishment, grades have the effect of heightening competition and of eliminating a co-operative spirit. The better students lord it over the weaker students and are made to feel superior while the poorer students are confirmed in their position of hopelessness and inferiority and are pushed down in terms of status, esteem, and self-worth. Poor grades seldom improve the learning process and result in teachers adopting approaches to children which are harmful and discouraging.

There can be no harmonious functioning in a class which uses competitive or norm-referenced grading. Those who receive good grades are confirmed in their belief that they belong by being the best, while those students who receive poor grades are convinced of their inadequacy and are forced to belong through various useless ways of behaving such as clowning, bullying, stealing. Many of these so-called 'poor' students are, in fact, extremely able but, when they cannot do as well as others, they see no value in continuing with their studies. Frustrated ambition is perhaps the most frequent cause for giving up (Dreikurs, 1968:184) and students turn away from any activity which does not provide them with an opportunity of proving their superiority. School failures are convinced that they have no chance of doing well which means 'as well as others (competition), as well as they ought to do (pressure), or as well as they want to do (over-ambition)' (Dreikurs, 1968:184). It is clear that students are at the same time co-operative and competitive. The question is which is to be preferred. Because students are basically social beings, it is only in a co-operative classroom can they find a true sense of belonging, by contributing and co-operating. Hill and Hill (1990:3) have concluded that:

> Recent theory, experimental evidence and studies conducted in classrooms all suggest that if schools are to provide for the optimal intellectual development of their students, relationships amongst children and the kind of co-operative activities children engage in will need to be taken seriously. Teaching the skills of collaborative learning, group management and organization will become more important than instruction and imparting knowledge.

Negative expectations

Many teachers convey to children the belief that they are not expected to do well in school. Bloom (1968:1) indicated this belief when he wrote:

> Each teacher begins a new term (or course) with the expectation that about a third of his students will adequately learn what he has to teach. He expects about a third of his students to fail or to just 'get by'. Finally, he expects another third to learn a good deal of what he has to teach, but not enough to be regarded as 'good students'. This set of expectations, supported by school policies and practices in grading, becomes transmitted to the students through the grading procedures and through methods and materials of instruction. The system creates a self-fulfilling prophecy such that the final sorting of students through the grading process becomes approximately equivalent to the original expectations.

The author recently asked a teacher how her Year 12 students had performed the previous year. She replied: 'Good, I got one through'. Being an all migrant school, her expectation was negative, an expectation which was clearly transmitted in all her transactions with the class. The work of Rosenthal and Jacobson (1966) substantiates the disastrous effects of negative expectations on student performance. Students' performance will invariably reflect their teachers' expectations. If the expectation is low, the performance will be low, and a self-fulfilling hypothesis is confirmed.

HOW TO ENCOURAGE STUDENTS

To a degree, encouragement is communicated by the attitude of the teacher. Teachers who accept and value students as they are now, who convey faith in their ability to learn and develop, and who recognise and acknowledge genuine effort or improvement will create a learning environment which is conducive to the development of relationships based on mutual trust and respect — the essential ingredients for encouragement.

In an excellent publication concerned with the nature and sources of encouragement and discouragement, Dinkmeyer and Dreikurs (1963.50) have indicated that the teacher who encourages:

- places value on the child as he is;
- shows a faith in the child than enables the child to have faith in himself;
- has faith in the child's ability; wins the child's confidence while building his self-respect;
- recognises a job 'well done' and gives recognition for effort;
- utilises the group to facilitate and enhance the development of the child;
- integrates the group so that the child can be sure of his place in it;
- assists in the development of skills sequentially and psychologically paced to permit success;
- recognises and focuses on strengths and assets;
- utilises the interests of the children to energise instructions.

Glasser (1969), and Dinkmeyer and Dreikurs (1963) have suggested the following methods and attitudes which will facilitate the development of confidence in others:
- accept and have faith in the individual as she is (not her potential);
- expect her to handle her tasks and show this by your actions;
- when confronted with misbehaviour, separate the deed from the doer;
- confirm the fact that mistakes, defeat, or failures are common to life and not catastrophic;
- emphasise the joy of doing and the satisfaction in accomplishment rather than evaluations of how one is doing;
- recognise progress and provide ample encouragement for genuine effort;
- show confidence in the child's ability to be competent and avoid comparisons with others;
- allow for differences such as rate of learning, patience, neatness, or interest;
- never give up on the child, no matter how persistently she tries to defeat the encouragement process.

While attitudes are important in encouraging children, there are a number of techniques which are designed to translate the above attitudes into useful classroom practices. 'While our intention is to help others have confidence in themselves, to be self-reliant, and to have the courage to be imperfect, we can show this by what we do' (Sweeney, 1975:36). Two such procedures are:
- to build on assets and strengths and minimise mistakes and deficiencies;
- to emphasise the activity not the result, the process not the product.

Build upon assets and strengths

The primary responsibility of a teacher is to promote in students more adequate ways of behaving. Whether in the area of cognitive, affective, or psychomotor domains, the role of the teacher which emphasises the expedition of learning is the most crucial. In performing this role, teachers tend to make one basic error; they believe that the most effective way of obtaining higher levels of student performance is to point out and correct current deficiencies, weaknesses, or inadequacies in student performance. This procedure is one of the most damaging processes in education as it invariably worsens the situation by providing an additional source of discouragement.

Consider the case of Robert, a seven-year-old boy in second grade who is having trouble with his reading. Robert knows that he is not reading well as he observes that his classmates read better than he does, that his parents show concern over his slow progress particularly in relation to his third-grade sister who reads fluently, and that his teacher spends more time with him than with other children. Robert's teacher, in her attempt to assist him, invariably focuses upon his weaknesses. A typical session consists of frequent corrections such as: 'Not "cause" but "case" '; 'Not "them" but "then" '; 'Not "roast" but "coast" '. The teacher's philosophy reflects a position that children will not improve unless their deficiencies are revealed to them. She may use diagnostic tests which reveal a weakness in phonics, reversals, or substitutions. Corrective measures are then implemented to counteract these deficiencies. By focusing on mistakes and weaknesses, the teacher reinforces Robert's belief that he reads poorly and provides an additional source of discouragement to an already discouraged child.

Why does Robert read poorly? Apart from the children who choose to read poorly for reasons discussed earlier, the most common cause of inadequate performance is a lack of skill. Skills are acquired through practice. Which skills do students practise? Those which they feel confident of being able to attain. By concentrating on deficiencies and weaknesses, the teacher begins to erode Robert's confidence and leads him to believe that he will never read well. Once students begin to lose faith in their ability to cope with learning, their progress is jeopardised, and the likelihood of disturbing behaviour is increased.

Consider another example in which a fourth grade is being taught place value. The teacher has worked several examples on the board for the children and they are now solving their four problems which have been set. Janet completes the four but has three wrong. Her teacher immediately focuses on the errors which Janet has made. It is little

Robert's teacher, in her attempt to assist him, invariably focuses upon his weakness.

wonder that many children drop mathematics at the first available opportunity. Janet simply lacks skill in place value and will acquire the skill through practice. However, by the teacher's constantly focusing on her deficiencies, Janet's courage and confidence to continue with mathematics are weakened.

What should the teacher do? In the case of both Robert and Janet, recognise that the students lack skill, a condition which will be corrected through practice. The likelihood of practice is increased when the students are confident of their ability to cope with their tasks. By focusing on strengths and assets, the teacher provides the necessary incentive for the students to continue improving. In the case of Janet, the teacher might tick the problem which is solved correctly and say: 'That is a good start to place value'. How does Janet interpret that remark? 'If that is a good start, then I will do better tomorrow.' Teachers must keep students thinking that they can cope with all learning tasks, a belief which current approaches to mastery learning would support. Similarly, Robert's teacher might ask Robert to read aloud for her, ignore any errors which he made and, on completion of the exercise, ask Robert a question about the story he read. The teacher then expresses pleasure with the answer, enjoys the activity with Robert, acknowledges his effort and any improvement, and builds up his confidence in his ability to read. Nothing is said to Robert about his errors as they simply reflect a lack of skill, a condition which will be corrected with practice.

In all teaching situations, stay positive and acknowledge the students' strengths and assets rather than highlight their weaknesses. A painting of 'Our home and family', presented by a first-grader to her teacher, might receive the comment: 'What a lovely garden you have painted' rather than: 'How can the children be as tall as the house?'. A sheet of handwriting, poorly executed by an unskilled writer, might be greeted with: 'Look how well you have written the capital letters'. The teacher who encourages is the one who builds on strengths rather than one who attempts to eliminate weaknesses. If a student's attention is directed towards the avoidance of errors, he has little incentive to develop. Recognise strengths and ignore weaknesses. In this way children are encouraged to bring academic performance to full strength as their energies are released for this purpose.

We live in a 'mistake-centred' society in which individuals are afraid of making mistakes. Part of the attitude may be accounted for by the traditions of the past where mistakes implied non-conformity and carried with them an element of worthlessness. In a competitive society such as ours where people are uncertain of their belonging, where they feel that they have to be better than others, or have more wealth, power, or status, people are trying desperately to be right all the time as they fear the humiliation and loss of status which mistakes incur. As a result, people make every effort to avoid mistakes, an attitude which invariably leads them to mistakes. When we focus on error, we discourage ourselves and are then led into error. Further, when we expect to behave in a certain way, there is a strong tendency to confirm that expectation. If we expect to make mistakes, we probably will. A student who is writing a notice to take home should not be subjected to: 'Careful now, no spelling errors' or 'Only your best writing now'. Mistakes under these circumstances are likely to result from the teacher communicating to students that poor spelling and poor writing were expected.

There is nothing wrong in making mistakes. In many learning situations, they are unavoidable. Students who are afraid of making mistakes cannot function effectively because the only time they know whether they are right or wrong is after an activity is completed. If they are afraid of making mistakes, they cannot move, develop, or make decisions because they fear they may be wrong. Students should be taught that mistakes are unimportant, that they are part of learning, and that it is more important to decide what to do about correcting mistakes than avoid making them. The past is gone and cannot be changed but there is always something one can do about the future. Mistakes can teach students a great deal provided they are not embarrassed or ridiculed for having made mistakes.

This is not to suggest that teachers do not take the opportunity of correcting student errors. For example, if a teacher observes that a number of students are spelling 'agriculture' incorrectly when reporting on their visit to the Agricultural Show, she might say: 'I see that Sandra has spelt this difficult word correctly' and proceed to write it on the board. Students who have spelt it incorrectly will become aware of their own error but will have avoided being subjected to criticism or negative feedback. The same procedure could be followed in relation to Janet, the student who makes errors in place-value problems.

The teaching of English provides numerous examples of the belief which teachers hold regarding the need to eliminate error from students' work. A class may have been on an excursion to 'Puffing Billy', a small steam engine which runs through the hills near Melbourne. The teacher asks the class to write a two-page description of the train ride. David submits his report, which contains five or six spelling errors. What would the teacher do who understands the encouragement process? She might point out his excellent description of the train, the correct use of some difficult phrases and acknowledge the correct spelling of several difficult words. What about the spelling errors? She would ignore them because she knows that they reflect a lack of skill in spelling, a skill which will be acquired as long as David continues to read and to write. She might take the opportunity of assisting with spelling by writing some of the commonly mis-spelt words on the board but always relating them to students who have spelt them correctly. The same procedure could be applied to syntax, descriptive phrases and the like. In short, the teacher's procedures have focused on assets and strengths, have minimised mistakes and deficiencies, and have strengthened her students' faith in their ability to learn. In her sequential teaching of communication skills, the teacher will allow students ample opportunity to apply those skills and will acknowledge their achievement and efforts. Eliminate negatives from teaching — vocabulary, attitudes and actions.

Take one final example. Sally was learning to weave. She had been working happily with a small group of friends. Her pattern required a procedure with which she was unfamiliar. She asked the teacher for assistance. The teacher looked at her weaving and said: 'Before I show you how to proceed, you must undo the last three or four centimeters because they are so uneven. It would be a pity to spoil your woven rug'. Sally went slowly back to her seat, put the weaving away, and began to draw aimlessly in her workbook. Our concentration on mistakes is devastating. A child's interest, co-operation, enthusiasm, and confidence are shattered in mistake-centred classrooms. The particular teacher, no matter how well-intentioned, has lowered a heavy boom on Sally. In all probability, Sally will show little interest in weaving in the future and her chances of acquiring skills in this area are minimal. A teacher who encourages would show Sally how to do the new process and enter enthusiastically into the activity: 'I am sure that this rug will look attractive in your bedroom' and finally, and most importantly, focus on Sally's weaving strength. For example: 'What beautiful colours you have chosen for your rug'. She would recognise that the unevenness of Sally's weaving is the result of her lack of skill and, therefore, requires no comment. The teacher maintains an environment in which Sally will quickly develop the necessary weaving skill, an environment which reflects a faith in Sally's ability and desire to learn.

Emphasise the activity not the result

There is a strong tendency in students to evaluate themselves in terms of their achievement. They identify what they are with what they do. Some students will complete a task for the sole purpose of winning the teacher's praise. Others will strive to obtain praise by producing the best work because they feel worthless unless they are on top. A teacher's praise becomes a reward and students feel worthwhile only when they are praised. Praise, being tied to a competitive system, is given only for a well done or a completed task. Consequently many students come to believe that their worth depends upon the judgment of others. 'I am worthwhile only when I please the teacher' is a typical evaluation of a student whose worth is judged against his achievement. When the child becomes an adult, his effectiveness, his ability to function, his capacity to cope with life's tasks will depend entirely upon his estimation of how he stands in the opinions of others. He will live constantly on an elevator — up and down (Soltz, 1967:65). 'I belong only when I am pleasing others.'

It is important for students' development for them to feel that they are accepted unconditionally by the teacher and that their acceptance has nothing to do with the quality of their performance. While teachers may reject certain levels or types of behaviour, they must never reject the students whose performance is unacceptable. It is necessary for teachers to separate the deed from the doer, the activity from the result, or the process from the product. Teachers fail to do this when they make statements such as:

'You have the tidiest workbook. Good boy.'
'I am pleased to see that your spelling was all correct.'
'You have done very well with a 93 per cent. Good girl.'
'I am delighted to see that you obtained all A's.'
'You are the best library assistant we have ever had.'
'You were wonderful in the play last night.'
'Two gold stars for your work today.'

What is wrong with this type of statement
on the end product or the doer and teach
judge their worth by the amount of praise
Students who receive praise have met the tea
dards and are, therefore, worthwhile. Students wh
mance is not praised judge themselves as fail
decision as to whether praise is given or not is
external to the child and is usually based on the de. ands
and values of others. Thus a teacher who uses praise,
communicates this message to his students. 'Because you
have done something which I regard as good, you are to be
rewarded and valued by me.' In contrast, students whose
work is not praised believe that they are worthless. 'How do I
measure up?' becomes of central concern to children who
live in this up-and-down cycle powered by praise or its
absence.

Our emphasis upon the end product of an activity will
cause many children to give up because they are not able to
meet the standard of others. If children's efforts fail to bring
the expected praise, they may assume that what they have to
offer is not worth the effort and give up in despair. Yet
discouraged students, needing recognition the most, are
rarely praised because their performance is usually below
the level required by the teacher. As they feel unable to
please the teacher, they judge themselves as worthless and
begin to contribute less and less.

A better procedure is to concentrate on the activity itself
rather than on its outcome, to acknowledge the deed rather
than the doer. Emphasise the task rather than the student.
For example, a student who approaches the art teacher with
a completed sketch might receive the comment: 'I see that
you have put a lot of work into that sketch' rather than:
'What an excellent sketch. Good girl'. A student who has
completed a mathematics problems sheet might be told by
the teacher: 'I see you have worked very hard on your
mathematics'. The child who tidies the science bench:
'Thanks for your help; that makes things a lot easier'.
A student who reports to you that he kicked six goals in the
house match: 'I see that you really enjoyed the game'.
Elevate the status of the activity rather than the product of
the activity; acknowledge the act rather than the actor. In

way, we remove any idea that students' worth is dependent upon how they measure up to the demands and values of the teacher.

What does a student learn in the following incident? A teacher, on handing back a spelling test, comments: 'Ten out of ten, good boy'. The message is clear. 'My worth as a person depends on pleasing the teacher. 'I am a "good boy" when I receive ten out of ten. If I receive less than that, then I am a bad boy.' Consider the number of times teachers compliment students, give classroom privileges, gold stars or house points. Such practices teach students that they are worthwhile only when they are excellent or pleasing the teacher.

A type of student for whom this principle of encouragement is particularly important is the over-ambitious child. These children set impossibly high goals for themselves and they believe that their belonging depends on being the best, on being something special. Consequently they fail to complete activities which they feel will not be done well enough (perfectionism) or they will not engage in activities when they feel they cannot be the best (over-ambition).

> If a child has set exceedingly high standards for himself, praise may sound like a mockery or scorn, especially when his efforts fail to measure up to his own standards. In such a child, praise only serves to increase his anger with himself and his resentment at others for not understanding his dilemma (Soltz, 1967:66).

The effect of frustrated over-ambition may be observed in the student who, when the teacher commented on the excellence of his model aircraft, smashed it to the floor in anger and left the room. Why? The student is a perfectionist who judges himself against what he does. Because he is a perfectionist, nothing he can do is ever good enough. He became angry when the teacher praised his model because it indicated to him that even the teacher did not understand what a failure he was. 'How can it be good? Nothing I do is good enough.' If the teacher had concentrated on the activity and said: 'I see that you enjoy making model planes', she would have shifted the emphasis away from the product to the activity, from the actor to the act, and her comment would contain no implication regarding the worth of the student.

When the teacher commented on the excellence of his model aircraft, he smashed it on the floor in anger and left the room.

Many teachers will find it difficult to accept the proposition that the child who refuses to attempt tasks or gives up before the completion is an ambitious child. Yet, as previously pointed out, frustrated ambition is perhaps the most frequent cause for giving up. Children who feel that they must be the best will turn away from any activity in which they cannot excel. A child who shows no interest in art does not lack ability or interest in this subject, but believes that he or she cannot prove superiority by pursuing this activity. It is amazing to note the very large number of students who are extremely able in certain areas but appear to have no interest or ability in others. In almost all cases, this lack of participation is attributable to the over-ambition in youngsters who have been trained by parents and teachers to compete and made to feel inferior if they do not excel.

principle of acknowledging the process rather
ict is the distinction between praise and
Many teachers believe that by praising stu-
timulate them into appropriate behaviours.
ct is likely. Praise is reserved for well-done
...rpreted by students as meaning that they
...c measured up to another's standard. Therefore, praise
gives false values to children as it indicates that they have
worth only when they gain praise.

The basic differences between praise and encouragement
have been summarised by Dinkmeyer, McKay, and Dinkmeyer (1980:51).

Praise	*Encouragement*
1. Praise is a reward given for a completed achievement.	1. Encouragement is an acknowledgment of effort.
2. Praise tells students they've satisfied the demands of others.	2. Encouragement helps students evaluate their own performance.
3. Praise connects students' work with their personal worth.	3. Encouragement focuses on the strength of the work, helping students see and feel confident about their own ability.
4. Praise places a cold judgment on the student as a person.	4. Encouragement shows acceptance and respect.
5. Praise can be withheld as punishment or cheapened by overuse.	5. Encouragement can be freely given because everyone deserves to receive it.
6. Praise is patronising. It's talking down, as if the praiser enjoys a superior position.	6. Encouragement is a message between equals.

Additionally, praise always involves the student rather
than the student's behaviour, the actor not the act. Typical
statements of praise and their equivalents in encouragement
are:

Praise	*Encouragement*
1. 'I am pleased that you topped the history test.'	1. 'I see that you enjoy studying history.'
2. 'Ten out of ten. Good girl!'	2. 'You must really enjoy maths!'
3. 'You were the best of the violinists at the concert.'	3. 'You have really practised hard on your violin this year.'
4. 'You are the best monitor we have, Sandra.'	4. 'I appreciate your help in the classroom, Sandra.'
5. 'You have the neatest writing in the class.'	5. 'Looks as though you're enjoying your writing.'
6. 'I am so proud of your artwork.'	6. 'It is nice to see that you enjoy art.'

To conclude this chapter on encouragement, teachers may like to consider the language of encouragement. While the process of encouragement is largely non-verbal, an attitude of teachers towards children which communicates respect, trust, faith, and belief in oneself, it can be practised verbally by teachers. Clint Reimer lists ten verbal approaches to encouragement (Reimer, 1967:71-73):

1. 'You do a good job of ...'
   Children should be encouraged when they do not expect it, when they are not asking for it. It is possible to point out some useful act or contribution in each child. Even a comment about something small and insignificant to us may have great importance to a child.
2. 'You have improved in ...'
   Growth and improvement is something we should expect from all children. They may not be where we would like them to be, but if there is progress, there is less chance for discouragement. Children will usually continue to try if they can see some improvement.
3. 'We like (enjoy) you, but we don't like what you do.'
   Often a child feels he is not liked after he has made a mistake or misbehaved. A child should never think he is not liked. It is important to distinguish between the child and his behaviour, between the act and the actor.
4. 'You can help me (us, the others, etc.) by ...'
   To feel useful and helpful is important to everyone.

Children want to be helpful; we have only to give them the opportunity.

5. 'Let's try it together.'

   Children who think they have to do things perfectly are often afraid to attempt something new for fear of making a mistake or failing.

6. 'So you do make a mistake; now, what can you learn from your mistake?'

   There is nothing that can be done about what has happened, but a person can always do something about the future. Mistakes can teach a child a great deal, and he will learn if he does not feel embarrassed for having made a mistake.

7. 'You would like us to think you can't do it, but we think you can.'

   This approach could be used when the child says or conveys the impression that something is too difficult for him and he hesitates to even so much as try it. If he tries and fails, he has at least had the courage to try. Our expectations should be consistent with the child's ability and maturity.

8. 'Keep trying. Don't give up.'

   When a child is trying, but not meeting much success, a comment like this might be helpful.

9. 'I'm sure you can straighten this out (solve this problem, etc.) but, if you need any help, you know where to find me.'

   Adults need to express confidence that children are able and will resolve their own conflicts, if given a chance.

10. 'I can understand how you feel (not sympathy, but empathy) but I'm sure you'll be able to handle it.'

    Sympathising with another person seldom helps him, rather it suggests that life has been unfair to him. Understanding the situation and believing in a child's ability to adjust to it is of much greater help to him.

In summary, encouragement recognises effort and improvement, shows appreciation for contribution, accepts students as they are now, minimises mistakes and deficiencies, focuses on assets and strengths, and separates the deed from the doer. Above all, encouragement is a process which communicates to children respect and self-worth through accepting them as they are. Encouragement is not a unitary process but a combination of attitudes and techniques which help prepare students for self-sufficiency. Basically, it is any action which conveys to the child that the teacher respects, trusts, and believes in him and that his lack of skills in no way diminishes his value as a person (Dreikurs, Grunwald, and Pepper, 1971:68).

Principles and language of encouragement

Consider the following principles of encouragement and how they might be expressed verbally, especially in forms other than questions, and non-verbally. Next reflect on the incidents of the last week and record examples of the language you used or could have used to encourage your students.

Principle	Language	Your example of language
Accept students as they are Convey acceptance that is genuine and not conditional.	'I really enjoy teaching this class.'	
Use listening skills Invite a student to talk without your demanding, interrupting, or taking over.	'Tell me more about it.'	
Convey empathy Recognise how student may think or feel.	'It looks as though you are really enjoying that.'	
Express gratitude Let children know when you appreciate their efforts, without dwelling on or moralising about it.	'Thank you. That really helped.' Or, a non-verbal smile.	
Encourage social impact Stimulate student to share skills and efforts with others.	'Others in the class might like to know how to do this.'	
Foster material impact Encourage students to develop skills that influence and beautify the world.	'Your drawing makes our classroom more pleasant.'	

Principle	Language	Your example of language
Offer choices Present options to students when whatever the child decides is acceptable to you.	'Would you rather paint at the easel or join us for a story?'	
Acknowledge effort Consider what the student does, instead of the product.	'I would like to know how you obtained that effect.'	
Emphasise strengths Identify students' assets, talents and uniqueness.	'You have a talent for caring for animals.'	
Acknowledge contributions Share with students how their efforts helped improve the situation.	'Your coming early this morning really helped me.'	
Encourage self-impact Help students to nurture themselves.	'What do you think you can do now?'	
Invite sharing Help children share with you.	'Would you like to show me how you did that?'	
Show confidence Let students know that you have faith in their abilities when it appears that they can handle it.	'Yes, it is a tough topic. But I know that you can work it out.'	
Encourage when it is not expected Encouragement is an expression of growth for both the giver and the receiver.	'I have learned a lot about being a teacher from you.'	

Try these

(1) Classify the following statements as either praise or encouragement.

Praise   Encouragement

A 'You have taken a good deal of care with your assignment.'

B 'That's a difficult problem but I am sure you will work it out.'

C 'I am proud of you for behaving so well at the sports.'

D 'Sally and Jane are such great helpers to me.'

E 'You are the smartest one to have worked out that problem yourself.'

F 'I certainly appreciate your help in the library, Bob.'

(2) Read the statement on the right-hand side. Which principle is relevant to each?

A Build upon assets and strengths.

1. 'You are writing much better but you must improve your spelling.' ( )

B Minimise mistakes and deficiencies.

2. 'That's a good start to logarithms.' ( )

C Emphasise the activity not the result.

3. 'I see you enjoy woodwork.' ( )

D Separate the deed from the doer.

4. 'Jan has the tidiest desk in the class.' ( )

Answers

(1) Praise: C; D; E
Encouragement: A; B; F

(2) 1 B; 2 A; 3 C; 4 D

6
Development of Responsibility in Students: Self-discipline

INTRODUCTION

Our school system is in a dilemma regarding discipline. Society is in a similar position as debate rages over the effectiveness of corporal punishment in dealing with offenders. Visiting experts suggested that parents who smack their children be charged while a politician advocates the return of the lash. Teachers vacillate between domination and submission, between authoritarianism and permissiveness, and between order and freedom. The problem of discipline dominates, in schools, in homes, and in society.

The problem of classroom discipline has been highlighted by the many governmental enquiries into the area and the recommendations which are currently being implemented in the schools. Without exception, the recommendations have included the abolition of corporal punishment, the reduction in externally imposed discipline, and a total support for self-discipline and individual responsibility.

Many teachers and parents have reacted strongly against

such legislation, the strength of their response reflecting their concern that the growing number of defiant, apathetic, and unco-operative students will prove unmanageable without physical punishment. Such is the bankruptcy of interpersonal relationships in schools and homes. Many teachers and parents who know no approach to motivation other than the threat or use of punishment feel that without external control they will be powerless to influence the behaviour of young people.

No one would deny that the maintenance of order is essential in any school. While freedom is a desirable attribute, order prevents a school from degenerating into chaos. The major technique traditionally exercised by teachers to maintain order has combined the use of rewards and punishments. Students who conform to the demands made on them by teachers are rewarded while those who deviate are punished. Given the long history of rewards and punishments, it is not surprising to find that many teachers regard their use as inevitable.

> Tradition dies slowly and teachers have not shed the slave
> mentality of subordinates who need to be kept in line
> through fear and who use intimidation to keep others in line,
> particularly our children (Dinkmeyer and Dreikurs, 1963:
> 118).

In a democratic society, characterised as it is by social equality and mutual respect, there is little doubt that rewards and punishment have lost their effectiveness. Teachers who persist with their use are finding that they create more problems than they solve. Rewards and punishments are products of, and necessary to, an autocratic society which is based on force, power, and fear. This type of society reaffirmed the traditional superiority of teachers over students and allowed teachers to make all decisions concerning the behaviour of students. Pupils who complied were rewarded while those who resisted or failed to meet certain criteria were punished. A teacher who uses rewards and punishments communicates a clear message: 'Because you have done what I wanted, I will reward you', or 'Because you have not done what I wanted, I will punish you'. Both approaches showed a lack of respect for students. There is no disputing the fact, however, that rewards and punishments were effective in an authoritarian school or classroom. The roles of both teacher and student were clearly defined as those of superior and inferior respectively and each knew what was expected of the other in each situation.

With the weakening of the authoritarian system and the strengthening of democratic processes, the vertical continuum of superiority–inferiority gave way to a system of social equality, a relationship which respected the rights of individuals to decide for themselves rather than being imposed upon. As Dreikurs (1968:26) points out:

> Regardless of individual differences in race, sex, money, age, education, or any other individual trait or quality, each individual has to be recognized in his equal value, commanding respect for what he is. Equality is not an ideal or a hope for the future; it exists.

Students are now recognised as having a new status which relates to their right to determine and direct their own behaviour. Any approach which ignores this status, such as rewards or punishments, domination or imposition, will invite the stoutest opposition and will invariably fail.

Within a democratic society, the use of rewards and punishments is both ineffective and inappropriate. They are inappropriate because they are based on the assumption that one group of people knows what is best for another. Reward is given by the superior to the inferior on the whim of the former while punishments are administered for failure to satisfy the arbitrary criteria of those in the superior position. Among social equals, rewards and punishments have no validity. Does any person really know what is the best behaviour for others? Does any person have the right to make others behave in certain ways? In an authoritarian society or school, the answer to both these questions was 'Yes'. Whatever the teacher decided upon was right and students were required to accept it. Today students refuse to be treated as inferiors and teachers are required to justify their demands in ways which were not required in the past. Defiance and rebellion are becoming commonplace in schools as students fight the authoritarian demands made on them by schools and teachers.

Not only are rewards and punishments inappropriate in today's schools, but they are no longer effective. Teachers who continue with rewards and punishments will find that their use has a number of disadvantages:

> Rewards and punishments make teachers responsible for their students' behaviour. Rewards and punishments prevent students from learning to make their own decisions. Rewards and punishments result in behaviours which are displayed only in the presence of the authority figures. Rewards and punishments invite resistance by attempting to force students to conform. (Dinkmeyer and McKay, 1976:7).

Specific problems which are likely to be encountered when punishment is used by teachers as a control technique are described below.

1. Punishment has the effect of temporarily suppressing behaviour but not of eliminating it. A teacher who punishes a boy for calling out in class will find that, for a short time, the punishment will be effective. However, observe the same student some weeks later and he will be seen calling out as frequently as he was before the punishment. Further punishment will again be necessary to suppress the undesirable behaviour temporarily. As punishment fails to weaken behaviour but only serves to suppress it, teachers who control through the use of punishment will need to punish students continually, a practice which would not be acceptable to most teachers. As Good and Brophy (1977:117) indicate: 'Punishment is a stopgap measure to suppress misbehaviour, and is not a solution to a problem by itself'.

2. Punishment has the effect of inviting retaliation. A teacher who punishes a pupil for lateness may find that her carefully prepared board drawings are erased. A science teacher who gives a detention may find that valuable equipment is damaged. A librarian who orders a noisy student from the library may discover a number of mutilated books. In each case, the student is responding to punishment with behaviours which say: 'If you have the right to hurt me, I have the same right to hurt you'. Revenge and retaliation are characteristic of students whose teachers choose to control through punishment.

3. The use of punishment requires that teachers assume the responsibility for their students' behaviour. Rather than

allowing students to make their own decisions and to accept responsibility for them, teachers make all the decisions concerning student behaviour and threaten or use punishment as a means of obtaining compliance. There is no respect shown to students, equality is violated, co-operation undermined, hostility generated. If schools wish to prepare students who are responsible for their own behaviour, then learning opportunities must be provided for students to take responsibility for their actions.

4. For those students whose goal is power or revenge, the use of punishment will invite and strengthen resistance and defiance. A teacher who tries to make a power-conscious student tidy up his desk, put books away, complete an assignment, sit quietly, or stop talking will find that his or her request will simply intensify the student's resistance. The threat or use of punishment will only aggravate the situation as it helps the student to develop greater powers of resistance and defiance. Further, a display of power by the teacher exercised through punishment confirms the student's faulty belief in the value of power. No amount of punishment will deter students whose goal it is to defeat others or to seek revenge.

5. The effects of punishment are unpredictable. While a reward given following a particular type of behaviour has the effect of inviting the student to repeat that type of behaviour, punishment is unspecific as it is given to suppress an undesirable behaviour rather than to strengthen a particular way of behaving. If the hypothesis is accepted that individuals always make the most appropriate response in view of their perceptions of a situation, then there is little value in punishing that response. Rather, a teacher should assist a student to re-assess or re-interpret the situation and develop more appropriate responses to the newly structured situation.

6. Another unfortunate effect of punishment is that students learn to avoid both the punisher and the punishing situation. If mathematics periods are viewed as occasions when students encounter a wide variety of aversion, they will tend to drop or avoid mathematics. Similarly teachers who are viewed as a source of aversion, in that they use punishment freely in the classroom, will find that students tend to avoid

A teacher who punishes a pupil for lateness may find that her carefully prepared chalk-board drawings are erased.

them. Any situation which is associated with punishment will create anxiety in students which can be avoided or relieved by avoiding the situation.

As one of the main aims of the educational process is to

encourage children in their educational progress, there can be no room for practices such as punishment which have the effect of discouraging children.

> There is no way that punishment can be encouraging. If an optimistic child comes to school and is punished, he loses his optimism. If a negative, pessimistic child comes to school and is punished, he is reinforced in his pessimism (Manaster and Corsini, 1982:241).

A strong case can be argued against the use of rewards, which are as detrimental in their application as is punishment. Reward, like punishment, is a product of a system which assumes that others know what is best for particular individuals and grants them the prerogative to dispense rewards for behaviours which please them. Students who are rewarded for certain classroom behaviours soon acquire an attitude of 'What's in it for me?'. They refuse to participate or co-operate unless they are rewarded for they have come to believe that they have a right to be rewarded.

Students who work only for a reward derive no pleasure from achievement; the reward is the goal, not the satisfaction which comes from learning. Extrinsic motivation replaces and destroys intrinsic motivation. Activities are judged not in terms of their interest or value but in terms of their external reward value. A number of studies have substantiated the destructive effects of external rewards on learning. For instance, a student who enjoys reading does not need to be externally rewarded for this activity. A teacher who begins to reward the student will find that the student now reads in order to obtain rewards. If rewards are discontinued, the student no longer reads. Reporting on a series of studies, Greene and Lepper (1974:54) concluded:

> The use of intrinsic rewards and controls can undermine the intrinsic interest of a child in the activities for which he received a reward.

Students do not need to be rewarded in order to act responsibly or to learn; they prefer to belong and contribute through co-operative and constructive behaviour. Teachers should respect and capitalise on this desire by providing opportunities for its expression rather than distorting it by offering rewards or threatening punishment.

Although Adler originally stated that the fundamental motivation was a striving for perfection, emphasising that personal 'minus' feelings were to be overcome by striving for personal 'plus' attainment, he finally concluded that the basic motivation was to belong to the human community, to have a place, to contribute to the welfare of human society. Whereas society strives from a minus to a plus and towards perfection, individual striving is to contribute.

The use of rewards and punishments in school tends to maintain order but provides no freedom for students. When some progressive schools decided to discontinue rewards and punishment, students were given freedom but order was sacrificed. The results were disastrous. Being democratic does not mean simply stopping being autocratic. Because there was no one to teach teachers the new skills of becoming democratic leaders, they have become permissive anarchists. Many classrooms are chaotic and students do what they want, learn what and when they like, care nothing for the needs of others, have little respect for the teacher, school or others. The challenge today is to provide an orderly system in which student freedom is respected. This requires that students exercise self-discipline rather than an externally imposed discipline.

To develop responsible or self-disciplined students requires an alternative approach to discipline. There is an alternative approach to rewards and punishments which is more effective and relevant to the classroom, in which the values of co-operation, social equality, self-discipline, mutual respect, and encouragement are accepted. The concept of behavioural consequences has many advantages and none of the unfortunate disadvantages which are associated with rewards and punishments.

BEHAVIOURAL CONSEQUENCES

Few would argue that a major task confronting our schools is to induce individuals to behave responsibly and to demonstrate a degree of self-control. Traditional methods adopted to achieve this aim have emphasised pressure from without, the use of rewards and punishments which attempted to make students behave in certain ways. In the presence of teachers, students behaved appropriately in order to earn a reward or to avoid punishment. The challenge facing teachers today in a democratic society is to stimulate students to behave more responsibly, not because of external pressure, but because they have decided that there are ways of behaving which are more appropriate than others. 'Stimulation from within' rather than 'pressure from without' is the major thrust of the new discipline.

The most powerful technique which is available to teachers who aim to induce responsible social behaviour in their students is the use of behavioural consequences. The rationale of this approach is that all behaviour is shaped and maintained by its consequences and that individuals will not continue to behave in ways which distress or harm nobody but themselves. Young children soon learn respect for a hot stove, a sharp knife, or a bicycle which tilts too far from centre, because they learn the consequences of their own behaviour if they behave inappropriately. Children associate the consequences of being burnt, cut, or bruised with their own behaviour rather than with the intervention of another person. Nobody is making them do anything but, if they violate order, they know that their behaviour will produce unpleasant or hurtful consequences.

Life is a series of choices in which individuals make decisions and experience the consequences. If gas bills are not paid, the gas supply is discontinued. Arrive late at the airport and the flight leaves without you. Over-eat and put on weight. Choice–decision–consequences is the series of events which teaches us all to be responsible for our own behaviour. We cannot blame others for what we have brought upon ourselves. Next time, we will make a more responsible decision because we have experienced the consequences of irresponsibility. The logic of the social or natural order impresses the individual rather than the authoritative demand of another.

There are two types of consequences.

1. Natural behavioural consequences

In nature there are neither rewards nor punishments; there are only consequences. Natural consequences represent the 'routine effects of reality or the natural flow of events without interference from parents or teachers' (Baruth and

Eckstein, 1976: 83). For instance, a child who refuses to eat goes hungry; a child who leaves off a pullover on a winter's day suffers from chill; a child who stays up too late at night suffers from tiredness next day. It is the natural order or the reality of the situation which impresses the child; the teacher is not involved and adopts the role of a friendly bystander. 'I am sorry that you are cold but you know what to do about it' would be the response of a teacher to a student who leaves his pullover in the classroom when students are outside at play. The technique of applying natural consequences involves doing nothing. Information is given by the teacher to the student about the consequences of behaviour; the student acts or does not act properly and the teacher permits the student to receive the natural consequences of the behaviour. Teachers do not scold, threaten, argue, or preach but simply express their regrets.

2. Logical behavioural consequences

There are, unfortunately, few natural consequences available within classrooms while some which are would involve an unacceptable element of physical danger. However, the application of logical behavioural consequences is completely feasible and acceptable. These consequences are guided and arranged by the teacher, the group, or another adult and are designed to let the reality of the social order impress the child rather than the authority of the teacher. A student who gets up late in the morning will experience the consequences at school; a damaged library book is repaired by the student; students who do not practise are not considered for selection; homework not completed precludes a student from participation in a particular lesson; a science bench left untidy will result in a student's missing out on a subsequent period; a uniform left home will result in a home economics student's missing practical work; or a latecomer will not be given the problem sheet or details of a desk assignment. In all cases, students have a choice of behaviours and the consequence of unacceptable behaviour has a logical relationship to the choice.

Many teachers find it difficult to distinguish between punishment and behavioural consequences. There are a number of important distinctions between the two.

Punishment	*Behavioural consequences*
1. Teachers are responsible for student behaviour.	1. Students are responsible for their own behaviour.
2. Concerned with the past and always retaliatory.	2. Concerned with the present and not retaliatory.
3. An arbitrary connection between the behaviour and its consequences.	3. A logical connection between the behaviour and its consequences.
4. Based on superior– inferior relationship between teachers and students.	4. Based on the concept of equality and worth between teachers and students.
5. Always personalised and involves moral judgment.	5. Impersonal and involves no moral judgement.
6. No alternative or choice of behaviours is given by the teacher.	6. Students always have the right to decide between several behaviours.
7. Voice, relationship, and atmosphere reflect anger and resentment.	7. Voice, relationship, and atmosphere are friendly when consequences are invoked.
8. Expresses the power of a personal authority.	8. Expresses the reality of the social order or the situation.
9. Implies that teachers know what is best for students.	9. Implies that students are capable of managing their own lives.

Try these

To clarify the differences between punishment and behavioural consequences, read the following incidents and indicate whether the teacher used natural consequences (NC), logical consequences (LC), or punishment (P).

1. The teacher gave John a detention because he arrived late.
2. Although warned, Tim used the saw carelessly and gashed his hand.

3. The teacher refused to accept Jane's assignment which was offered one week after the due date.
4. The teacher would not allow Harold to use the box of mathematics games because he had failed to put them away yesterday.
5. Tim left his lunch at home and the teacher refused to lend him money to buy lunch. Tim became hungry.
6. When Sam slammed his desk top, the teacher made him write out 50 times, 'I must not slam my desk top'.

Answers

1 P; 2 NC; 3 LC; 4 LC; 5 NC; 6 P

APPLYING BEHAVIOURAL CONSEQUENCES

A teacher who wishes to use behavioural consequences will find many classroom situations which lend themselves to this approach. Regardless of the type of student behaviour, the aim in applying consequences is to stimulate individuals to become more responsible for their own behaviour by allowing them to experience the consequences of their own behaviour. It is not the intention of an authoritarian punitive teacher to impose values and standards on students and demand compliance but, rather, to allow the reality of the natural or social order to impress students with the desirability or otherwise of certain behaviours.

The use of behavioural consequences can be demonstrated by considering some typical classroom situations and the manner in which consequences are applied. It is important to note that many consequences are determined by the class rather than by the teacher. When rules or routines are decided by the teacher without consultation, many students will feel inclined to ignore them. The imposition of arbitrarily decided consequences will be viewed by students as a form of punishment and a product of an authoritarian system which many of them are fighting. For example, Tim spray-paints on a wall. The teacher rebukes him and makes him clean it up. The class discusses the spray-painting incident and decide that the culprit is responsible for cleaning it up. Even though the outcome is the same, the latter is now a logical consequence. When students are involved in problem ownership, formulating consequences, they learn the value of maintaining and respecting order. Further, they are willing to accept the consequences and support the teacher in the application of these consequences with non-conforming students.

Homework

The failure of students to complete homework assignments is a constant source of irritation to most teachers. Corsini believes that it was created by the devil in view of the amount of friction it creates. Many parents take on the responsibility of ensuring that their children complete homework while teachers and parents threaten, cajole, scold, and punish students with respect to homework. How might consequences be applied to this problem?

> A high-school mathematics teacher raised the question of homework with her Year 9 students. She pointed out that it was important for students to complete the mathematics homework and gave a number of reasons to support her view. She said: 'I expect that there will be times when some students fail to complete the assignment. What should we do about that?' After some discussion it was agreed that students who did not complete homework should not be permitted to participate in the mathematics lesson that day. Some weeks later, John failed to complete his homework. His teacher said: 'I see that you have not finished your assignment, John. I am sorry that you will not be able to participate in the lesson today. Would you please sit over there?'

The above incident highlights several features involved in the use of behavioural consequences. First, nobody is making the students do anything; they have freedom to decide whether to complete the homework or not. If they fail to complete the assigned task, they experience the consequences of their behaviour, a consequence which they themselves helped to determine and agree upon. Secondly, the teacher is not involved in scolding or punishing but she maintains a pleasant relationship with John and simply expresses her disappointment that he is not able to participate in the particular lesson. Thirdly, behavioural consequences are more effective when good relationships exist between teacher and students. If John were involved in a power struggle, he would use the homework issue to defy the teacher and her request that he move to the rear of the room would be a further signal for him to attempt to defeat her. Finally, the consequence came from the group rather than from the teacher. If the teacher had announced, 'Students who do not complete homework will not be permitted to participate in the class', students would view the decision as arbitrary, involving punishment, and reflecting the personal power and authority of the teacher.

Lateness

A persistent problem which confronts many teachers is the student who is a frequent late-comer to class. Lessons are interrupted, time is wasted in repeated explanations, and attention-seeking behaviour is strengthened. The problem may be corrected by the use of consequences as demonstrated by the following incident.

Tim is often late arriving at class in the morning and can be relied upon to be several minutes late following recess breaks. His teacher rebukes him but gives him details of the work which he missed because of his lateness. She decided to apply behaviour consequences. Tim arrived late for the first period after lunch. His teacher ignored him and did not give him details of the task she had set for the class. When Tim asked for details of the task, his teacher told him that she did not have time to give a second explanation but would detail the task for him at the end of the period and he could complete it in his own time.

Although the above example illustrates a logical consequence not necessarily decided by the class, it features the essentials of behavioural consequences. Tim is required to accept responsibility for his own behaviour; the consequence is logically related to the behaviour; a choice of behaviours is given; the needs of the learning situation are emphasised rather than the personal power of the teacher, while the consequences are impersonal, involving no element of moral judgment. It is now up to Tim to decide whether he will continue to come late to class and experience the consequence or whether he will come to class on time.

Damaging school property

Most schools have ample evidence of the damage which students inflict on school property. Initials are carved on desks, library books are torn and written on, equipment misused, and class texts damaged or stolen.

Such acts are increasing and huge sums are being expended on restoring property to a functional level. Almost no measures are successful in decreasing the number of delinquent acts in schools. How would behavioural consequences approach the problem?

Sam was working in an art and craft room with the rest of his class. He was engaged in woodwork which involved the use of an electric drill. He decided to drill his initials into a benchtop and, when completed, stood back to admire his handiwork. His teacher, who had not observed the incident, came to check Sam's progress and noted what he had done. In a matter-of-fact tone of voice, the teacher said: 'I see that you have damaged the bench, Sam. Would you like to repair it yourself or would you like the school to do it for you and charge the costs to your parents?' Sam said nothing but went to the cupboard, took out some glass paper, and began to sand the initials.

The above incident illustrates a successful application of logical consequences. A choice was given; the consequence was logically related to the behaviour and was impersonal, involving no moral judgment or blame; the teacher was respectful to Sam; the tone of voice was friendly; and the consequence was concerned with the present and was not retaliatory.

Quietness in the library

Whenever rules of order are required, the group which will be affected by the rules should be involved in their making. This procedure not only teaches students the need for order but also assists teachers when the need arises to apply the consequences. Behaviour in the library is used to demonstrate this procedural aspect of logical consequences. A librarian might hold a discussion with each class on the occasion of the initial visit to the library. She would point out the importance of a quiet working environment if students are to gain the maximum benefit from their library visits. During the discussion, the librarian might invite students to discuss the possible courses of action which are available if particular students disregard the need for silence in the library. A consensus is reached that only students who are quiet may be permitted to remain in the library. On a subsequent occasion, should it be necessary, the librarian would approach a child who is violating the particular rule regarding silence in the library and say: 'I am sorry, Stephen. Only people who are quiet may stay in the library'. What is the librarian making the child do? Nothing. It is up to Stephen to decide whether he wishes to stay in the library. The element of choice exists; the librarian and her tone of voice are friendly; the consequence is logically related to the behaviour; and it is Stephen who must accept responsibility for his own behaviour.

Team practice

The need for team rules in sporting activities is an excellent opportunity for the group to determine its operating rules and the consequences which will be used to stimulate the acceptance of the rules.

> *Mr Mathews is the football coach at a metropolitan high school. He has been worried by the poor attendance of his players at practice and decides to raise this issue at a team meeting. He said: 'We play our matches on Friday afternoon. We practise after school on Tuesday. Do you think that students who don't practise should be allowed to play on Friday?' After some discussion, the team reaches a decision that the team will be selected from those students who attended practice. Two weeks later, Peter chose not to attend practice. Mr Mathews approached Peter on Wednesday and said: 'I see that you didn't practise yesterday. I am sorry that you will not be playing on Friday'.*

Again the elements of a behavioural consequence are present. It is up to Peter to decide his own behaviour: whether he wishes to attend practice or not. Mr Mathews did not make him do anything and his manner and voice remained calm and friendly. The consequence is logically related to the behaviour and it is a consequence which Peter himself helped formulate. Mr Mathews has respected Peter's

Quietness in the Library.

right to decide and has used an effective method to stimulate him.

It is not difficult to envisage similar incidents occurring in schools. The home economics teacher could discuss with her class the need for protective clothing and the possible consequences which could be used if students failed to dress appropriately. The trades teacher might discuss the need for safety in the workshop and the consequences which might follow unsafe behaviour. The librarian could discuss the need for orderly borrowing and return of books and the consequence for students who violate order by failing to follow the rules. An English teacher may wish to formulate rules for group discussion and the consequence to be used in the case of a student who dominates the discussion.

In all the above cases, the element of choice is present for the students. Nobody is forcing them to do anything. The student chooses to do homework or not, to return library books on time or not, to practise or not. If a student chooses to behave in an unacceptable manner, logical consequences immediately follow. These consequences are known to the students and their application is a direct result of the student's decision. Teachers who use behavioural consequences are not abdicating their responsibility but are attempting to induce more responsible behaviour in students by methods which respect the individual and give the right to the individual to decide. While students are free to decide, they will experience the consequences if their behaviour violates order. Through the use of consequences, freedom and order are successfully combined while order without freedom (autocratic) and freedom without order (laissez-faire) are rejected. Needless to say, consequences must never be used when safety or danger is involved. In the case of school crossings, handling of dangerous equipment or school bus travel, no choice is offered.

A final word: the application of behavioural consequences is a technique for dealing with immediate behavioural problems but does not provide students with an understanding of their goals if they choose to behave irresponsibly. Classroom discussions, to be described later, are necessary to assist students to gain insight into the purposes of their behaviour and of alternative ways of behaving. Students who steal from the lockers may be seeking attention, displaying power, or seeking revenge. Consequences may preclude them from entering the locker area but will not assist them in understanding the purpose of their behaviour or in changing their perception of the situation which may then result in more adequate behaviour. Nevertheless, behavioural consequences are among the most important techniques which teachers may use to improve relationships with their students and to develop self-discipline in them.

Try these

(1) For each of the following incidents, indicate whether it is an example of punishment (P), natural behavioural consequence (NC), or logical behavioural consequence (LC).

1. John misses the camp because he has not completed his homework.
2. Susan misses out on craft because she has not brought her materials.
3. John is asked to repair the library book which he has damaged.
4. Sally mishandles a Bunsen burner and burns her hand.
5. Robert arrives late for a class and is given a detention.
6. The teacher corrects only assignments which are submitted on time.
7. Jane leaves her workbook lying on a locker; subsequently she is unable to locate it.
8. Charlie complains that the test questions are covering topics he hasn't learned.
9. Harry steals from the lockers and is expelled from the school.

(2) John requests and receives permission to borrow a tape recorder. Because of his carelessness in handling it, he runs the batteries down. Which approach by the teacher would be advocated by the author?

A 'That is the last time you will use the tape recorder.'

B 'You can take yourself up to the principal and explain what happened.'

C 'The batteries will cost you $2.50. Do you have it or will I put it on your book account?'

(3) Consider the following incident. Does it indicate the use of punishment or of behavioural consequences?
The teacher said: 'Just remember this, young man. Nobody is indispensable and because you did not practise last night you will not be playing today. Remember, that was the team decision'.

(4) Harold, a Year 9 student, has been caught cheating in an examination. His teacher wishes to use behavioural consequences rather than punishment. On which of the following aspects would she concentrate?

A   the moral aspect of cheating
B   what she will do now rather than what Harold has done
C   implementing an aversive reaction
D   exerting her power of authority over Harold
E   humiliating Harold to prevent him repeating it
F   logically relating a consequence to the cheating
G   maintaining a friendly relationship with Harold
H   accepting responsibility for Harold's behaviour

(5) Consider the following statements made by students when asked by the teacher to account for their inappropriate behaviours:
'Why didn't you tell me that the assignment date was near?'
'The boys made me mess it up.'
'They made me so angry that I couldn't help it.'
'What do you expect from me? I'm dumb.'
'How can I write well with this old pen?'
'What do you expect? My parents don't care.'
Question 1: How do the above students avoid responsibility?
Question 2: How can teachers help students to accept responsibility?

Question 3: Why do students avoid responsibility?
Question 4: How much responsibility as students should
students accept for their own behaviour?

(6) The following examples are given in the Canter model as consequences which teachers may use when students misbehave.
- Loss of privilege, e.g. miss a film.
- Loss of preferred activity, e.g. miss playing basketball.
- Visit to the principal; must be 'unpleasant'.
- Detention, e.g. staying after school.
- Time out, e.g. isolation.

Are the above examples of consequences or punishments?

Answers

(1) 1 P; 2 LC; 3 LC; 4 NC; 5 P; 6 LC; 7 NC; 8 NC; 9 P
(2) C
(3) This is an example of punishment. Although the teacher is applying a behavioural consequence which has been decided by the group, his phrasing is harsh and angry. Consequences are indicated in a firm, friendly and impartial statement.
(4) B; F; G
(5) 1. They blame others for their inappropriate behaviour.
    2. Avoid blaming or punishing but allow consequences to follow.
    3. Because they are afraid of being blamed or punished.
    4. Total responsibility.

(6) They are punishments. They are not relevant to the behaviour; they are disrespectful; they express the power of the teacher; they are concerned with the past and are retaliatory, expressing anger and resentment.

7

Group Dynamics: Integrating a Class

INTRODUCTION

In a pair of challenging questions, Dreikurs and Cassel (1972:73) asked: 'Do you regard your class as a mirror of your own personality, feeling confident only when they obey and inadequate when they disturb? Or do you really feel that you belong to your class as a group member?'. It is a tradition in teaching that teachers are single-handedly to teach and correct a given number of students in their class. Today, given the concepts of shared responsibility and participatory decision-making, it is important that teachers see themselves as group leaders of one class, be it comprised of 10, 20, or 30 students. The use of group dynamics, the ability to integrate a group and to establish a group atmosphere in which all students are willing to co-operate and contribute, is a skill which must be developed.

Previous chapters have suggested a number of techniques which may be appropriate for particular individuals who are creating management or learning problems in the classroom. Teachers whose students engage in various forms of misbehaviour, such as attention seeking, power, revenge, or withdrawal, must first render such behaviours ineffective by refusing to be caught in the act–react cycle. By going against their first impulse, teachers will have taken the first step towards implementing an effective corrective program.

When a student's behaviour does not achieve its intended goal, it is likely that the disturbance will intensify. That in itself is an indication that the teacher's action is proving to be successful. However, there is no reason to believe that student behaviour will improve simply by rendering goals ineffective. On the contrary, positive corrective action must also be undertaken. The application of the techniques of encouragement and of behavioural consequences will tend to reduce the incidence and intensity of most behavioural problems which teachers encounter, and prevent new problems from arising. This is particularly true for primary school children but less so for post-primary students whose behaviour reflects a growing degree of autonomy.

In both primary and secondary schools, problems are invariably linked to faulty relationships between students and teachers or between students themselves. Group approaches are necessary if problems arising from faulty relationships are to be corrected and new, more satisfactory relationships established. There is no escaping what Adler called the 'iron logic of communal life'. Humans are social beings. Their behaviours express social movement and interaction. All problems are social problems and can be resolved only in a social context for it is within the group that the behaviour is meaningful.

With the huge upheavals of the 1960s and 1970s, the traditional relationship between teachers and students changed markedly. The classroom took on a new aspect and the roles of teachers and students changed accordingly. Teachers have traditionally been regarded as absolute authorities in their classrooms. All decisions regarding school organisation, curricula, conduct, classroom rules, and patterns of relationships were made by teachers and their authority was largely unchallenged.

Societal changes of the past two decades which have been described as a shift from an autocratic attitude to a democratic attitude have challenged the authoritarian role of the teacher, and the newly accepted value of social equality is one which must be faced by all teachers. Unfortunately very few teachers have recognised the nature of the problem or are aware of consequences of these social changes. Many still attempt to enforce compliance and press students into submission, practices which result in defiance, hostility, animosity, and open warfare.

With the development of democratic patterns, the authority of the adult diminished while the authority of the group became increasingly important. 'The approval of his peers becomes more important for the child than that of adults, parents, or teachers' (Dreikurs, Grunwald, and Pepper, 1982:130). In no area is there one person who, by virtue of a superior position, knows what is best for others and has the right to impose values on them. Values have become relative and the group now replaces the authority as the value-forming agent. The right of a teacher to decide the behaviour of students has been weakened by the development of democratic social patterns. No practice which perpetuates a superior-inferior relationship is acceptable in today's society. Those who have gained so much ground in the last decade or so — women, coloured people, the labour force, children, and students — are not about to surrender these hard-won gains. Calls for firmer discipline, a return to more autocratic control, or to increased punishment, will be spectacularly unsuccessful.

Like other societal institutions, schools have been greatly affected by these changes. Teachers are beginning to understand that their role has changed and the need to share responsibility with their students is a necessary and inevitable outcome of the changes. The class group — the peer group — has become increasingly important and teachers must, accepting the role of group leader, learn to utilise the group to their advantage. Failure to do so will result in the group becoming unhelpful, an obstacle, and supporting individual students in rebellion against the teacher.

A deliberate and conscious decision will need to be taken by teachers if they are to cope with the problems generated by societal changes. It is a decision by the teacher to consider, for each situation, not what the teacher wants, not what the student wants, but rather what are the needs of the situation. For example, a teacher may believe that students in class should have permission to speak before doing so;

students may feel that they have the right to speak without permission. The needs of the situation, however, require that class discussions should be orderly and that students who wish to speak should be able to do so provided they do not interrupt others or dominate the discussion. The focus is not on the teacher's or student's wishes but on the needs of the situation. The teacher and students explore these needs and establish procedures for meeting them. These procedures may be quite different from those reached in another class but that difference reflects the relative nature of values today. There is no right way to conduct a group discussion but the procedures decided by a particular class become the guidelines for that class. The teacher, acting as a group leader, involves the group in decisions which concern them. What does the situation require in the library? What behaviour is appropriate in a small outside playing area? What is required when viewing a film? The teacher and students determine, for each of the above, the needs of the situation. Gone is the authoritarian demand of the teacher; gone also is the natural resentment and struggle by students against this authoritarian demand. Instead, in an atmosphere of social equality, mutual respect and shared responsibility, decisions are made co-operatively in terms of the needs of each situation.

Not only is the group the most appropriate body to make decisions in a democratic society, but it is also the most powerful agent for dealing with problems which might arise within the group. Teachers have been taught to believe that they are personally responsible for the behaviour of each student in their classes. Patterns of student behaviour and performance are decided by the teacher; those students who meet them are rewarded while those who transgress are punished. This is the typical authoritarian practice in which children were coerced into accepting externally imposed patterns of behaviour through the threat of punishment or the promise of reward. In this type of classroom, the peer group supported the authority of the teacher and developed conforming and submissive behaviour with only indirect signs of resentment.

The responsibility for student behaviour in a democratic classroom now belongs to the group. The class, under the leadership of the teacher, formulates a behavioural code for a particular class and it is the responsibility of the class to enforce the code. Students who deviate become the responsibility of the group rather than the teacher. The group identifies the problem and formulates the solution. The group 'owns' the problem and solution. Until teachers develop procedures which utilise the group for the benefit of each individual student, they will find that the group will often support the student who rebels.

> The individual power of a teacher is no longer sufficient to restrain a recalcitrant pupil or to move him in the desired direction unless group pressure can be mobilised for that purpose. (Dreikurs, 1960:1).

The group can be particularly helpful to a teacher or can create innumerable problems. Teachers who can solicit peer group support have a powerful ally to support them in their dealings with difficult children. Many students who oppose the educational process have a superior ability to create group cohesiveness which is directed against the teacher. Without the ability to influence groups positively, teachers will be seriously impeded in their work. The group is the reality in which students operate and the practice of dealing with students in a one-to-one relationship discourages children from facing their problems in a social context. All student problems encountered in a classroom reflect an unwillingness to co-operate. The use of the peer group to promote and reinforce co-operation in individual students not only constitutes an effective way to teach and to exert corrective influence, but is imperative in our democratic classrooms where the authority of the peer group has replaced the authority of an individual teacher (Dreikurs, 1968:69).

A teacher who utilises the group in dealing with individual students is freed from disciplinary or corrective action as that responsibility is delegated to the group. The emphasis is not, 'What am I going to do about it?' but rather, 'What are we going to do about it?'. A student who constantly interrupts or argues with a teacher will become the responsibility of the group when the teacher invites its assistance with a statement such as, 'I am having great trouble teaching this

'Helen knew that she could help James if she could spend more time with him... but at whose expense?'

class because of Jim's frequent interruptions. What can we do about it?'. It is not the teacher's problem; it is not Jim's problem; it is a problem for all. Shared responsibility is one of the most powerful and important ingredients in a democratic classroom. Teachers do not teach 10, 20, or 30 individual students; they teach one group of 10, 20 or 30 students. The ability to utilise this group will determine a teacher's effectiveness in a classroom; an inability to do so will result in the perpetuation of procedures which have lost their effectiveness and are responsible for many of the problems encountered in schools today. It is not surprising that so many teachers complain of stress and burn-out; they still think in terms of 27 individual relationships rather than in terms of shared influence.

The suggestion has been made that the teacher's role is now that of a group leader who assists the class in making decisions which affect the group and the individuals who comprise it. The class is not only the value and decision-making unit but it is also the judicial agency. It is necessary, therefore, that the group be integrated, with individual students working co-operatively and harmoniously to achieve group goals. The extent to which this is achieved depends very much on the skill of the teacher. Unfortunately very few teachers possess the skills necessary to achieve group cohesion. This is not a reflection on teachers but on their training institutions which still concentrate on providing teachers with the technical skills of instruction and knowledge acquisition and with a view of the class as a collection of individuals with whom the teacher relates on a one-to-one basis.

Ineffective and unskilled handling of group procedures is the major problem facing teachers. Indeed Dreikurs (1960:3) goes so far as to suggest:

> The success of a teacher depends to a large extent on his ability to unite the class for a common purpose. His ability or his failure to do so will often determine not only what the children learn, but how they develop and grow, intellectually and socially.

Lindgren (1956:30) also highlights the importance of the teacher working with groups rather than with individuals and suggests that the relationship between a group and a teacher is different from the relationship between a teacher and an individual child.

> Classroom groups are, as a rule, not mere collections of individuals, but have personalities of their own. Failure to recognise the separate psychological existence of the group will result in the teacher dealing and thinking of a one-to-one relationship or of a sub-group relationship. Such an approach emphasises divisiveness that interferes with learning, communication, and social functioning.

A typical classroom is far from integrated. One can identify a number of cliques such as the social group, the scholarly group, the sporting group, the nuisance group, the 'hopeless' group, the power group and so on. A learning task which appeals to one sub-group will have little appeal to the others; a sub-group which is praised by a teacher will be scorned by the other groups; the success of one sub-group will further discourage the others. Students fail because they cannot do as well as others. The tendency of students to form opposing camps, to set up antagonistic sub-groups of the 'good' and the 'bad', the advanced and the slow, and capable and the deficient, the boy and the girl, and the established Australians and the recent arrivals, represents the greatest challenge to teachers. Their success or failure in meeting this challenge is the major determinant of teaching effectiveness and of student learning.

The above discussion of the changing nature of inter-personal relationships between teachers and students has highlighted the need for teachers to develop the skills of group dynamics. Traditional teacher education programs have assumed an authoritarian pattern of classroom interaction and have emphasised the individual learner. Management and instructional strategies were taught within this framework. As the classroom and the interpersonal relationships within the classroom have taken on a democratic aspect, teachers are unprepared to fulfil their new role.

Teachers who are to be effective in today's school must view themselves as group leaders, recognise the increasing influence of peer pressure compared with adult domination, think and act in terms of the group rather than of individuals, and develop the techniques that lead to the establishment of cohesiveness within the class. The value of sociometry must be recognised, the indispensable technique of group discussion must be practised, the divisiveness of competition recognised, and the compelling influences of classroom climate on morale and cohesiveness be realised. The above imperatives represent a major challenge to teachers and to those who train them but, as Corsini (1977:296) correctly observes, 'a good system of education must be based on a correct theory of personality and upon a proper philosophy of life'. Values which are fostered in a democratic community, such as mutual respect, co-operation, shared responsibility, and social equality, must be those which are developed, practised, and modelled in the schools of today.

In a discussion on the importance of a teacher operating as a group leader, Dreikurs, Grunwald, and Pepper (1982:135) observe:

> The skilled teacher, who is sensitive to the group atmosphere, will sense the type of atmosphere that her new class has and plan a constructive program through which she can gradually change the children's attitudes. The climate of the classroom reflects the personal characteristics of all and influences in turn the development of each child emotionally, and socially. Therefore, the teacher must know not only the individuals in the class but also how they interact with one another, since this determines how they feel in the class. Without some knowledge of group dynamics, a teacher cannot have the necessary insight into the group's problems. She can understand the functions of the group only by examining the interactions that take place and the perceptions, goals, and frustrations of the individual students.

To integrate a class successfully, a teacher will find the following approaches and techniques of group dynamics helpful: (a) classroom atmosphere; (b) classroom discussion; (c) sociometry.

CLASSROOM ATMOSPHERE

Regardless of the position taken by teachers in relation to the degree of freedom which they allow students in all aspects of learning and behaving, teachers create a definite classroom atmosphere which is decisive on the extent to which they can integrate a class and on the level of social and intellectual learning of students which they promote. One teacher may assume total responsibility for deciding what students do and how they behave, and allow no freedom for students in respect to these matters. Another teacher may grant students total freedom to decide their own program and behaviour, and impose no rules of order. A third teacher might involve students in decision-making and will respect the students' right to decide within an orderly framework. The social climate which each of these three teachers creates is quite different and is decisive in determining the degree of class cohesiveness.

Autocratic leader	Democratic leader	Laissez-faire leader

Dominates, directs
Decides all issues
Encourages no
  participation in
  planning or control
  by members
Makes personal
  criticisms
Assumes all
  responsibility
Maintains wide social
  distance from
  members
Defines goals, imposes
  them on members
Initiates all activity
	Shares control with
	  members
	Asks for contributions
	Makes objective
	  criticisms
	Encourages group
	  initiatives
	Delegates
	  responsibility
	Participates in activity
	Has close relationships
	  with members
	Works for mutual
	  establishment of
	  goals
		Makes no attempt to
		  regulate or orient
		Allows complete
		  member freedom
		No restrictions imposed
		  on members
		No clear goals
		  established
		Allows complete non-
		  participation
		No participation of
		  leader with group

Figure 8   Characteristics of three types of classroom leadership

The three types of social climate described above may be classified:
1. Autocratic: orderly but no freedom; over-control
2. Laissez-faire: freedom but no order; under-control
3. Democratic: freedom with order; inner control
The characteristics of each type of leadership together with the typical reaction are described in Figure 8.

Many teachers find the concepts of Individual Psychology confusing, particularly when they are applied to leadership or classroom atmosphere. To many, the concept of freedom implies permissiveness while others have suggested that A.S. Neill's Summerhill is a prototype of Individual Psychology. Corsini (1977:322) has commented on these misconceptions:

> Individual Education (Adlerian) is no more like Summerhill in theory or practice than it is like West Point. West Point is essentially an authoritarian school; Summerhill is essentially a permissive school; Individual Education is essentially a democratic school.

Being democratic does not result merely by refraining from being autocratic. Anarchy results when one believes that the opposite of autocracy is democracy. Being democratic does not mean simply permissiveness or doing as one pleases; it is a system which re-affirms the values of respect and equality and operates on the principle of freedom with order.

Regardless of the objectives of a school, there is nothing which can be said in favour of the laissez-faire approach. A teacher who wishes to emphasise scholastic achievement, communication, social skills, co-operation, high morale, cohesiveness, responsibility, or whatever, will find no justification for a permissive approach, an approach frequently advocated by some of the so-called progressive educators in their mistaken belief that democracy is the opposite of autocracy. The only realistic choice of leadership is between autocratic and democratic, two patterns of behaviour which Dreikurs (1968:74) has polarised as follows:

Autocratic	Democratic
Boss	Leader
Voice, sharp	Voice, friendly
Command	Invitation
Power	Influence
Pressure	Stimulation
Demanding co-operation	Winning co-operation
I tell you what you should do	I tell you what I will do
Imposing ideas	Selling ideas
Domination	Guidance
Criticism	Encouragement
Fault finding	Acknowledgement of achievement
Punishment	Helping
I tell you	Discussion
I decide, you obey	I suggest and help you to decide
Sole responsibility of boss	Shared responsibility in team

Mindful of the major function of a teacher, the unification of the class, a major prerequisite for successful learning for all, which of the two 'climate zones' or types of leadership is the most effective?

One of the classic studies designed to answer this question was conducted by Kurt Lewin (1948). Working with young children, Lewin established three types of social climates — autocratic, democratic and laissez-faire — and studied the behaviour of students under each type of leadership. Using the same teacher, who displayed each type of leadership for three different groups of children who were in different rooms, Lewin found that on achievement measures, there was little to separate the authoritarian and democratic groups. When the criterion of social relationships was applied, very significant differences between the autocratic and democratic groups were evidenced.

The autocratic group was very competitive, functioned only when the teacher was present, fought and quarrelled in the leader's absence, and engaged in a high frequency of negative comments about each other's work. In contrast, the democratic group was co-operative, functioned well without the teacher, shared materials, commented positively on each other's work, and displayed characteristics of a well-integrated group. As expected, the laissez-faire group was chaotic.

Two particular aspects of Lewin's study are significant. First, when a third person, the janitor, wrongly accused a randomly selected student in the autocratic group of stealing an article from his store room, the other students made no effort to defend or assist their colleague even though they were aware of the erroneous nature of the charge. When the same accusation was made in the democratic group, the students defended their peer and pointed out the physical impossibility of the act. They were cohesive and integrated and demonstrated concern for others. The autocratic group was fragmented and their members self-centred, not caring about others as long as they were not affected.

A second interesting aspect of Lewin's study concerned the effect on students when the leader reversed roles in each group. What happens when a democratic leader assumes an autocratic role or when an autocrat becomes democratic? In the first situation, there was no initial change in the behaviour of the students. Having developed a trusting relationship with the teacher, students in the democratic group accepted the change and before long took on the characteristics of the children in the autocratic setting. In the autocratic group, the change in the teachers' behaviour from autocratic to democratic resulted in chaos. Freed from externally imposed discipline which relied on pressure from above, reward and

punishment, the students were disorderly, noisy, and difficult to manage. It took some time before they settled down
under the new leadership and began to exercise some
degree of responsibility for their behaviour. This aspect of
the study has tremendous significance for today as it accurately reflects the major social changes over the past two
decades. As applied to education, it suggests that, when
children move from an autocratic environment into a democratic setting, they tend to run wild and abuse their freedom
because they have not learnt to rely on their inner restraint
when the outside pressure has failed to force them into
submission (Dreikurs, 1968). While order without freedom
undoubtedly served the needs of an autocratic society, the
democratic values of respect, equality, and co-operation
made the model of freedom with order an imperative in
schools. Without a democratic climate or atmosphere in a
classroom, the values which we accept today, particularly
co-operation, are unobtainable.

Writing of the Lewin experiments, Dreikurs, Grunwald,
and Pepper (1982:76) observe:

> This observation has far-reaching significance for our entire
> culture. Whenever people move from an autocratic setting
> into a democratic setting, they become 'free', but they do not
> know what to do with their freedom. Freedom carries with it
> certain responsibilities. This holds true for adults as well as
> for children. Many of the events of our time — the confusion,
> misused freedom, the lack of responsibility — validate the
> observations of Kurt Lewin.

CLASSROOM DISCUSSION

A second approach which a teacher may use to integrate a
class is the use of classroom discussion. This indispensable
procedure should be a regular part of each student's program. While spontaneous discussion may occur as the need
arises, provision should be made for regular weekly discussion to occur at a definite time and place.

What is classroom discussion? It is interchange of ideas
guided by the group and directed towards particular problems. Whereas conversation is random, discussion is
focused and involves the teacher and students in talking,

listening, and thinking about some common problem or situation. Through discussion, students are involved as socially equal, responsible participants in the educational process, while the teacher's involvement is that of a group leader, guiding, stimulating, and functioning without concern for prestige or authority.

There are a number of goals which may be achieved through group discussion. Dreikurs (1968:79) has identified the following.

1. *Group discussion aims to help students to understand themselves and each other and, if necessary, change their motivations and concepts.* To achieve this purpose, discussion allows students to express themselves freely and for the teacher to make interpretations in terms of the goals of particular students. There is no preaching, moralising, or fault-finding involved; but an attempt is made to have students become aware of their motivations, their mistaken views of how they belong, and of alternative ways of behaving. When students begin to think about the problems of others, of the factors which contributed to these problems, of their own influence in creating problems in others, the classroom takes on the dimensions of cohesiveness, co-operation, and social responsiveness.

2. *Classroom discussion stimulates children to listen to others, to help each other.* Indeed, for many difficult students, discussion is the only way in which they can be reached. This is particularly true in adolescence when the group is the value-forming body which places subtle pressure on its members to accept the values of the group. Drug-taking, stealing, vandalism, and defiance are the types of problems for which the influential power of the group is indispensable.

The major concept involved is shared responsibility. No longer does a teacher view the group as 30 individuals but rather as one group of 30 students. Problems in relation to members of the group are not the teacher's problem but the group's problem. It is the class together with the teacher which has the responsibility for dealing with the bully, the truant, the clown, or the thief. For example, a teacher may raise a problem which she has in teaching a particular class. Although no names are mentioned, students will quickly identify their classmate who is causing the difficulty and will, under appropriate guidance, offer suggestions as to the purposes achieved by such behaviour. Further, some will volunteer information concerning their own goals, goals which were unknown to them before the discussion. Children learn to listen to others, to communicate their ideas and feelings, to understand others, and to accept responsibility for helping others. If teachers have learnt to understand students, they can help students better to understand themselves and others. Following the identification of a particular student's goal, the invitation to a class, 'What are we going to do about it?', demonstrates respect and equality while invoking the most powerful corrective influence which the teacher possesses: the group.

Some people may object to the practice of discussing a particular student's problem behaviour in front of a group. However, if one accepts as a basic philosophy that all important problems are social problems and that failure to resolve them implies a lack of co-operation, the classroom is the logical place in which to discuss and solve problems. The advantages of dealing with problem behaviour in the group far outweigh any possible harm. Dreikurs (1960:9) is of the opinion:

> The beneficial effects of providing a feeling of togetherness in discussing difficulties and deficiencies and using them as projects for understanding and improvement, rather than as objects to scorn, outweigh any possible harm. For this reason, the average teacher can be safely encouraged to experiment with this kind of group discussion.

3. *Classroom discussion establishes the group rules and consequences which will follow their violation.* It is clear that there are many school rules over which teachers and students have no control — uniforms, bus times, grading, timetabling, starting time, examination requirements, and the like. However, in each classroom, there are many procedures which can be worked out co-operatively by the teacher and the students. By involving students in these decisions, teachers increase feelings of belonging, foster a spirit of togetherness, and promote an evolving co-operative attitude.

There is no issue which cannot be raised by teachers or students in classroom discussion. All problems become common problems which have to be resolved by the group. Failure to involve students as responsible equals in decisions which concern them is to invite resistance. While traditional practice has permitted teachers to impose their decisions and commands on students, the need today is to win student understanding and acceptance of classroom procedure.

In employing classroom discussion, a teacher might begin by involving students in decisions which relate to procedural matters in the classroom. For example, a teacher might raise the question of homework in the following way: 'There will be times when I will give the class homework. It is important that it is completed. However, I expect that there will be times when some students do not complete the homework. What do you think we should do about them?'.

After some discussion, the class might agree that students who fail to complete their homework should not be allowed to participate in the particular subject on the day when the assignment would be due. At some subsequent stage, Robert fails to complete his mathematics homework. His teacher would say: 'I see that you have not completed your homework, Robert. I am sorry that you will not be able to participate in the lesson today. Would you please sit over there this period'. Robert is not taught that period nor does he participate in the class activities.

What is the teacher making him do? Nothing. It is up to Robert. If he wishes to complete his homework, then he does so; if he does not wish to complete his homework, then he experiences the consequences, consequences which he himself has helped formulate and which will be implemented by the teacher with the full support of the class. What is the teacher's role? He or she acts as a group leader to help the class formulate rules for classroom procedures. When it is necessary to implement the consequences, the teacher does so with no personal involvement. In fact, the teacher expresses some regret that Robert will not be allowed to participate in the class that period but it has nothing to do with the teacher. Robert has freedom to decide whether he will or will not complete the work. If he chooses to violate the

Robert is not taught that period nor does he participate in the class activities.

classroom order, then he will experience the consequences of that violation.

Similar discussions will be held to formulate other aspects of classroom procedure. Topics may include library borrowing, use of audio-visual equipment, lockers, uniforms, movement to and from rooms, bus travel, excursions, and the like. The emphasis is always on the needs of the situation rather than on the personal desires of either the teacher or the students. In formulating rules of order, classroom discussion takes place in an atmosphere of mutual respect, shared responsibility, social equality, and co-operation. In this democratic setting, students participate as responsible partners in educational decisions rather than as involuntary participants with varying degrees of consent.

Not only are the rules of order established by the group, but the interpersonal problems which arise in any classroom are more effectively resolved by the group than by the individual teacher. Many teachers still see themselves as being personally responsible for the behaviour of each student in the class. This is a legacy of the authoritarian society which expected the teacher to deal individually with and correct each individual student. As stated earlier, the classroom has taken on a democratic aspect and the role of the teacher has changed accordingly. As adult domination diminished the peer group influence became more marked and the ability for the teacher to use the group in dealing with individuals became a necessary and desirable procedure. Through classroom discussion, a class may be effectively integrated, used to deal with the personal problems which arise in a group, and taught those critical human relations skills which are so essential in a democratic society.

In a regular group discussion, the teacher may raise a problem concerning a particular student who is creating a problem for others. It has been established that Jim, a Year 9 student, has been stealing from the lockers and from clothes left hanging in the gymnasium change room. The tenor of the discussion might be as follows:

Teacher: I wonder why it is that Jim needs to steal from other students?

Student: Because he want to hurt us.

Teacher: Do you feel hurt when somebody steals from you?

Student: I feel hurt and angry.

Teacher: Why would somebody want to hurt others?

Student: Perhaps because he wants to get even with them.

Teacher: Why would somebody want to get even with others?

Student: Because he feels that they dislike him.

Teacher: You think stealing is his way of retaliating?

Student: Yes.

Teacher: Does it make sense to you to hurt or get even with somebody whom you think dislikes you?

Student: Yes. And it would also make sense to damage that person's books or personal possessions.

Teacher: Could it be that Jim feels that we dislike him and that he steals in order to get even with us?

Student: Yes, I think so.

Teacher: Do we want to show Jim that we like him or not?

Student: I think we should. If we don't he will keep stealing from us.

Teacher: How do you suggest that we show Jim that we like him?

Student: We work in groups of four in class for the next three weeks. I would like Jim to be in my group.

Another: We play house matches on Friday. Let Jim be captain of one of the teams.

Student: (And so the discussion continues.)

There are a number of important points to be observed in the above discussion.

- The teacher focuses the discussion on the purpose of Jim's behaviour rather than on the morality of the behaviour. There are no judgements being made and no attempt at scolding, preaching, punishing, or fault-finding.

- The teacher emphasises the nature of 'shared responsibility' by referring to 'our problem' and 'What are we going to do about it?'. The group, rather than the teacher, is responsible for generating and exerting a corrective influence on Jim. It is not the teacher's problem; it is not the student's problem; it is not Jim's problem; rather it is 'our' problem.

- Jim is involved throughout the discussion. Would this not embarrass him? On the contrary. Students would prefer to behave appropriately but they do not know how to stop behaving inappropriately. Most approaches to stealing emphasise the moralistic aspect of the behaviour and use threats and punishments. They do not seek to determine the purpose of the behaviour but rather concentrate on futile attempts to locate causes. By concentrating on the purpose of Jim's behaviour, the teacher assists him and others to become aware not only of Jim's goals but also of the goal of a number of other children. Students cannot change their past or their present but they can change their future, that is, their goals. Instead of Jim simply believing that he is disliked, ostracised and unacceptable, he now begins to see the purpose of his behaviour and the possibility of change. Through listening to the classroom discussion, Jim will begin to think: 'Maybe I am wrong. These students don't dislike me'. Once he begins this line of thinking, there is no logic in going on hurting or getting even with them.

162 UNDERSTANDING CLASSROOM BEHAVIOUR

- The need to deal with all problem behaviour within the group is apparent in this example. To remove Jim from the class and talk to him about his stealing or refer him to special services would be futile. Jim's behaviour is meaningful in the classroom and the class is the appropriate group to help Jim re-evaluate his decision to seek revenge. After all, his stealing reflects a judgement he has made about his peers, and they are the ones to convince him that his judgement is wrong. Both Jim and the class have decisions to make. The students must decide whether or not they want to show Jim that they do like him and whether they are prepared to help him. Jim must decide whether or not he wishes to change the goal he selected in view of his perception of the situation. Given the possibility of choices, a satisfactory resolution to Jim's problem is likely. Where no choice is apparent, such as when the view is held that Jim is 'just no good' or 'incorrigible', then there is no possibility of change.

The classroom discussion provides the forum for all problems which concern the teacher or the students. Everybody is entitled to raise issues which concern them and to seek a group response to their solution. One student may raise the problem of the unavailability of library books caused by certain students failing to return them on time. Another student may query the excessive amount of homework being set. A teacher may raise a problem which he has in teaching a particular class. For example, the teacher may say:

Teacher: I have considerable trouble in teaching this class. Do you know why?

Student: Would it be because Harry and Michael argue with you so much?

Teacher: You have noticed it? Yes. I wonder why they need to do that?

(And so the discussion would continue with the emphasis on the purpose of the behaviour — probably power — and solutions co-operatively arrived at for overcoming the problem.)

Some teachers who feel a reluctance to begin discussing the problems of particular children in their class may prefer to use a number of stories as a means of helping children analyse social problems, of understanding behaviour, and of relating the characteristics of the story to themselves. There are some excellent stories written specifically for these purposes. A list of titles which are useful for effective group discussion is available in Baruth and Eckstein (1976). English and history teachers will find no problem in selecting characters from novels and plays and from history, to demonstrate the goals of behaviour (particularly power), of faulty life styles (for example, Richard Nixon's belief that he belonged only by controlling), and of the sources of discouragement which resulted in a failure to develop social interest, the society's barometer of normality.

A typical story which could be used with primary school students is one written by Maurice Bullard (1963) entitled 'Bo, The Ball Player'. The teacher may use the story to assist students to determine the purpose of behaviour and, when appropriate, to identify with the characters portrayed in the story. For example, the teacher might begin as follows: I will read to you a story about a French poodle. Later we will discuss how you feel about this little dog'.

Bo, The Ball Player

Bo was a beautiful young silver-grey French poodle dog. He was friendly, liked to play ball, and quickly made friends with everybody.

Bo had two very nice owners, father and mother Johnson. They had many friends who often came to visit. Bo was a fine ball player. He could catch a ball rolling across the floor, on the first bounce, or even high in the air. He would carry it back in his mouth and toss it into the lap of any one who looked like a ball player. Bo thought all people looked like ball players.

Whenever father and mother Johnson's guests met Bo for the first time, they always said, 'What a cute dog, and how clever he is to catch and bring the ball'. Bo wagged his short little tail. No matter what direction they threw the ball Bo would scramble and catch it. Everybody admired Bo.

But Bo never seemed to get tired. Nobody could quit playing ball because Bo wanted everybody to see how well he played. He played ten minutes, or half hour, or even a whole hour. Everybody got tired of playing with Bo. They had come to talk and have fun with father and mother Johnson. But Bo tossed the ball on their laps, wagged his tail, sneaked up on the ball, and even turned half-circles in the air when he jumped for the ball.

After reading the story, the teacher will lead the discussion by asking the following types of questions:
1. 'How do you feel about Bo?'
2. 'Why did Bo wag his tail?'
3. 'Do you like every thing about Bo? Do you always like his behaviour?'
4. 'Why does Bo want to play all the time?'
5. 'Why was Bo bothering the guests?'
6. 'What does Bo need to learn?'
7. 'Are little dogs the only ones who want so much attention and who don't let their parents talk when they have guests?'
8. 'Do children in the classroom ever behave like Bo?'

The ability to manage classroom discussion is an essential skill of a teacher. It is advisable to begin class discussion using a three-phase approach. The phases for establishing class meetings and their purposes and procedures are indicated in Figure 9.

PHASES IN ESTABLISHING CLASS MEETINGS

Phase 1:   Begin with low-key planning sessions.
Phase 2:   Introduce problem-solving when you feel the group is ready.
Phase 3:   Set up regular, formal class meetings.

In all classroom discussions, the teacher's role is that of a leader, listener, adviser, and consultant who aims to assist students to participate co-operatively in the interests of the group. While the forms of the classroom discussion will vary from teacher to teacher, Dreikurs, Grunwald, and Pepper (1971) have made five suggestions for group discussion which teachers might find useful.
1. Group discussion may be held on any subject at any time of the day.
2. Sometimes it is valuable to stop everything and have a discussion concerning a particular child's action or to share a particular event or happening.
3. Certain discussions should take place at a definite time and place. For example, the last period on Wednesday afternoon could be set aside to discuss classroom and personal problems and to share thoughts and feelings.

Phase	Purpose	Procedure
1. Informal planning discussions	To provide initial training in making co-operative decisions	Discuss low-key issues: room arrangement, bulletin board committees, sharing classroom jobs, planning field trips and parties, deciding on the order of studying subjects. Then move to more complicated issues: units of study, learning activities, methods of evaluation.
2. Introduction of problem solving	To give students practice in solving group-owned problems	Begin with general problems by appealing for students' help: 'We have a problem about cleaning up after art' ('I have a problem and I need your help'). When the group is ready, discuss the misbehaviour of individual students.
3. Setting up of regular class meetings	To get students involved in classroom management and planning, and to provide a safe environment to discuss personal concerns	Discuss how to set up the meetings: rules and procedures. Stress that students, not just you, will have the opportunity to bring up topics. Hold the first class meeting soon after the planning meeting. Train students in leadership so they can take charge of meetings.

Figure 9 Phases, purposes and procedures of class meetings

4. Teachers can use stories as a basis for discussion in helping children to understand behaviour.
5. The class council may be used as the framework for group discussion. The class council consists of two or three members regularly selected by the class to form the council which will meet weekly to deal with grievances and suggestions brought to it by students. The council may deal with each problem or arrange for discussion with the entire class.

The crucial point in class discussion is that all children are involved in decisions which concern them. They learn to listen to and understand each other; they become involved

The class council may be used as the framework for group discussion.

in establishing and maintaining rules necessary for functioning in an orderly group; they co-operatively solve problems through democratic procedures; they become integrated for a common purpose with each student gaining a sense of belonging to the class; further they are accepted and respected by their teachers who model the values of shared responsibility, co-operation, social equality, and mutual respect — values which are indispensable in a democratic classroom.

SOCIOMETRY

A third method of promoting class integration is the employment of sociometric techniques, an approach developed by Moreno (1953) and described in his classic book, *Who Shall Survive?*. Sociometry is a means of assessing specific group structures and, as applied to education, of determining the relationships of individual students to others within the class and of highlighting the roles which they play in relationships to one another.

The group is the focal point in education as students, being social beings, can realise their potential only in interaction with others. Accepting this Adlerian principle, Jennings (1959:4) states: 'Individuals can fully develop only in interaction with their fellows'. The social atmosphere which individual students and teachers create through their interactions in a group is a decisive factor in the degree of learning and level of integration of each member of the class. While many approaches have been designed to study the individual, reliable procedures of determining the social interaction of students are relatively new in education and not widely used. As a consequence, teachers are not well prepared to study group relationships and are frequently ineffective in creating a unified and co-operative class.

It has been a basic assumption throughout this book that individual students can be understood and assisted most effectively within the group setting. As the social context provides the environment within which each individual develops, a knowledge of this environment and the ways of influencing it are essential for all teachers. Approaches which deal with students individually or in isolation rather than as members of a group within the group are counter-productive and frequently have the undesired effect of intensifying the existing problem. The consequences of individual approaches to students, so strongly condemned by Dreikurs, have been described by Jennings (1959:45):

> The more a child succeeds in learning exclusively by and for himself, the greater the loss to him as an individual. Those who are successful learn not only to individualise all achievement and responsibility, but they also learn to cherish exclusiveness in their social relations and to keep others

from undermining their position and prestige. In other words, they are learning how to keep group life as sectionised and divided up as possible in order to safeguard their own standing in some part of it. Other less successful children are learning to withdraw and suppress their rebelliousness, to give up trying to exercise their talents, and to acquiesce in a social situation that is largely responsible for their own failures. They may be afraid to enter social doors that are actually open to them and pass up opportunities where their contributions would really be welcome. Both are apt to get distorted views of themselves as individuals and as members of society.

There are other reasons why the group is a more valid teaching unit than is the individual. Almost without exception, these reasons can be traced back to the nature of a society of which the school is a part. Our society requires that individuals play different roles, experience achievement as a joint effort, learn to deal with interpersonal conflict, develop social skills, deal with social diversity, and demonstrate those qualities embodied in respect, responsibility, resourcefulness — the three Rs of the school today. These ends must be planned for by the provision of curricular experiences conducted in an appropriate social milieu in which the teacher, employing the skills of group dynamics, integrates and unifies all for a common purpose.

The process of class unification is impossible unless teachers are aware of the social structure of the group. Each class typically consists of a number of sub-groups or cliques which support or reject particular types of behaviour. Until the nature and extent of these sub-groups are known, teachers will act to intensify differences within the class and lessen their influence on all individual students. However, once the structure of a class is known and the sub-groups identified, teachers can begin the process of unification by establishing contact between different sub-groups, by developing group spirit through positive interactions, by breaking down antagonisms between groups, and by building on positive elements designed to establish a co-operative and cohesive classroom.

A number of texts have been written specifically on the use of sociometric information (Gronlund, 1959; Jennings, 1959; Moreno, 1953). Basic to all sociometric approaches is

the practice which allows students to express their preference for other students in the class by allowing them a
choice of partners for a particular activity. Sociometry has
been defined by Jennings (1959:11): 'The study of the patterns of interrelations between people and the process of
their measurement'. In an attempt to determine the psychological significance of relationships, a sociometric test is
given which 'discloses the feelings which individuals have
regarding one another in respect to membership in the
group in which they are at a given moment' (Jennings,
1959:11).

The results of this test are represented graphically as a
sociogram, a visual representation of the structure of the
relationships among the students in the class. The results of
such an approach will often surprise teachers as it is almost
impossible to understand the group structure of a class
without the use of sociometry. As Dreikurs (1960:5)
observes:

> The existence of sub-groups is usually not visible, even to the
> keenest observer. Some sensitive and perceptual teachers
> may 'feel' and sense existing positive and negative relation-
> ships between their students. However, experiments indicate
> that, without sociometric methods, a teacher cannot be fully
> aware of the nature and extent of sub-groups, nor of the
> sociometric status of individual children. A sociogram alone
> may enable him to arrive at a diagnosis of group relation-
> ships and to provide corrective efforts to change them.

The initial step in constructing a sociogram is to obtain
each students' preference for other students in relation to a
particular short-term activity. For example, the situation
might involve sitting together, working in small groups,
committee work, or a sporting activity. Once the situation
has been decided, each student is asked to list the names of
two or three individuals with whom they would like to share
the activity.

A number of criteria have been developed to improve the
usefulness of the sociometric data.
1. The situation must be actual rather than hypothetical; the
test must never be used as an end in itself. 'You are going to
work together in groups of four in social studies for the next
three weeks.'

2. The results of students' choices must be implemented and groupings made, as far as possible, on the basis of these choices.

3. The situation for which preferences are to be included should be for immediate activity rather than a distant or remote situation. 'Next Monday' rather than 'next term' will produce a more reliable response.

4. Students may be asked to indicate their first, second, and third preferences.

5. Results of the sociometric choice are always confidential.

It is convenient to ask students to record their preferences on a card and for the teacher to record the data on a sociometric tabulation form similar to that illustrated in Figure 10. Each child has been asked to select three other children and to indicate a first, second, and third choice.

While the sociometric tabulation form gives a total picture of all students' responses, the educational and psychological

Chooser	Allen	Brian	Colleen	Deborah	Ellen	Fran	Graham	Harry
Allen		2		3			1	
Brian			1				2	3
Colleen					1	2		3
Deborah			1		2		3	
Ellen			1				2	3
Fran	2		1					3
Graham			3	1			2	
Harry			2			3	1	
Choice								
1st	0	0	3	2	1	0	2	0
2nd	1	1	1	0	1	1	3	0
3rd	0	0	1	1	0	1	1	4
Total Choices	1	1	5	3	2	2	6	4

Figure 10   Sociometric tabulation form

significance of the data is best portrayed by a sociogram which visually displays the social structure of the class as a whole. A typical sociogram is presented in Figure 11.

Three configurations are significant in this sociogram.

1. There are very few lengthy sociometric chains — strings of one-way choices which connect different students. Lines of communication are indicated by chains, and their absence in this sociogram indicates that friendships in the class are based on cliques. Consequently the class does not act as of one accord, will show little concern with problems requiring group consideration, and the teacher is likely to experience problems in obtaining co-operation from certain students.

2. The class is far from integrated as patterns of choices are largely self-contained. A number of clearly defined sub-groups such as M, N, P, and D, E, F, G, which mutually choose each other and have no preference for, or by, other students, are indicated. In such a class, antagonism, lack of co-operation, and disciplinary problems would be expected.

3. The class is sharply divided on the basis of sex. Very few girls have chosen to work with boys while boys have also been exclusive in their choices. This may indicate a school practice reflected in curricula which keep the sexes apart, a physical arrangement such as separate playgrounds, or maybe a school expectation. The dichotomy of sexes can only be understood in relation to a knowledge of local conditions.

Individual reactions in sociometric interpretation focus on students who are not chosen, most chosen, mutually chosen, and, if the data permit, rejected by others. In Figure 11, C and T have received no choices and are referred to as isolates. K and A comprise an example of a mutual pair, each having chosen each other. M, N, and P constitute a clique, a closed group who choose each other. A has received a significantly larger number of choices than could be expected by chance and is referred to as a star. Perhaps the most interesting student is H. She has received only two choices but they came from A and K, the two most popular students in the class. In other words, H is powerful but not popular; she is a potent force in the group and the teacher would need to be aware of her potential influence.

In considering the above configuration, a teacher would

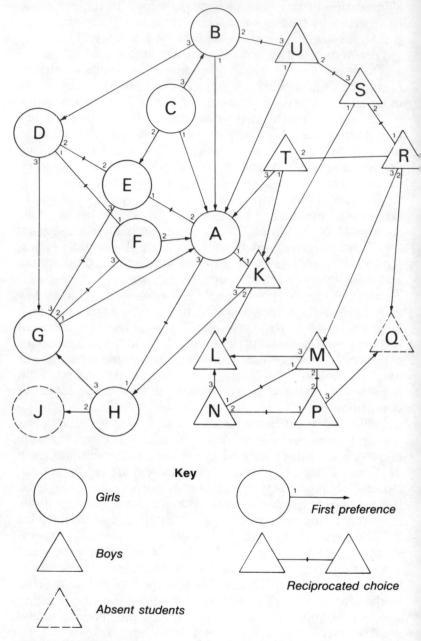

Key

Girls ⬤

Boys △

Absent students △ (dashed)

⬤——1——→ First preference

△——●——△ Reciprocated choice

Figure 11 Sociogram

need to follow up the cues indicated by the above interpretation. Why is H so powerful? Are the cliques disruptive or facilitative of the classroom goals? What is the basis of the cliques — nationality, proximity of homes, interest in sport, sociometric level, religious background, scholarly interests? Why has nobody chosen C or T? What do A and K have in common which makes them so popular? Why is there such poor communication between sub-groups? Why is there such a strong sex division? Are the patterns revealed similar to those expected by the teacher? Would a similar pattern of interactions be obtained if the criterion of choice was shifted from 'working together' to 'playing together' or 'sitting together'?

The sociogram indicates the structure of relationships but offers no explanation. It is the teacher's responsibility to follow up the questions raised by the sociogram and, through interviews, classroom discussions, and staff meetings, attempt to understand and influence the group and its members. The first step a teacher must pursue is to carry out the original agreement as indicated when the choices were made by the students. The class must be organised into working groups as quickly as possible and the activity commenced on the day indicated. A major principle for translating sociometric data into action is the same for all types of activity: 'Each individual should be given the highest degree of satisfaction compatible with maximum happiness for everyone else and maximum stimulation for all' (Jennings, 1959:48).

The above principle may be achieved by a set of procedures which group students according to the following criteria.
1. Start with the pupils receiving the smallest number of choices and work up to those receiving the most choices.
2. Attempt to satisfy the chooser's mutual choices first and her highest level of unreciprocated choices next.
3. If there are conflicts, satisfy the choice of the child who is in a weaker position in the group.
4. Do not put unchosen children with those who have rejected them, into a closed cluster, or with a mutual pair. Usually an unchosen child should have her first choice. (Some teachers ask students to indicate whether there are

any particular individuals with whom they would prefer not to work. Such children are referred to as rejectees. Asking students to provide such information is not acceptable to the author.)

5. Make sure that pupils who reject each other are kept apart.

6. Make sure that every child has been placed with at least one of her choices.

7. If there is a cleavage or undesirable clique, social contacts should be broadened by intermixing. However, new relationships must be built gradually; there should always be at least two pupils from each sub-group in the resulting sociometric groups.

In the example presented earlier, the teacher's major problem is the presence of distinct and non-interacting subgroups such as D, E, F, and G and M, N, P. Integration of the class would require that the teacher establish contacts between sub-groups by establishing sociometric chains. One way of doing this would be to include a number of outsiders in each clique. For example, if groups of four students are to be formed, two original clique members and two other students who are not rejected by the original clique members would constitute the group. This allows for a widening of influence and a spread of ideas which would be impossible under the original structure.

The problem of the cleavage between the sexes would require that the teacher should implement all the girl–boy choices irrespective of their priority. Further, administrative changes could be made to rectify the situation. Physical arrangements such as separate playgrounds, locker, lunch area, and curricula could be changed so as to encourage integration.

Finally, given the situation indicating sharp divisions between groups of students, the teacher is faced with the problem not only of extending the networks between the cliques but also of investigating the reasons for these divisions. Until these are determined, it will be difficult to decide appropriate learning experiences which will aid in reversing this trend to group disintegration. Many possible explanations exist, including economic background, academic ability, religion, race, nationality, employment after school, prestige, and sporting ability. While restructuring of relationships through the strengthening of sociometric chains requires time and planning, the benefits resulting from increased student co-operation make the effort very worthwhile.

The teacher's role as a group leader whose major task is to integrate a class for common purposes has been emphasised. Sociometry has been suggested as an indispensable technique for a teacher who wishes to develop positive group relationships and better group integration. Until unification of a class has been achieved, a teacher will continue the counter-productive and damaging practices of ability grouping, withdrawal programs, establishment of special classes or schools for the handicapped or gifted, homogeneous grouping, differential curricula setting, and the like. A teacher who is skilled in integrating a class will find the above practices unnecessary, particularly when the teacher is willing to implement a group-based mastery learning strategy. When this latter strategy is used by a teacher who has the skills to unify a class, an optimal academic and social learning environment is provided for all students.

8
Mastery Learning: A Preventative Approach to Discipline

INTRODUCTION

In recent years, policy makers in education have begun to re-examine questions of equity in student learning, levels of student attainment, equality of educational outcomes, the relationship of schools to the economy, teacher stress, burnout, and effectiveness. All of these issues are being raised against the background of restricted educational budgets, increasing costs of the educational enterprise, and a general tightening of resources available to education.

Over the past two decades, a body of research has begun to emerge which has embraced the above issues within the framework known as mastery learning. The group of researchers who have worked on the questions of excellence in learning, equity, teacher renewal, and effective resource utilisation has reached the conclusion that 'school education can be equal and excellent for the vast majority of students and can be economical and personally exciting for most professionals' (Block, 1989:2).

Based on the ideas of Benjamin Bloom (1976), a holistic set of instructional ideas, beliefs and strategies have emerged which are collectively referred to as mastery learning. This approach is an optimistic and generous theory of school learning which suggests that schools can provide not only equality of educational opportunity but equality of educational outcome. In a classic statement, Bloom (1976:16) wrote that:

> Where conditions for learning in the home and school approach some ideal, we believe that individual differences in learning should approach a vanishing point.

Bloom presents a very precise message to educators which suggests that virtually all students can learn to a very high standard if instruction is approached systematically, if students are given appropriate assistance in learning when they need it, and if some clear criterion exists of what constitutes mastery.

The view that 'what any child can learn, all can learn' was received cautiously by many educators who waited until some of their colleagues produced evidence supporting or rejecting Bloom's thesis. Two decades of research has now been completed and the evidence is clear: 'Mastery learning has helped reshape the face of contemporary educational practice, research, and theory' (Block, 1979:114).

It is appropriate to ask why an instructional strategy is being discussed in a book which is devoted to classroom behaviour or management. It is the author's belief that disciplinary problems can be largely prevented through effective teaching. 'At the heart of a disciplinary problem is an educational failure by the school' is a hard model for teachers but one which has been demonstrated over and over. A great many disciplinary problems arise because instruction and management are deficient, causing pupils to lose interest and turn their attention to troublesome behaviours. If most students can achieve a similar level and rate of learning and motivation for further learning, then the current concern with discipline will become a non-issue.

Further, the benefits of mastery learning will be permanent. Evidence is beginning to emerge that early and successful application of mastery learning can effectively immunise students against future emotional health problems and stress related problems. It is clear that the success-oriented nature of mastery learning has a major impact on self-esteem, self-concept and worth, factors which are central when considering the nature of student behaviour.

In discussing mastery learning, Bloom has written a number of important papers spanning a twenty-year period. The early papers, 'Learning for mastery' (1968) and 'New views of the learner' (1978), indicated a new understanding of the great potential of virtually all students to learn well whatever the schools have to teach. In a 1980 article entitled 'The new direction in educational research: Alterable variables', Bloom identified those variables which are causally related to learning and which can be influenced by teachers. For too long teachers have been hindered in their work by the existence of assumptions regarding students and learning which have no validity or which cannot be varied by teachers. These would include intelligence and home background. Bloom discussed this limitation on teachers in a most interesting article, 'Innocence in Education' (1972).

More recently Bloom (1984) has written a most influential paper, 'The search for methods of group instruction as effective as one-to-one tutoring'. On the basis of a series of related investigations conducted over the previous five years, Bloom outlined six strategies currently available to teachers which will enable almost every student under group instruction to attain levels of achievement which were formerly attainable only under good tutorial conditions. The success of these strategies as judged by student learning, motivation, self-concept, mental health, social responsibility, and co-operation suggests that teachers cannot continue to remain 'innocent'. 'What you do once your innocence is threatened can have profound effects on the future of curriculum and instruction in our schools' (Bloom, 1972:129).

Even, more recently, Block, Efthim, and Burns (1989) have presented compelling evidence on the effectiveness of mastery learning. The following conclusions may be drawn from the past two decades of research:

1. Mastery learning provides a model of instruction that is effective for a wide range of students. Essentially the same system of instruction has resulted in rapid gains for under-achievers and has provided a means for allowing gifted and talented students to move through two levels of instruction in a year.

2. Mastery learning has reduced the spread between the lowest achiever and the highest, without slowing down the fastest students.

3. The skills and concepts taught in a mastery learning format have been internalised by students so that they are transferred to the other curriculum areas.

4. It is clear from observations that along with the achievement gains typical of mastery learning, there is also a remarkable impact on student attitude as reflected not only in decreased behaviour problems but in the pride students take in themselves and their school.

Like most developments in education, mastery learning was greatly affected by the reform movement in the 1980s. In that period, whole school approaches became the norm in many facets of schooling — disciplinary codes, curricula, philosophical orientation, assessment and the like. Mastery learning, essentially a classroom activity, needed a vehicle whereby it could be applied on a whole-school or regional basis. Under the auspices of the American Association of School Administrators (AASA), the Network of Outcome-based Education (OBE) was formed within the national Center for the Improvement of Learning.

The formation of the Network of Outcome-based Schools has resulted in a further spread of mastery learning ideas and the incorporation of mastery learning within the OBE movement. Outcome-based education is an approach to reform in all aspects within the total school system designed to promote maximum learning in all students. Mastery learning is the main vehicle upon which to begin the change process in instructional strategies, curricular organisation, and belief systems of teachers, students, and parents. Block, Efthim, and Burns (1989) have presented an analogy whereby OBE is the canopy of an umbrella, mastery learning is the centre pole supporting the umbrella, while the hinged ribs radiating from the central pole are the many effective school movements and/or strategies available to teachers.

Spady (1985) has identified the basic philosophical premises underlying OBE and the essential operations of OBE.

Key philosophical principles of Outcome-based Education

1. *All students can learn and succeed.* Successfully learning the things that lead to literate, self-sufficient, well-informed adults is within the grasp of virtually all students. Schools exist to foster those capabilities, to ensure their accomplishment, and to recognise formally and reward them whenever they occur. Designing and organising instructional delivery that directly builds on the capabilities students bring with them to the learning situation reinforces their motivation for learning and their opportunity to succeed.

2. *Success breeds success.* How students experience their learning progress affects their self-concept, motivation, and approach to later learning experiences. Providing students with the opportunity to learn and succeed and formally acknowledging and recording their learning success in its own terms encourages students to seek further learning experiences. Learning success is not a scarce commodity reserved for a small group of superior achievers, but the deliberate goal of quality instruction for all students.

3. *Schools control the conditions of success.* Schools directly control the structure and availability of the curriculum, student learning experiences, instructional time, assessment measures, grading and credit options, and opportunities for program advancement — all of which have an enormous bearing on the learning success of students. How schools organise and implement these elements either promotes or inhibits student learning, motivation, and formal success.

Essential operations components of Outcome-based Education

1. Using clearly defined outcomes for all students:
   a. to define and develop curriculum content, structure, and articulation
   b. to establish criterion-referenced measures of student and program success

c. to establish record-keeping and reporting systems for student progress.
2. Organising instructional delivery based on the performance capabilities and learning needs of students.
3. Adjusting instructional time and learning opportunities to enable all students to reach outcome goals successfully.
4. Formally acknowledging and documenting student learning and success whenever they occur.
5. Modifying the instructional program on the basis of documented student learning results and available data on instructional effectiveness.

ALTERABLE VARIABLES IN LEARNING

Before outlining the strategies involved in mastery learning, it would be useful to consider the variables which Bloom has identified as being causally related to learning and which are capable of being manipulated by teachers. What amounts to a world-wide revolution in educational research and in our understanding of the factors which influence learners has taken place as a result of a shift in research emphases from the study of the actors (teachers and learners) to the study of acts (teaching and learning). Central to this shift are two changes:
1. A movement from what may be called static or fixed variables to variables which are alterable during the teaching–learning process.
2. A concern with establishing causal links between teaching processes and student learning rather than determining correlations between variables.

The importance of this shift in research emphasis has been highlighted by Bloom (1972:2):

> If parents, teachers, and other educators are really convinced that a good education is absolutely essential for all who live in modern society, then we must all search for the alterable variables and processes which can make a difference in the learning of children and youth in or out of the school. Such alterable variables will do much to explain the learning process, and they can do more to directly improve the teaching and learning processes in the school. The basic task of research is to further our understanding of how such

processes can be altered and what their consequent effect will be on students, teachers, and learning.

The alterable variables which Bloom has identified have resulted in a major change in our views of students and in their potential for learning. In contrast to static variables, alterable variables are capable of being influenced by teachers and, as such, greatly increase a teacher's ability to promote maximum learning in all students.

Five alterable variables which are described by Bloom and their equivalent non-alterable variables are as follows.

1. Intelligence versus cognitive entry behaviour

Teachers have frequently used intelligence and intelligence test scores to predict future academic success. Correlations of +.50 to +.70 were obtained for most school subjects and the conclusion was drawn that intelligence is a major factor controlling student learning. Intelligence test scores have been used widely for selection, prediction, streaming, and curricular decisions. If we accept that intelligence is a highly stable trait and highly predictive of school success, there is nothing the school can do to improve learning. Rather the school's role is to eliminate the weaker students and to provide further learning opportunities for the more able students.

A variable which is alterable and highly predictive of school success is cognitive entry behaviour. This variable refers to those skills, specific knowledge, and abilities which are the essential prerequisites for the learning of a particular learning task. These entry behaviours are highly alterable because they represent particular content and skills which may be learned, while they typically correlate +.70 with measures of school achievement. While cognitive entry behaviours are alterable, have an obvious causal effect on later achievement, and correlate with current achievement, intelligence is non-alterable and adds nothing to cognitive entry behaviour in predicting success in learning. As Bloom (1972:5) accurately observed:

> Much of the variation in school learning is directly determined by the variation in students' cognitive entry characteristics. When means are found for ensuring that students

reach adequate levels of competence on the essential cognitive entry behaviours, most students can be assured of high levels of school learning with very little variation in their achievement. The alterability of cognitive entry characteristics has the most profound implications for instruction, curriculum, and our views about the learning potential of almost all students in the schools.

2. Time available for learning versus time-on-task

Teachers will often argue that if they had more time available for teaching, students would be able to learn more effectively. Yet time, in the sense of years, days or hours available for school learning is relatively fixed. Each term, each year level, each assignment is associated with a fixed period of time and there is little which teachers can do to lengthen learning time without considerable administrative changes or additional costs.

Time available for learning can be contrasted with time-on-task, the time that students are actively engaged in learning. It is logical that if one student spends 85 per cent of a classroom hour actively engaged in learning while another spends only 20 per cent, there will be a large difference in the achievement between the two students. Time-on-task is strongly related to the quality of instruction and the extent to which students possess the necessary entry level behaviour for each new learning task. What is important is that time-on-task can be altered during a sequence of learning tasks by high-quality instruction. It is possible for teachers to greatly increase the time-on-task of each student, a variable which has a direct causal influence on student learning and attitude to learning.

3. Parental status versus home environment processes

Many studies have documented the fact that children coming from families of high socio-economic status or professional families, with parents with high levels of education or income, tend to have considerable school success. Such findings are not helpful for teachers as there is nothing they can do to alter the parental status of these students.

In contrast to the non-alterable variable of parental status is the view that it is not the characteristics of the parents which are important in student learning but rather how parents interact with their children. It is not what parents are; it is what they do. A number of home process variables have been identified which are significantly related to student learning. They include the ways in which time and space are organised in the home, the aspiration of the parents for their children, the provision of help in learning when the child most needs it, the contribution of the home to the development of the mother tongue, and the encouragement of the child to do well. These processes correlate +.70 to +.80 with measures of school achievement. What is important is that these processes can be taught to all parents and, as such, are alterable variables which can do much to improve the school learning of children. The alterable curriculum of the home is twice as predictive of academic learning as is family socio-economic status.

4. Teacher versus teaching

The huge effort made in attempting to determine the personal characteristics of successful teachers has produced almost no useful findings. Bloom (1980:10) concludes that, on the data available, 'the characteristics of the teachers have little to do with the learning of their students'. Even if significant findings had been obtained, there is little teacher education programs can do to develop personality characteristics in teachers.

A more promising approach has been to identify the behaviours involved in successful teaching. Again, it is not what teachers are; it is what teachers do. A number of interactive factors have been identified which have been classified under cues, participation, and reinforcement. It is the manner in which teachers use these variables that influences the degree of learning. These facets of teaching can be altered through in-service education thus permitting all teachers, irrespective of personality characteristics, to provide quality instruction for the students.

5. Summative versus formative testing

Most teachers employ tests to measure or summarise student achievement for the purpose of grading students. The basic notion is that the students have had a common learning experience and are to be assessed in terms of what they have learned. As test results obtained in this way are highly predictive of subsequent school achievement, many teachers have inferred that differences between students in school achievement are non-alterable, being influenced by factors such as intelligence and home background rather than variables within the learning process.

In contrast to summative testing is the use of tests as an integral part of learning. Formative tests are used primarily for feedback purposes to determine the extent of a student's knowledge and to pinpoint those areas which require further learning. When corrective procedures are made available to students to strengthen their weaknesses as revealed by the formative tests, almost all students reach the standard of achievement set by the teachers.

Formative tests are not used for the purpose of grading but to improve the learning of students. Their use 'ensures that most of the students have the necessary cognitive prerequisites for each new learning task, that students have increased interest in the learning, and a greater confidence in their own ability to learn, and that they use more of the classroom time to engage in the learning process' (Bloom, 1972:7).

Bloom has presented a new view of the learner which suggests that teachers have the potential to promote high levels of achievement in all students. By replacing stable or fixed variables such as intelligence, elapsed time, teacher characteristics, and home background with alterable variables such as cognitive entry level, time-on-task, and formative testing, Bloom has indicated the ways by which teachers can develop strategies whereby most students (perhaps over 90 per cent) can master what we have to teach them.

TYPES OF LEARNING STRATEGIES

There are many types of mastery learning strategies. They include the individualised programs such as Individually Prescribed Instruction, Individually Guided Education, Project PLAN, the Keller PSI, and learning packages. Group-based methods of mastery learning centre around the model developed by Block and Anderson (1975) and are referred to as Learning for Mastery (LFM).

Although there is considerable support for the effectiveness of the individualised strategies, they have not been widely adopted by teachers who generally prefer a group-based, group-paced, approach to teaching. Group instruction is a basic fact of life in most classrooms and Block and Anderson have chosen to improve the effectiveness of that means of teaching rather than advocating a procedure which teachers find too different from their traditional approaches.

This chapter will not present a detailed description of the LFM strategy but will refer readers to Block and Anderson (1975) and Block, Efthim, and Burns (1989) for a full description. Rather, the basic outline of LFM will be presented.

Group-based mastery learning

Block and Anderson have translated Bloom's theory into a teaching strategy, a strategy designed to supplement and better individualise the teacher's traditional group-based techniques which are employed with a given curriculum to be covered in a fixed period of time. The strategy consists of the following steps:

1. The course or subject is broken down into a series of learning units covering one or two weeks of instruction.
2. The instructional objectives, representing a wide range of learning outcomes (for example, knowledge, comprehension, and application), are clearly specified for each unit.
3. The learning tasks within each unit are taught using regular group-based instruction.
4. Diagnostic-progress tests (formative tests) are administered at the end of each learning unit.
5. The results of the end-of-unit tests are used to reinforce the learning of students who have mastered the unit and to diagnose the learning errors of those who fail to demonstrate mastery.
6. Specific procedures for correcting learning deficiencies (for example, re-reading particular pages, using programmed materials, and using audio-visual aids) and additional learning time are prescribed for those who do

not achieve unit mastery. Retesting may be done after the corrective study.

7. Upon completion of all the units, an end-of-course test (summative test) is administered to determine the students' course grades. All students who perform at or above the pre-determined mastery level (set at course's outset) receive a grade of A in the course. Lower grades are also assigned on the basis of absolute standards that have been set for the course.

8. The results of the unit tests (formative tests) and the final examination (summative tests) are used as a basis for improving the methods, materials, and sequencing of instruction.

THE TWO SIGMA PROBLEM

A more recent paper by Bloom (1984) challenges teachers to go beyond mastery learning. Bloom refers to the '2 Sigma Problem' which is this: 'Can researchers and teachers devise teacher-learning conditions that will enable the majority of students under group instruction to attain levels of achievement that can at present be reached only under good tutoring conditions?'.

Bloom has clearly gone beyond the LFM which aimed to raise the average student's performance by one standard deviation (1 sigma) over conventionally taught students. Bloom is now looking for ways of raising the average student's performance by two standard deviations (2 sigma) over conventionally taught students. Of this challenge, Bloom (1984:6) writes:

If the research on the 2 sigma problem yields practical methods (methods that the average teacher or school faculty can learn in a brief period of time and use with little more cost or time than conventional instruction) it would be an educational contribution of the greatest magnitude. It would change popular notions about human potential and would have significant effects on what the schools can and should do with the educational years each society requires of its young people.

The gap between theory and practice, reflected in sigmas of 1.0 compared with the targeted 2.0, has generated major research programs designed to solve the 2-sigma problem. Seven options have been identified which will make conventional group-based motivation as effective as one-to-one tutoring. They are:

1. Initial enhancement of cognitive prerequisites.
2. Improve the quality of teaching to provide effective learning cues, more equal participation and reinforcement, and systematic diagnosis and correction of errors.
3. Improve student processing of conventional instruction.
4. Improve instructional materials and technology.
5. Improve the teaching of higher mental processes.
6. Improve the home environment through parent education.
7. Control the peer group.

By mixing the above strategies with mastery learning, teachers can effectively develop the potential talent of all students to levels which conventional teaching does not begin to approach. The effect on students will be dramatic, particularly in relation to problems of classroom management, discipline, and self-esteem.

9
Adolescence

INTRODUCTION

A major problem in secondary schools is the large number of adolescents who feel alienated, who do not share common values, common ideas, or ideals and who are not able to gain a sense of belonging in the typical school community. While most primary school children are generally easy to influence, many of these children become difficult to manage during adolescence. Children 'play games' and try to please their primary school teachers but when offered the independence and autonomy of adolescence, they suddenly 'cast off the false mask they have been wearing and become themselves' (Manaster and Corsini, 1982:93).

Dreikurs (1968:33) has highlighted the problem of adolescence by referring to the rebellion of youth as the generation gap in which adolescents and adults live in two different worlds.

In the past, during this period, the teenager had one foot in adolescence and the other in adulthood. He slowly became an adult. He got a job, drove his own car, contributed to the family income, and took on the responsibility for his younger brothers and sisters. All this has changed. At present, teenagers are at war with adult society. Their freedom from responsibility induces them to continue their adolescence far beyond the age customary for this period of life. They do not want to assume the responsibilities of adults. Teenagers have become a powerful subgroup, living in a different world, distinguishing themselves from adults through their long hair, untidiness, odd clothing, noisy music, and use of drugs.

While adolescence has generally been considered a difficult period, today's teenagers seem more troubled than those of previous generations. Concern is increasing as the percentage of young people involved in aberrant or illicit behaviour grows. Statistics on drugs, alcohol, substance abuse, juvenile crime, suicide, and sexual activity indicate an increase in the frequency and number of individuals involved. Whereas adolescents are very critical of adults, they see nothing wrong with their own behaviour.

Young people today have grown up during a period of affluence where even the poor have been cushioned against severe poverty. Electronic media, computers and cars are commonplace to them. They were also born and brought up during a period of great social and political upheaval with extensive media coverage of soaring crime rates, high-technology revolution, high levels of youth unemployment, the arms race, runaway inflation, rapidly rising divorce rates, two income families, increasing violence, sexual revolution, overt homosexuality, women's liberation, black power, the Gulf war, and terrorism. All have helped shape juvenile behaviour and are factors which are related to the problems which teachers experience in relation to their adolescent students.

There are a number of practices, insights and approaches which the author has found to be most valuable in dealing with difficult adolescents. Typically, adolescents who create problems in schools have as their goal power or revenge, goals which are often expressed through drugs, stealing, delinquency, defiance, violence, alcohol abuse, school failure, bullying, and sexual permissiveness.

Almost without exception, difficult adolescents have been humiliated in school, at home and in the community and are placed in a position of inferiority. As humiliation and inferiority are painful conditions, adolescents act to relieve pain in one of two ways. One is to seek temporary relief through drug-taking and alcohol abuse. The other is to make an exaggerated attempt at superiority. They will wreck a monument, a train, a school, or property. So well will they do it that they stand back in admiration and conclude: 'They say we are not good at anything. Let them do a better job of destruction than that. How great I am'. Consider the following extracts from the *Northern Territory News*:

A gang of children went on a wild rampage at St Paul's primary school on Saturday evening. 'It was like a tornado had been through the place', said St Paul's parish priest.

18 February, 1985

Vandals used bricks to smash 20 windows at the Darwin Institute of Technology on Saturday. Police said a half brick was found at the site of each of the 20 smashed windows.

9 April, 1985

Similar items can be found in almost any daily newspaper. The behaviours they describe are designed to ease the pain of humiliation, of feelings of inferiority, by an exaggerated show of superiority. While papers suggest a number of causes such as parental neglect, educational failure, economic and social disadvantage, and boredom, the rejection of causation and the acceptance of the belief of individual responsibility would suggest that most programs designed to overcome these 'causes' are ill-founded.

PRINCIPLES FOR ASSISTING ADOLESCENTS

It is important to note that the principles which are discussed in relation to adolescents are no different from those which are appropriate to individuals of all ages. Probably the most important difference in adolescence compared with childhood is the increasing degree of autonomy and independence which teenagers experience. What does not change, however, is the need to establish and maintain relationships between teachers and adolescents which are based on equality, mutual respect and trust. Without such relationships, teachers can abandon hope that adolescence will be anything other than a war between the two generations. The author knows of no difficult adolescent who is not being treated disrespectfully or is not being treated as a child.

Prevent further humiliation of the adolescent

The first task of a teacher who wishes to redirect the behaviour of a student who is causing concern is to teach the adolescent how not to be humiliated in future situations. Recognise the importance of the principle of self-determination which suggests that one cannot be hurt unless one chooses to be. The adolescent has a choice and an individual who feels humiliated has made a faulty choice.

How do you correct faulty thinking? Ask an adolescent to describe an actual situation when he was last humiliated. The adolescent might say: 'My father made me furious last night when he criticised my friends'. This statement could be stated: 'When my father criticised my friends, I became furious'. Who is making you furious, your father or yourself? 'I am'. 'My English teacher made me angry when she said that I was the worst student she had this year'. This becomes: 'When the English teacher said I was her worst student she had this year, I became angry'.

Adolescents must learn that they have a choice, that they are active in the process of being humiliated or not. Working in groups, adolescents can learn that there are ways of feeling other than being the victim of perceived unfair treatment. When there is no humiliation, there is no pain; when there is no pain, there is no need for drugs, alcohol, vandalism, delinquency and the like. When there is no sense of inferiority, there is no need to defeat others. For the adolescent, like everybody else, *alles kann anders sein*: everything can be something else. To empower youngsters with the ability to improve their lives is a challenge facing teachers in their task to win co-operation. We cannot change what was, but we can change what is.

Go along with adolescents' views of themselves

It is necessary for teachers to establish some rapport with difficult students if they are to influence them positively. To achieve this rapport it is necessary to accept what an adolescent says and not to oppose the opinion or feelings expressed. In other words, 'go with them'.

A high school student might say to a teacher: 'I just can't stand Miss Jones; she just keeps picking on me'. A teacher who responds: 'Well, she is only trying to help you' will immediately lose the student. 'Oh, you too' will be the reaction of the student who is at war with those who might oppose him. A more appropriate response by the teacher would be: 'She probably is'. 'My parents can't stand the sight of me.' 'Could be.' 'The principal thinks that we are a disgrace to the school.' 'You are probably right.' 'I am just so stupid in maths.' 'Maybe.' 'The phys. ed. teacher has banned me from sport.' 'He did that?'

Remember, it is essential to establish rapport with young people who see many adults as a source of frustration, humiliation, or discouragement. Rather than attempting to convince them that their views of teachers, parents, or principals are wrong or that they deserve the treatment they are receiving, teachers aim to establish themselves as people who can accept and identify with the feelings expressed by the student. We are not condoning behaviour but attempting to help the adolescent develop more appropriate ways of behaving by first establishing rapport.

Three faulty beliefs

There are three faulty assumptions which troubled youngsters hold and which are the basis for all corrective measures. These beliefs are:
1. I am a failure (negative self-concept).
2. Life holds nothing for me (pessimism).
3. It is futile starting anything (low risk-taking).

Teachers need to work on these three areas aimed at developing optimism, courage and risk-taking. The aim is to have an adolescent believe:
1. I can cope with the problems of living (positive self-concept).
2. Eventually things will turn out for the best (optimism).
3. I will take a chance (risk-taking).

To achieve these aims, the following suggestions are made to teachers.

1. The courage to take a chance

Discouraged adolescents have been humiliated so often that they act to avoid further hurt. To initiate constructive action by the student is the teacher's goal, remembering that we have taught the adolescent that no further pain or humiliation is possible. The most important message for the teacher is this: 'Life is today'. There is no talk about the future such as: 'If you don't complete your homework, you could fail at the end of the year'. Or, 'If you don't pass mathematics you might not get an apprenticeship'. Life is today for the troubled youngsters and that is where the teacher begins: 'What do you have to do today or tomorrow?'.

A teacher might ask a student: 'What do you have to do

today apart from attending class?'. 'Study for a chemistry test.' 'What will that involve?' 'Two hours of study.' 'Is that all you have to do? Can you do it?' 'Yes.' Similar discussions could be held on matters such as writing up an experiment, joining a club, arranging an appointment with the guidance teacher or booking computer time. The important things to emphasise are now, today, activity, movement, commitment — extend an invitation which the adolescent would be unable to resist. 'Fill in one form.' 'Write one letter.' 'Go to one meeting.' 'For goodness sake, is that all?'

2. Optimism

Teachers must recognise that many adolescents perceive that their current situation is difficult and that the future in home, work, school or the community is not promising. What we must work towards is establishing a conviction that, although life is difficult now, eventually it will turn out for the better. Whether it does or does not depends on the adolescents' willingness to do something today. Movement, however small, is the goal.

The author has found that it is far more effective to work with a small group of adolescents rather than with individuals. In individual discussion, an adolescent can advance reasons to avoid responsibility or action, reasons which have no validity but cannot be refuted by the teacher. For example, 'I have too much homework this evening', or 'I haven't got any friends to help me with the assignment'. When such excuses are advanced in a group, the group will quickly point out the fallacy of such arguments and make it impossible for a student to resist a particular invitation. They know the reality of an adolescent's life much better than the teacher.

Further, by making the group responsible for the behaviour of each member in the group, it becomes difficult for a group member to opt out of a particular responsibility. The two-hour study preparation required by John to pass his chemistry test tomorrow becomes the responsibility of the group. Each student is given the responsibility to make sure that John does his study and presents for the test. The power of the group to influence members of the group has to be recognised and capitalised on by teachers.

3. Establishing faith in themselves

The negative self-concept which adolescents have is the result of a whole series of discouraging experiences which began in the home and are continued into the school. This negative view has to be reversed so that adolescents can say to themselves: 'I am what I am and I am OK. I will do my best and I do not have to run, hide, be better than others, or feel hopeless'.

One approach to assist in this process is to help adolescents separate the reality of the situation from their individual personal conclusions. Often these personal conclusions give rise to expressions of negative worth. For instance, an adolescent turned out for cricket practice but was not selected in the team. A teacher is told by the student: 'I wasn't selected because Mr Myers does not like me'. The teacher asks the student to describe the reality of the situation. 'I went to practice but wasn't selected in the team'. The self-defeating statement is omitted. The teacher asks the student to generate alternative explanations for the situation which triggered the faulty conclusion. 'My fielding is not too good.' 'My bowling is very loose.' 'I tend to swing pretty wildly.' The teacher now invites the student to work on one of the weaknesses. Similarly, 'I only received 40 per cent in the maths test; I must be dumb'. What other explanations are there for the poor results and what positive courses of action can the students engage in to correct the actual situation?

The encouragement process which was described in Chapter 5 forms the major basis for restoring adolescents' faith in themselves — 'I can do a job; I belong; I am useful'.

TYPICAL ERRORS MADE BY TEACHERS IN HELPING ADOLESCENTS

In their relationships with adolescents, teachers typically make two mistakes. One is to resort to permissiveness in the belief that there is little which can be done during this 'stage'. The other is to increase their authority believing that the increased independence of the adolescent is a threat which must be dealt with by increasing domination and control.

Permissive relationships

Schools have traditionally emphasised order at the expense of individual student freedom. When the major social upheavals occurred in the 1970s, teachers were urged to give students more freedom or involvement. Many granted freedom to students at the expense of order. The results were chaotic, not only in schools, but in families, factories, racial relations, and marriages.

The permissive teacher views adolescence as a stage through which students pass and that disturbing behaviour is normal and unavoidable. Teachers feel that they have no power to influence adolescents and, while not condoning irresponsible behaviour, feel powerless to influence. Adolescents interpret this attitude as an open invitation to do as they wish.

When teachers allow freedom without order, they lose the respect of their students who see them as weak, unable to provide guidance, and as poor models. Further, adolescents who are taught by permissive teachers begin to lose respect for themselves as they recognise that teachers have given up on them, do not value or respect them as they are, and are simply waiting for the adolescent to leave school or become more mature.

Autocratic relationships

At the other end of the continuum is the autocratic teacher who, while respecting and implementing order, refuses to allow students to exercise their right of choice. Such teachers believe that their teaching effectiveness is judged by their ability to control students and that they have the right to impose values, beliefs, and standards on students.

Adolescents have learned that they have the power to withhold co-operation from such teachers and do so in matters such as being apathetic towards school work, drug taking, refusal to do homework, being rude, and general disobedience. The increased efforts by teachers to force their students into compliance through coercive methods only serve to invite further retaliation and greater levels of unco-operative behaviour.

The following activities are examples of each of the two types of teacher.

Autocratic teacher	*Permissive teacher*
Demands that homework be done	Takes no action regarding late-comers
Accepts no contrary opinion	Ignores offensive language
Resorts to punishment	Provides materials for students who have forgotten
Uses criticism	Does not check classroom offenders
Promotes competition	

Teachers need to recognise that all problems of classroom management or discipline are basically problems of faulty student–teacher relationships. Teachers will have little problem with adolescents when they form relationships based upon respect and equality. The characteristics of a relationship based on equality have been described by Dinkmeyer and McKay (1983:7) as:

- mutual respect
- mutual trust
- mutual concern and caring
- empathy — sympathetic understanding — for one another
- a desire to listen to one another
- emphasis on assets rather than faults
- a commitment to co-operation and equal participation in resolving conflicts
- sharing of thoughts and feelings rather than hiding them and bearing resentment
- mutual commitment to common goals, but with freedom to pursue independent goals
- support for an acceptance of one another as imperfect people in the process of growing.

It is important to recognise how deeply young people are involved in a conflict with adults. It is not only the obviously violent, vicious, or delinquent student who is involved but a vast number of young people. If the solution were simply a matter of good teacher example and guidance or firm school discipline, we would not find so many problem adolescents coming from schools which are characterised as possessing 'good discipline'. No teacher or school is secure against the possibility of its students joining the army of active rebels whose protests about unemployment or Austudy changes evoke fears of LA-style riots.

Previous chapters have suggested a framework for understanding student behaviour. While this framework is appropriate for all relationships — parent–child, husband–wife, teacher–student, white–coloured or management–labour — there are a number of aspects which are particularly relevant to the adolescent.

As suggested earlier, adolescent students who are regarded as being behavioural problems by teachers share certain common characteristics.

- They view themselves as failures.
- They are pessimistic about their future.
- They lack the courage to take a chance.
- They have been humiliated frequently.
- They see themselves in a position of inferiority.

These faulty views and their correction are the basis of helping the difficult adolescent. It is essential to recognise that 'everything can be something else', that anything is possible, that young people are not victims of upbringing, of heredity, of emotion, or schooling or of society. They do not behave badly at school because they come from single-parent families, from poor homes or from uncaring parents. Students decide on the way they will behave and contribute very much to their own lives; they are not victims of circumstance. 'Individuals are responsible for their behaviour. One has considerable control over one's life' (Manaster and Corsini, 1982: 161). It is essential to recognise the potential of any student to change because faulty behaviour simply reflects faulty decisions. Think through the implication of the following question: 'Could James behave well if his life depended on it?'. The answer is always 'Yes', indicating that students can always improve their behaviour by changing their beliefs, decisions, or viewpoints.

Consider the positive view on living expressed by a young unemployed person in a letter published in the *Age* of 3 February, 1983.

Making the best of life without employment

from C. Milne

By contributing to the myth that unemployment necessarily equals misery 'The Age' is doing the Recession Generation a great disservice. Negative thinking has a habit of becoming self-fulfilling.

May I, from direct experience, argue that life for some frustrated young job seekers can indeed be happy and rewarding. The trick lies in creating for oneself the sense of purpose and belonging, and the pride in achievement, which flow from being employed.

Step 1. Each night decide on the next day's activities. Every hour must be covered and normal working hours must be adhered to.

Step 2. If you are receiving the dole, 'work' for it. Assuming a rate of $7 an hour, clean a park, help a pensioner, mind a child for a centre for homeless children.

Step 3. Improve your health by running and exercising every day.

Step 4. Make an effort, through community agencies, to meet and befriend other job seekers.

Step 5. Undertake some regular recreational work such as coaching the local under-12 football team.

As a suggestion, a typical 'working' week might include: writing job applications, attending interviews, growing vegetables in the back yard, working for the dole, exercising, reading, cooking, coaching the under-12s, fishing from a pier.

Happiness is a function of attitude, not of circumstances. In fact, to be unemployed can be seen as a privilege. If one thinks of it as a temporary phase during which one has the time to exercise more compassion (through community/ social work), these times may turn out to be the most rewarding of all.

A basic principle in dealing with adolescents is to recognise that their basic need is to belong, to feel a part of, to identify with the school, the peer group, the home, and the community. However, the competitive nature of most secondary schools encourages teachers to instil high ambition and achievement into students. This attitude is expressed in grading practices, curricular choice, streaming, and teacher expectation. Consequently, many students are denied the opportunity to obtain a sense of belonging through contributing and co-operating, because, in competitive schools, there must be winners and losers. For each student who achieves significance through scholastic, social or athletic success, many thousands are denied such opportunities. As a result, they turn to behaviours which are admired by their peers but rejected by teachers. These include smoking, taking drugs, driving wildly, indulging in sexual activity, stealing, defying authority, or resorting to personal abuse of teachers.

Make no mistake, adolescent students are looking for guidance but they find few teachers who will treat them as equals. The more difficult a student is, the more he is punished, threatened, lectured to, admonished, discriminated against and made to feel inferior or worthless. Nothing will be effective with adolescents until teachers change their relationships with their students and begin to win their co-operation.

Change your behaviour first

Teachers who try to change the behaviour of a difficult adolescent will invariably fail. When teachers suggest to teenagers how they should behave in relation to study, friends, TV watching, dress, homework, and the like, they set themselves up to be defeated. Adolescents have the absolute power to say 'No' and they exercise it frequently. Teachers are naturally concerned about such behaviours as rudeness, stealing, drug abuse, school failure, neglect of responsibility, violence, or disobedience. Faced with such unacceptable behaviours, teachers will frequently resort to punitive methods such as detention, time-out, withdrawal of privilege or physical punishment. Such activities are totally ineffective as they generate hostility, invite retaliation, worsen relationships and minimise the possibility of winning the student's co-operation. What these measures teach young people is that those who have the power, win. From then on they become more skilful in how they use their power.

Probably the most powerful message coming from modern psychology is this: 'If you wish to change the behaviour of another person, change your own behaviour first'. Teachers are always full of good intentions provided that their students are prepared to change. As long as teachers are convinced about what students should do, they will overlook the only influence which they can use to resolve conflict — themselves.

Teachers, interested in learning about approaches which they can use to change student behaviour, generally fail to realise that students will change only when teachers are prepared to change. As Dreikurs (1972:205) pointed out:

We all try to change the other one and have no luck. Stop thinking about what the other one should do; the only one we can change is ourselves.

As applied to the goals of misbehaviour which were discussed in Chapter 3, the above suggestion would result in the following teacher reactions to typical adolescent behaviours.

Behaviour	Goal of behaviour	Teacher response
Clowning Showing off Lateness	Attention seeking	1. Refuse to give special attention on request 2. Allow consequences to take place
Stubbornness Apathy Disobedience Untruthfulness	Power	1. Refuse to fight 2. Admit your inability to make students do anything 3. Allow consequences to take place
Stealing Delinquency Moodiness Personal abuse	Revenge	1. Refuse to be hurt 2. Avoid retaliation 3. Maintain order 4. Allow consequences to take place
Truancy Inability to learn Giving up easily Indolence	Withdrawal	1. Avoid criticism 2. Look for slight improvement 3. Acknowledge effort 4. Never give up.

The following comments by Dreikurs (1972:205) suggest that the only person for whom we are totally responsible for and can change totally is ourself.

I think this is the most important lesson, namely, that we begin to see what we are doing and could do differently, and stop thinking about what he should do.

As long as you continue to think about what your adolescent students should do, then there is no possibility of a resolution to the fighting between teachers and students. Recognise the enormous power of change which you possess merely by changing yourself.

ENCOURAGEMENT

At secondary school level, every student who is viewed as being a behavioural problem is a discouraged person who believes that he or she has no chance of being successful in school, lacks self-confidence, is pessimistic about the future, has a negative self-concept and refuses to take risks. The modification of these faulty views is the basis of all corrective work and the heart of such correction is the encouragement process.

Chapter 5 has discussed the nature of encouragement and the techniques of application. The importance of encouragement cannot be over-emphasised as, without exception, every difficult adolescent is a discouraged individual. While parents are the prime discouragers of children although their intentions are otherwise, teachers can use the encouragement process to correct the faulty view which many adolescents hold about themselves. The ability to encourage students is the most important single skill which teachers must develop.

The sources of discouragement during adolescence include mistake-centred approaches, competition, grading, streaming, negative expectations, overly high expectations, perfectionism, overprotection, suppression or autocratic approaches, peer comparisons, and conditional acceptance. Statements which reflect the above sources are:

'You are still making the same mistake.'

'Come on, Helen. With your ability you should be doing much better.'

'That is a well-designed poster but you should have used more colour.'

'I doubt whether you will ever be able to cope with calculus.'

'Let's see who is the best on the vocabulary test.'

'John can do better.'

'Careful now. No spelling mistakes.'
'You are too young to try that.'
'You will sit the way I tell you to sit.'
'Please yourself about doing homework. I don't care.'
Methods of encouraging adolescents are similar to those used to encourage all people.

* Focus on assets and strengths while minimising mistakes, for example, 'Your stories have many original ideas'.
* Acknowledge contribution, effort and improvement, for example, 'Thanks for tidying up the science bench. It makes my job easier'.
* Communicate confidence in students' ability to solve their problems, for example, 'Speaking in front of the whole school is a big task but knowing you, I am sure that you will do it well'.
* Comment on processes rather than on products, on acts not actors, for example, 'I see from your report that you have worked hard in science'.

When students know that their teachers have confidence in them, they can begin to develop confidence in themselves.

Specific methods for encouraging teenagers aim to convey the message to them that you have faith in them as they are. Looking for signs that they have what it takes to bridge the gap between childhood and adulthood, adolescents are encouraged by a teacher's quiet confidence in their ability to handle the problems of living. Specifically, teachers may encourage adolescents by:

* seeking their advice about a problem that faces you in the school;
* being interested in their activities;
* inviting their opinion on matters of current social, economic or political concern;
* inviting them to handle a task formerly done by the teacher;
* accepting mistakes and failures as matters of fact;
* emphasising their strengths;
* using the group as a means of solving problems;
* dispensing with as many school rules for them as possible;
* inviting them to share lunch in a common room;
* supporting their participation in a wide variety of activities;
* inviting your friends or acquaintances to talk with them during a school-related activity.

INDEPENDENCE, RESPONSIBILITY AND DISCIPLINE

Adolescence is a time of increased independence coupled with increased responsibility. To grant one without the other is to court disaster. While the increasing autonomy of the adolescent must be recognised and respected each independent action by an adolescent will produce a consequence which must be allowed to follow. This is the basis of self-discipline which is the only acceptable basis for schools in today's society.

Traditionally teachers have used rewards and punishments in an attempt to teach students to behave responsibly. The detention room is well known by most of us. The use of punishment is completely ineffective with adolescents and only teaches them to retaliate and generates rebellion and hostility. Adolescents are autonomous people and teachers cannot make them do anything.

Rewards are similarly ineffective in teaching adolescents to be responsible. The message communicated by a reward is 'Never do anything for nothing'. Students initially have a strong desire to belong to the school and to contribute to it, a desire which should be respected rather than destroyed by the use of rewards. Again, can you really make an adolescent do something by offering rewards? As with punishment, 'no'.

As suggested in Chapter 6, an alternative to rewards and punishment is to allow students to experience the consequences of their own behaviour. Homework not done means that the student does not participate in the lesson that day. Students who miss cricket practice are not chosen. Youngsters who arrive late make up the lost time in their own time. Library books not returned preclude the student from borrowing for a period of time. This is the basis of self-discipline. The adolescent's right to decide is respected, no attempt is made to make the adolescent do anything, yet the adolescent is held responsible for the decisions made.

Teachers will need to negotiate consequences with teenagers. Consider a 15-year-old who wishes to use a school computer at lunch time. The student and teacher agree that when the student finishes with the computer, it is to be closed down and the manual filed away. On a subsequent day, the student simply leaves the room without closing down or filing away. On the next day the teacher might say to the student: 'I see that you are not able to keep to your agreement. Ask about using the computer in two weeks' time'.

The above procedure highlights a number of points:

- A choice is presented. Either use the computer as agreed upon or have no access to it for two weeks.
- Teachers follow through. Consequences must be experienced or the student learns that agreements count for nought.
- Behaviours and consequences are negotiated. Adolescents are more likely to accept decisions if they have been involved in making them.
- Conflict is avoided. Nothing is said to the student at the time the agreement is broken but the teacher waited until the next day to raise the matter. At the time of the transgression, when the 'heat' is on, it is not the time to discuss anything.

The whole aim of the above procedure is to teach young people to become responsible. It is an approach which respects young people, treats them as social equals, fosters co-operation, avoids power contests, and balances independence with responsibility.

Shared responsibility

The autonomous nature of the adolescent is the major difference between the primary and secondary school student. Whereas the primary school child is far more dependent upon teachers, the adolescent is capable of deciding and acting independently of the teacher. Indeed, the peer group is a far more influential factor in the adolescent's life than is the teacher.

It is necessary to win adolescent co-operation by involving them in decisions which concern them. Failure to do this will frequently result in the adolescent refusing to accept decisions made by teachers. While teachers of primary school children may force them to conform, the adolescent knows that the teacher's power has been diminished by recent social events and will see a teacher's demand as a signal to defeat the teacher. A librarian who demands of a

Year 9 class that there will be no talking in the library can expect considerable resistance as can the teacher who announces to the Year 8 social studies class that assignments must be submitted by Friday. Telling adolescents what they must or must not do is to invite defeat. However, when young people are involved in making decisions regarding assignment dates, library behaviour, and the like, adolescents feel that they are being respected and treated as equal members of the school community. These are a necessary prerequisite for effective relationships between teachers and students in secondary school.

If you would like to know how successfully you are involving students in decision making, ask the students this question: 'Whose responsibility is it to run this class?'. If students respond with 'Yours', then they do not see the class as being 'our class'. If they respond with, 'All of us', then you are assured that the students will contribute to 'our' class.

The concept of shared responsibility implies that every member of the class, and that all classes within the school, should participate in the planning of the entire educational process. Even when confronted with administrative demands which constitute the reality in most schools, teachers can involve students in carrying out those obligations. Neither abdication nor imposition will prove effective with adolescents. By identifying the needs of the situation, the nature of the problem and possible solutions and consequences, students and teachers resolve conflicts and difficulties, without fighting or yielding, by respecting others and respecting themselves.

Try these

(1) Consider the following incidents. Classify them according to the criteria of:
    i. Which teacher is coercive?
    ii. Which teacher is permissive?
    iii. Which teacher encourages the students?
  a. Teachers invite students to discuss appropriate behaviour on school excursions.
  b. Teachers allow students to use offensive language without comment.

c. Teachers consistently criticise the way in which the students dress.

d. Students are permitted to come and go from class without permission.

e. Teachers give detentions to students when homework is not completed.

f. Teachers use classroom discussions as a means of solving particular problems.

(2) An adolescent back from a job interview reports 'I didn't get the job because the person did not like me'. How might the teacher respond and what actions could be taken to encourage the student?

(3) A State Minister of Education announced, after the abolition of corporal punishment: 'The working party on Discipline is studying alternative forms of punishment to make sure that they are adequate'. What mistaken belief is held by the Minister?

(4) A class decided that only students who completed the geography assignment would be permitted to attend the geography excursion. David failed to complete the assignment and, on being told that he could not come on the excursion, refused to stay at school and walked home, a journey which took two hours. On reaching home, his mother said: 'I am sorry that you missed the excursion but you know what to do about it'. What mistakes did the teacher or the mother make?

Answers

(1)

Coercive	Permissive	Encouraging
c; e	b; d	a; f

(2) a. Have the student state the actual situation. 'I went for an interview but didn't get the job.'

b. Have the student generate possible reasons, for example, 'I lacked the skills' or 'I didn't interview well'.

c. Ask the student on which of those reasons he would like to work.

(3) The Minister believes that punishment is an effective and appropriate form of control.

208 UNDERSTANDING CLASSROOM BEHAVIOUR

(4) Neither the teacher nor the mother made any mistake. The student was involved in the decision, given a choice, and experienced the consequences. The teacher followed through and was firm without being punitive. The mother minded her own business, recognising that the problem was between the child and the teacher.

10

Teacher Stress: A Cognitive View

INTRODUCTION

Stress in teaching has become a topic of increasing concern over the past decade. The problem has been highlighted by the size of the Workcare claims by teachers for stress-related illness. In the State of Victoria alone, teacher stress claims topped $100 million in one year. It is not only the financial cost that is of concern, but also the personal, professional, and social implications which are associated with the stress.

A considerable research effort has attempted to isolate those factors which may lead to stress. Yet it is true to say, as the Applied Psychology Research Group concluded (1989:14): 'It would seem that despite the many studies and many thousands of teachers that have been tested for stress over the past few years, we still lack a fully satisfactory picture of teachers stress and its determinants'.

In line with traditional approaches to behavioural problems, researchers have sought to determine the 'causes' behind teacher stress. As pointed out in Chapter 2, causalistic approaches are rejected by the author who views individuals as self-determining, as active participants in the making of their environment rather than victims of hereditary and environmental influences. Teachers do not simply react to events going on in schools but act upon them in accordance with their life style. In a sense, teachers choose their own problems in accordance with the faulty views which they hold regarding their means of belonging or their life style. The teleological approach suggests that potential environmental stressors become actual stressors through the operation of the life style. While teacher A is stressed by the involvement of parents in the teaching program, teacher B welcomes their presence. Students who are disruptive in class stress Teacher X but not Teacher Y. Why is this? Because there are no external causes of stress. No teacher can be stressed who chooses not to be stressed. This is not to suggest that stressful situations are not important influences upon wellness, but they do not cause illness. What forces converge on us or whatever situations we find ourselves in, are less important than what we decide to do.

FACTORS INFLUENCING TEACHER STRESS

Although the view taken is that stress results from one's response to stressors, it is useful to consider those factors which teachers report as being stressful.

Dewe (1986:145) in an investigation into the causes and consequences of teacher stress, identified the global nature of the problem: 'Teaching provides many situations which can induce stress'. From the multitude of demands that teachers encounter, a good proportion of them appear to be continuously perceived as stressful. It is interesting to note that many sources of stress relate to those situations where teachers felt they had little or no control, such as parental expectations, work overload, disruptive students, lack of administrative support, and the physical and mental demands of teaching. Dewe (1986:155) maintained that:

> Teacher stress is not just confined to the classroom. The lack of support from colleagues and senior staff, poor school organisation, a lack of effective consultation or participation in decision making, inadequate support for curriculum changes and inadequate equipment and resources all have the potential for causing stress.

Friesen and Williams (1985) also emphasised the inherent difficulty in the teaching situation where the teacher's role is becoming diverse and often in excess of their training. Many teachers feel that they cannot fulfil the growing expectations, yet they seem to be under a compulsion to engage in activities over and above their teaching role. Friesen and Williams highlight the potential for teacher stress when teacher training institutions give the impression that teachers should see themselves as:

> ... programmers, evaluators, counsellors, helpers, planners, learners, school representatives, supervisors, role models and builders of social conscience. Add to this, teachers are expected to serve as managers, reporters, surveyors, researchers, and custodians, and be punctual. Teachers are also expected to be both helper and disciplinarian towards students' (p.31).

Numerous studies have isolated a number of potential sources of teacher stress. The sources are included here because of the frequency with which they are reported.
1. Classroom discipline and the management of unco-operative, aggressive and unmotivated students.
2. Lack of administrative and leadership support and the absence of meaningful communication with the school principal.
3. Major and rapid organisational and curriculum changes and developments which increase the possibilities of role conflict and role confusion.
4. Absence of equitable rewards in relation to the demands of the position and the lack of promotional prospects.
5. Excessive clerical work, unproductive staff meetings, lack of time, and resources difficulties.
6. Lack of public and parental respect and support for education.

The above findings are evidenced in the 1989 Applied Psychological Research Group survey of teacher stress in Victoria. This survey of primary, secondary and technical schools, achieving a response rate of 92 per cent, found that the principal sources of teacher stress were as follows:

212 UNDERSTANDING CLASSROOM BEHAVIOUR

	Frequency of Responses
Student misbehaviour	97
Self doubts/lack of recognition/lack of promotion and career progress	91
Negative attitudes and lack of motivation in students	91
Discipline policy and problems	74
Problems with other teaching staff	74
Time allocation and determining priorities	55
Demands and expectations of parents and community	55
School administration and the principal	32
Changes: too many, too often	28

Most teachers would agree with the above summaries and findings and would probably add to the list. What they fail to see is that they are not passive victims of stressful situations but that they create their own stress by the meaning they give to events. A request for a time-table revision, an increase in teaching hours or class size, curricular change or assessment demands are not stressful in themselves. They become stressful through the mediation of the life style which generates stress symptoms in order to safeguard the self-esteem. All symptoms of stress are in the service of the life style. Symptoms such as migraine, anxiety attack, compulsion, procrastination, pathological pedantry, anorexia nervosa, impotence, constipation, neurosis, frigidity, paranoia, hyperactivity, depression, tears and complaints, fainting spells, and inability to concentrate are purposeful and represent inadequate ways of dealing with potentially stressful situations which arouse in teachers the fear of failure. Rather than deal with the symptoms of stress, it is necessary to deal with the faulty views which teachers hold.

Life style and stress

Life style is a cognitive blueprint, a set of rules by which values can be assigned, a hierarchy can be established, priorities set.

It permits individuals to maintain a certain stability and consistency in the way they approach the problems of living.

Life style is pervasive, performing a number of functions such as selective perception, decision making, control of experience, guiding action, self-protecting, reinforcing and predicting actions and outcome. For example, teachers who perceive themselves as weak and ineffective, will act accordingly. A teacher who feels that he must control, will find himself in frequent power struggles with others. Those who believe that 'life is unfair' will experience many events which reinforce that view.

An understanding of life style, the chief idiographic principle which accounts for one's uniqueness, is basic to understanding and the management of stress. Teachers become stressed when their life style clashes with the demands which teaching places upon them and they act to protect their life style. In their study of personality and illness, Matheny and Kern (1989:33) have observed:

> It appears that psychological factors in certain life styles may chronically trigger negative emotions, which in turn lead to neurological and hormonal adjustments predisposing persons to mental and physical illnesses.

From a variety of sources it may be concluded that there is a definite relationship between life style and an individual's potential towards the symptoms of stress. Each teacher's response to school situations can be seen in terms of a central theme, a theme based upon the conviction of each teacher, and a theme which at certain times will hinder him or her in efforts to cope with the demands of teaching. Adler initially described the central theme or life style as an individual's dominant method of interacting with others, which may be one of the following: 'ruling, getting, avoiding or socially useful'. Since then, extensive work has contributed to an understanding of life style typologies and their relationship to the way in which individuals respond to the problems of living.

LIFE STYLE TYPOLOGIES

Since each individual is unique, the use of typologies is contradictory. However, there are a number of typical life styles which appear when factor-analytical approaches are applied to life style inventories. Mosak (1977:183) has identified 14 typologies of life style which were described and elaborated on by Dewey (1978:17). They are:

1. The 'Getter'

   Feels *entitled* to receive and finds it difficult to 'do'. Their thought is always 'What's in it for me?' They may be charming but are usually passive, dependent individuals who are not self-reliant. Their outlook on life is pessimistic and they often feel that life is unfair to them. They are usually gregarious but may and manipulate others by putting them into their service. They may use temper, charm, shyness or intimidation as methods of operation. Sometimes they retreat into depression. Some cover up their basic pessimism by a super optimism to assure themselves that 'all is fine' or 'my luck is bound to change'.

2. The 'Driver' or 'Go-getter'

   Is an active, aggressive, forceful individual who always wants to be first, be on top, be better than others or be the centre. They have to win and when they don't they claim they were cheated. They must have their own way and power is important in all their relationships although they also feel they would like to please everyone. They believe it is important to be 'a real man' or 'a real woman'. Their over-ambition is counter-phobic for underneath they fear they are 'nothing'.

3. The 'Controller'

   Either wants to control life or not be controlled by life. They approach life with a hesitating attitude since their goal is that of perfection and they constantly test themselves and life. They need guidelines for everything so routines, schedules, order, and rules appeal to them. They are over-conscientious, punctual, and concerned with cleanliness, neatness, and correct dress. They are afraid of their feelings and favor intellectualisation. They deprive themselves of spontaneity, dislike surprises and find it difficult to relax and have fun. They may have good superficial relationships but find it difficult to develop close relationships with people. They often deprecate others, thereby exalting themselves. They may develop passive methods of controlling others, using tears ('water power'), weakness, shyness and charm.

4. The 'Person who needs to be right'
    Is an over-ambitious perfectionist with excessively high standards. They cannot tolerate .ambiguity and need guidelines for everything. They have trouble making up their minds and may ask for advice to an extreme degree. They are usually in a state of turmoil although they try to 'go by the book'. Right and wrong are the all-important issues; if they don't know what is right, they don't act. They are overwhelmed by the importance of the reactions of other people. They scrupulously avoid error but if caught in error, they rationalise that others are more wrong than they are.

5. The 'Person who must be superior'
    Feels inferior unless in a superior position. They strive for significance but have a basic feeling of insignificance. They must be the leader and are upset if their authority is challenged; then they try to 'get even'. They have little feeling for others although they use them as stepping stones for themselves. They are vain and frequently rude and arrogant, although they may maintain a demeanour of politeness that is not genuine. They deny their true feelings, may act 'tough' and are defensive. Some have to be master of everything and others emphasise keeping themselves under control and being above reproach. They may achieve the record for the number of days of underground burial. They won't enter a life arena unless they can be the 'centre' or 'best'. If they can't be first or best, they may settle for last or worst.

6. The 'Person who needs to be liked' or the 'Pleaser'
    Evaluations of others are the yardsticks of worth. They depend on the approval of others and are uncomfortable without constant praise. They are extremely sensitive to criticism. Because they are dependent on what is expected of them, they cannot be sincere. They cannot be strong leaders or efficient bosses or be effective in a catastrophe because they might be criticised.

7. The 'Person who needs to be "good"'
    Is a self-righteous person who looks down on others by pointing out their weaknesses. They may advertise their own goodness.

8. The 'Victim'

   Sometimes called the *schlimazel*, the victim is the one who always gets the dirty end of the stick. They are disaster-chasers and are accident-prone. They see life as abusive and full of suffering and tragedy. Although suffering is their goal, they are completely oblivious that it is they who provoke their own downfall. They may actually be courageous but see themselves as always losing out and seek pity. They are pessimistic about life and constantly complain about what is happening to them.

9. The 'Martyr'

   While the 'victim' merely dies, the 'martyr' dies for a cause. Martyrs have more arrogance than victims; martyrs feel that they are good and have value. Their goal is to suffer and thus enable and elevate themselves above others. They are highly critical, self-righteous and have high moral standards. They may complain bitterly or be cheerful, playing to their own audience but feeling sorry for themselves. They are 'injustice collectors'. Some martyrs advertise their suffering; others endure and suffer silently.

10. The 'Baby'

    Finds a place through charm, cuteness and the exploitation of others. They feel small, weak, helpless and unable to take care of themselves. Their goal is to get others to serve them. They may ask questions, seek help, try to be the centre of attention and expect special privileges. They are dependent on others and want to be loved or pitied. Their voices may remain high-pitched and child-like and they may continue to talk 'baby talk'.

11. The 'Inadequate person'

    Has an 'inferiority complex' and feels small and weak, that life is difficult and full of trouble or dull and unrewarding. Since they feel they cannot do anything, others should not expect anything from them and they don't expect anything from themselves. Their goal is to avoid demands and pressures and they try to get others to leave them alone. Through their default they indenture others. They avoid responsibility and are threatened by success because they fear that then others will expect more from them. They may be likeable and pleasant but they usually have trouble in an aggressive society. They were probably under-achievers at school, who had particular difficulty in mathematics and are likely to have difficulty handling money.

12. The '**Person who craves excitement**'
    Revels in commotion, feel rules are restrictive and ordinary life and routines are dull. They find fun in breaking rules and flirting with danger, often 'bite off more than they can chew', leave everything until the last moment, make 'messes', do things they should not do. They confuse others and become confused themselves. They may feel that they are someone special but there is considerable pessimism in their outlook on life. They are often attracted to inappropriate persons and frequently use sex to stir up excitement, or fall in love with someone who is married. Some find excitement through fears, masturbation, etc. not involving others.

13. The '**Aginner**'
    Opposes everything. They know only what they are against and do not stand for anything. They may be actively against or they may behave passively, circumventing the demands of others. They are extreme pessimists.

14. The '**One who avoids feelings**'
    Feels that reason can solve all problems, prizes rationality and the intellectual process and 'talks a good game'. They fear their own spontaneity lest they might move in a way that they have not planned.

Kefir and Kefir (1971) developed a mini-system of life style by classifying individual life styles as:

(a) Pleasers: those who endeavoured to get along with others.
(b) Superiors: those who attempted to always be best, first.
(c) Comforters: those who looked after their own comfort.
(d) Controllers: those who tried to maintain self-control.

Kern and White (1989), using the Life-style Scale (Kern, 1982, 1986), maintained that this scale appears to hold the most promise for the practitioner who wishes to acquire life style data rapidly in order to help individuals deal with their problems of living.

The Kern scale identifies five life styles which the author and his students have used in the study of teacher, management, and parental stress. The five life style themes/ typologies and their characteristics are:

(a) *Controller*

The life style indicates an individual who attempts to deal with life by being a logical, rational, problem solver; controlling emotions (especially anger, and thus may not get angry very often), and actively taking charge and leading others. Wants control of external events, and when cannot becomes stressed. Not afraid of confronting people; thus may have power struggles; may be autocratic and aggressive. May see life as win–lose situations, be a competitive, workaholic, Type A person, addicted on adrenalin, always in a hurry, (walking and talking). Others may perceive the individual as bossy, autocratic, opinionated, unwilling to listen, and more prone to confrontation than cooperation. Relationships with others may be a contest of winning and losing.

Assets that the person has are an ability to confront and solve problems rationally, and to meet conflict situations head on. Other assets include the ability to lead, organise and follow through with assigned tasks. A passive dimension of this scale may be characterised by an individual who appears cool, calm, collected, and unfeeling, and gives the appearance of having most situations under control. This person is quiet, shows few emotions, is seen as a very 'private' person, and seems to be a difficult person to 'get to know'.

(b) *Perfectionist*

The life style of the perfectionist attempts to deal with life's problems by wishing to control others or conforming to others' demands. Perfectionists like order and routine. A person who scores high on this scale may be one who likes to complete tasks alone, is conscientious and busy, and may be somewhat obsessive and conservative in response to life tasks. May see life in terms of right and wrong, and their goal is to be right. They are extremely sensitive to making mistakes; they are precise, and won't delegate as they fear others will make mistakes. This individual may portray characteristics of

conscientiousness, (may be a list-maker), thoughtfulness, sensitivity, and caution. The perfectionism may
also be a strategy for gaining control of situations or
others. Their source of stress is often within themselves.

Perfectionism may be combined with Control to produce an individual who is a driver, Type A personality, a
person whose life is out of balance between work and
personal relationships. When combined with Pleasing,
the perfectionistic individual is sensitive, a good listener
but pleases by not making mistakes. 'I never did anything wrong' is their epitaph.

(c) *Need to please*

A person with this life style theme will actively seek
approval from others, serve as a peacemaker or diplomat in interpersonal situations where conflict is involved. The individual will be very sensitive to others'
needs and avoid confrontation and conflict situations.
They will generally demonstrate caring characteristics
and most likely appear to possess high levels of social
interest. The passive dimension person follows direc-
tions, is flexible and easy to get along with. They may be
quiet, private persons rarely telling people what they
think, and on the surface appear somewhat shy. They
are sensitive and vulnerable, and can easily be hurt by
others. They are usually excellent listeners who have
difficulty getting their needs met because it is difficult
for them to use 'I' statements such as 'I want ...', 'I need
...', 'I prefer ...'.

The active or passive dimension represented by this
scale suggests individuals who are sensitive, quiet, good
listeners, shy, apologetic, and who may experience difficulties in the areas of confrontation, conflict resolution,
and getting their own needs met.

(d) *Victim*

A high Victim scale may indicate a person who has
feelings of low self-esteem, discouragement, may be
depressed, and have low energy levels. They may be
disappointed with their own abilities, trying hard but not
successful. This person may be over-sensitive to others'
feelings, have difficulties in problem solving, and is
interested in avoiding problems, stressful situations,

and conflict as much as possible. These individuals may feel an inability to control life situations related to career, relationships or peers; thus, may be highly stressed and unpredictable as too many things might be going on in their lives. Things may not be going well with the job, and difficulties may be encountered with completing tasks. They have an attitude of 'This always happens to me' and appear to have difficulties in 'keeping it together'.

(e) *Martyr*

A high Martyr factor may indicate individuals whose expectations of self and others are overly high, so that they continually set up problem situations at work, with others or with loved ones, that are characterised by criticism, frustration, feelings of unfairness, and falling short of personal expectations. Other behavioural characteristics may include criticism of self and others, overbearing expectations, tenacity, and high levels of frustration in one or more of the life tasks of career, social relationships or intimacy.

A high Martyr scale may indicate persons who are having difficulties or frustrations in a particular life task of family, work or friends, and could be depressed and extremely discouraged about this. They work very hard and will not give up (they will die for a cause). Life is a struggle, and things don't work out well for them. They are over-achievers who almost succeed and blame others when they are unsuccessful.

RELATIONSHIP BETWEEN STRESS AND LIFE STYLES

The importance of understanding one's life style in relation to teacher stress is highlighted by the following statement made by Kopp and Kivel (1990:139–140):

> The terms stress or stressors refer to examples of exogenous factors. Symptoms appear as part of that mistaken response to the exogenous factor; mistaken because, while they serve to safeguard the self-esteem and the life style, they also prevent an effective solution to the situation the person confronts.

In other words, while many teachers suffer symptoms of stress, they have a stake in maintaining the symptoms because they protect the life style. For example, the Perfectionist may continue to suffer from migraine rather than engage in activities which they feel may not be completed perfectly. Rather than deal with the symptom of stress, the migraine, the Perfectionist must be taught to have the courage to be imperfect.

Teachers are not stressed by events but by the view they take of them. The view they take may be positive or negative depending on their life style. While it is not suggested that teachers change their life style, they can become aware of their life style, the problems which it can create in their lives, and they can learn appropriate stress management strategies to prevent potential stressors becoming actual stressors.

Consider the following situation. A parent has come to the school principal to complain about the apparent lack of homework being set by you in Year 8 science. The principal has asked you to respond. Your immediate reaction might be one of the following:

(a) Thank the parent and agree to set more homework in the future.

(b) Indicate that you are already overworked, the request is unfair, but agree to take on this additional task.

(c) Suggest to the parent that you are running the science class and that you do not welcome parental intervention.

(d) Indicate that the homework could not be thoroughly checked by you because of the large class size.

(e) Simply accept what the parent says and wonder if anything will ever go right for you.

The above situation, which is a potential source of stress, becomes an actual stressor through the intervention of the life style. The Pleaser (choice A) will not be affected by the complaint and will act quickly to decrease the conflict. The Controller (choice C) will see this as a power context which must be won and immediately confronts the parent. Stress will only occur if the power struggle is lost. The Perfectionist (choice D) fears that the additional work will lead to a decline in standards and will express stress only if the homework request is implemented. Victims (choice E) expect to be placed in a no-win situation with the parent, and prefer not to be caught up in an argument. They will suffer stress because there is just too much happening in their teaching right now. Martyrs (choice B) expect criticism of themselves, believe that the request is unfair but will work hard to make sure the request is implemented. Stress will result when students do not complete the homework set by the teacher.

Consider the following profiles in Figure 12.

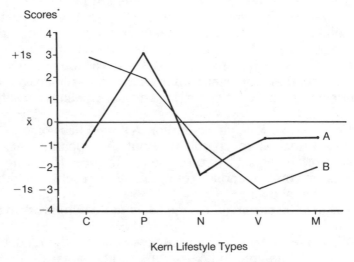

Kern Lifestyle Types

C = Controller   P = Perfectionist   M = Martyr
N = Need to please V = Victim

Figure 12:   Individuals profiles on Kern Life-style Scale

Scores* = scores in relation to the average or mean (x̄), and standard deviation (s) as designated by Kern (1982).

The dominant theme of A is Perfectionist. A high Perfectionist factor indicates an individual who attempts to deal with life's problems by wishing to control others or conforming to others' demands. A person who scores high on this factor may indicate a person who likes to complete tasks alone, is conscientious, extremely sensitive to making mistakes, and may be somewhat obsessive and conservative in response to life tasks. These individuals may see life in terms of right and wrong, and their goal is to be right. They may portray characteristics of conscientiousness, thoughtfulness, sensitivity, and caution.

As applied to teaching, these individuals will not tolerate errors in themselves or in their students. Their fear of failure is often transmitted to their students who become low risk-takers. Students begin to doubt whether their work will ever be good enough. Many give up because they cannot please the teacher, their parents or themselves.

The dominant theme of B is Control. A teacher who is high on Control tends to be aggressive, unwilling to listen, rational, unfeeling, autocratic and a confrontationist. In a classroom, Controllers will do just that — control the behaviour of students. 'Put that away.' 'Don't answer until I ask you.' 'Get on with your work.' 'Stop that noise.' Students are offered no choice as all authority is vested in the teacher. An environment of dependency or rebellion will result, the latter being very stressful for a Controller. It is no surprise that teachers who maintain an autocratic leadership style will be far more vulnerable to stress than a teacher who employs a democratic style.

It should not be thought that a particular life style is necessarily a negative characteristic. In their attempt to overcome feelings of inferiority, insecurity or incompletion, individuals can adopt either socially useful or socially useless strategies to express their life styles.

Victims, for instance, who operate on the useless non-constructive side seek to demonstrate how the world mistreats them and how much they must suffer in order to feel significant and secure. They will complain, whine, and point out disasters and injustices that happen to them, in order to show how much they suffer (Kopp, 1986).

Other victims, who operate on the useful or constructive side, act as diplomats. They help correct unjustice and oppression and gain a sense of significance and security from these behaviours. They will be activists and crusaders for equality and fair play in order to create more justice in the world.

The factor which decides whether a person pursues a life style in either a socially useful or socially useless way, is the level of social interest which the individual has developed. Thus, while life styles such as a Controller or a Pleaser may imply a non-constructive or useless role, an individual with high levels of social interest will turn the Controller's role into an organiser or a Pleaser into a diplomat.

Kopp (1986) has highlighted that aspect of Adlerian theory which suggests that individuals have the potentiality to express their striving for significance either positively or negatively. As the choice which the individual makes depends on the level of social interest, Kopp suggests that:

It is my hope that Adlerian educators, counsellors, and therapists will find it helpful in their efforts to encourage and 'reorient' others towards developing increased social interest (p.24).

STRESS MANAGEMENT STRATEGIES

The Applied Psychology Research Group (1989) has recommended several strategies for dealing with the problem of teacher stress. They include an increase in resources and remuneration, clarification of accountability, increasing prestige of schools and other measures which 'are intended to make life in school better for both teachers and students'. These recommendations will have no effect on reducing teacher stress. They are directed towards alleviating the causes of stress when it has been shown that there are no external causes of teacher stress.

In his classic *Who Gets Sick?*, Justice (1988:308) writes: 'You carry with you the most powerful medicine that exists. Each of us has it if we choose to use it, if we learn to use it'. Empowerment of teachers to improve the quality of their lives by cognitive stress management strategies becomes the goal. It is unrealistic to expect that teachers will change their life styles but they can become aware of the strategies which will help them cope with the variety of potential stressors associated with particular life styles which they will encounter in their daily work.

Most stress management strategies concern themselves with regular exercise, nutritional guidelines, deep breathing, relaxation, time management, and meditation. Research has shown that these approaches are effective in reducing the symptoms of stress such as high blood pressure, depression, insomnia, tension headaches, irritability, and bodily aches.

This chapter has suggested that teachers choose their own stress symptoms which result from inappropriate life styles. Stressful situations encountered in the school do not automatically produce physical or psychological distress. Causation is rejected because one's life style is a pervasive influence on wellness, physical and mental.

Current attempts to reduce the level of stress in the teaching profession are bound to fail for they are focused on symptoms. For example, the suggestion that a reduction in class size, teaching allocation, or clerical load will reduce stress fails to take into account the fact that teachers choose the stress which they experience. A Pleaser will be totally unconcerned about an increase in class size or teaching duties whereas a Perfectionist would be very stressed. Controllers who are removed from a potentially confrontational situation will find themselves even more stressed when there is nothing to confront.

Stress management strategies for the five life styles discussed above are:

Controller

- Positive self-talk and self-affirmation makes for positive thinking, and this helps with positive feelings. Accept responsibility for one's own thoughts, feelings, and behaviours, and the logical consequences of these. Talk positively to oneself and others, to give and accept encouragement. Smile.
- As a rational, logical problem solver, use thoughts to control feelings. Realise the usefulness of showing feelings to avoid presenting as a cold, unfeeling person.
- Due to the ability of confronting others, learn to confront oneself, and realise the importance of controlling anger.
- As one cannot control all external events, let go of some control. Avoid power struggles, being bossy and autocratic. Avoid the first impulse of fighting, and withdraw from the conflict. Accept what cannot be changed, and learn to relax.
- Use effective time management. Slow down and enjoy things in life: walk, talk, eat more slowly, allow people to finish sentences and avoid having the last word in conversations.
- Use self-control to listen effectively to others.
- Realise that some goals may be more effectively achieved through cooperation than competition.

Perfectionist

- Review the strategies for Controller.
- Positive self-talk and self-affirmation makes for positive

thinking, and this helps with positive feelings. Talk positively to oneself and others, to give and accept encouragement. Accept responsibility for one's own thoughts, feelings, and behaviours, and the logical consequences of these. Smile.

- Be able to accept some untidiness and disorder of self, students, and others.
- See that the courage to be imperfect is a strength.
- As the source of stress is in oneself, learn to relax, and take and enjoy a break with work colleagues, friends and family.
- Delegate responsibility to others.
- Realise that there is more than one right way of thinking and doing things.

Pleaser

- Positive self-talk and self-affirmation makes for positive thinking, and this helps with positive feelings. Accept responsibility for your own thoughts, feelings, and behaviours, and the logical consequences of these. Talk positively to oneself and others, to give and accept encouragement. Smile. Use positive self-talk to be less vulnerable and sensitive to being hurt and feeling rejected.
- Ignore other people's negative behaviours and talk. Accept oneself and others as they are, with their own thoughts, feelings, and behaviour.
- Be not overly concerned with the perpetual approval of others. Continual praise is not useful, whereas intrinsic feedback is.
- Take a course in conflict resolution, and/or assertion skills. Increase the use of 'I' and 'I prefer' statements. Practise saying 'no' in low-threat situations. Be courageous and voice an opinion.

Victim

- Positive self-talk and self-affirmation makes for positive thinking, and this helps with positive feelings. Accept and be responsible for one's own thoughts, feelings, and behaviours, and the logical consequences of these. Talk positively to self and others, to give and accept encouragement. Smile. Take responsibility to accept and 'own' one's feelings.

- Use positive self-talk to be less vulnerable and sensitive to being hurt and feeling rejected.
- Use positive self-talk to avoid feeling depressed and achieve more control.
- Become more satisfied with the accomplishments of oneself and others. Be more accepting and encouraging of self and others.
- Use time management, avoid procrastination and complete jobs. Learn to listen to others.

Martyr
- Positive self-talk and self-affirmation makes for positive thinking, and this helps with positive feelings. Accept and be responsible for one's own thoughts, feelings, and behaviours, and the logical consequences of these. Talk positively to self and others, to give and accept encouragement. Take responsibility to accept and 'own' one's feelings.
- Find good points in self and other people, and point this out. Be more accepting and encouraging of self and others.
- Place realistic expectations of self and others. Emphasise assets and strengths and minimise liabilities and deficiencies.
- Learn confrontation in low-threat situations.
- Associate with positive people to gain encouragement.

Stress, conflict and tension are a normal part of a teacher's life. Behavioural problems, changing curricula, lack of resources, lack of promotion, media criticism, and excessive time demands are examples of stressful events. It is not the events which produce stress but rather one's response to the events. Stressors from outside such as disruptive students, late-comers or administrative demands do not constitute stress. It is your response to them which constitute stress.

How teachers respond to stressors will be influenced by their life style, the belief which they hold about themselves, other people and the world. A number of life styles have been discussed including 'I must control', 'I must be perfect', 'I must be liked', and 'Life is just too much'. For each life style, a set of stress management strategies has been developed with aim to counter the effect of potentially stressful

228 UNDERSTANDING CLASSROOM BEHAVIOUR

structures or events which teachers encounter. While there are many things which teachers would like to change in schools, administration, curricula, assessment, choice of students and so on, the only thing that you can change with certainty is yourself. As the Roman philosopher Epictetus said: 'Men are disturbed not by things, but by the view they take on them'.

11
Conflict Resolution in Teaching

INTRODUCTION

Teachers will inevitably be involved in conflict situations involving students, colleagues, parents, and administration. The democratic society in which we live and which is now reflected in our schools will always generate conflict, as have previous types of societies. What has changed is the way in which these conflicts need to be resolved and the strategies which are necessary to resolve conflict, strategies which must become part of a teacher's repertoire.

Over the past two hundred years or more, conflicts have been settled in a rather simple manner. As conflicts were basically power contests, whoever had more power and was stronger won the contest while the one with less power was required to submit. In conflicts involving principals and teachers, principals won. Similarly, teachers defeated students while parents were decidedly stronger than their children. Industrial disputations were infrequent because of the invariable outcome, a win by management over labour. Conflict resolution simply reflected an inequality between individuals, a lack of respect, and an assumption that pressure from above was the most effective course of influence.

Certainly it made teachers' lives much easier because their position of superiority vested them with the necessary power to defeat students. However, for the winner, such a victory was a hollow one because the loser was not willing to accept the winner's superiority and refused to submit to it (Stagner and Rosen, 1965).

As discussed in Chapter 1, the advent of a democratic society profoundly affected relationships between groups such as teacher–student, parent–child and management–labour. Values began to emerge such as mutual respect, social equality, co-operation, shared responsibility and self-discipline. One effect of these social changes was to render ineffective and inappropriate traditional methods of resolving conflict. Conflict must be settled within a democratic framework in which the value of respect dominates.

Many strategies of conflict resolution suggest the need for better communication, more co-operation and the need for agreement. Communication, co-operation and agreement have nothing to do with conflict resolution. In fact, it is impossible to have conflict without these three variables being present. A teacher cannot fight with a parent unless both parties agree to the conflict, communicate their intention to fight and co-operate to keep the conflict going. What then are appropriate strategies for conflict resolution which are appropriate in our schools?

STRATEGIES FOR RESOLVING CONFLICT

The Adlerian approach to conflict resolution is represented opposite.

The Adlerian approach suggested does not attempt to avoid conflicts but seeks to resolve them in non-traditional ways. The procedures have been suggested by Dreikurs (1972) and Kopp (1987) and consist of five aspects.

1. Abandon the use of power

It is only possible to avoid fighting or yielding when parties in dispute respect each other. A teacher who attempts to

The Traditional Approach

Your Path / Their Path

The Adlerian Approach

A.   Your Path / Their Path

Both on collision course,

B.   Your Path / Their Path

you step aside and see where the other person is going

C.   Your Path / Their Path

You now continue on your way and

D.   Your Path / Their Path

the other person turns to see your direction.

Two approaches to conflict resolution (Adapted from Gerstein and Reagan 1986)

resolve conflict through the use of power will find that the other party is equally determined and is often a better fighter. As a result, teachers will be forced to fight, a procedure which will only maintain the conflict. An attempt by a teacher to dominate students has the effect of provoking resentment, rebellion, and retaliation.

On the other hand, teachers who give in show no respect for themselves and serve to maintain the conflict as the other party takes more and more advantage which will generate more conflict.

Dreikurs (1972:204) observed that it is necessary to:

> ... abandon all hope that anything can be settled in a power context. If you try to impress upon a child or husband or anyone else, what he should do, he will directly impress upon you that he won't do it. Fighting and giving in are the two resulting pitfalls.

Teachers who fight and impose their solution on students show no respect; teachers who give in violate respect for themselves. In schools today, conflict must be resolved by mutual respect.

2. Pinpoint the conflict

The vast majority of conflicts in schools are concerned with the consequences of the conflict rather than with the real issue. Curiously, what teachers fight about is never the issue. Regardless of the content of the dispute, both parties in the conflict use the dispute to demonstrate power, status or prestige.

The issue behind almost all conflict is rarely the issue of the disagreement but rather personal involvement, concern with status, with power, appearance, ambition and other personal goals. Teachers use matters such as work conditions, teaching hours, curriculum, discipline, assessment, and the like to involve others in a conflict; parents challenge school principals on discipline, uniforms, standards, and poor teaching while students use homework, lateness, smoking and behaviour to create conflict situations. No matter what the issue is which leads to the conflict, recognise that the main issue is always the same, winning or losing.

Students who are *actively* involved in power use a variety of situations to show teachers that: 'I can do what I like and you cannot stop me'. Their belief is that they only count when they are in control and they will choose any situation as a vehicle for confronting and defeating teachers.

Such students can be identified in a number of ways. Their behaviour is characterised by their refusal to follow rules, by lies, outbursts of anger and argumentation. Teachers react to these students by feeling angry and challenged. When teachers attempt to make these students comply, the students continue to escalate the problem. If teachers happen to 'win' the conflict, the students learn that power is important and next time they will be more skilful in how they use their power. No final victory is possible.

Students who are *passively* involved in power believe that their power and significance lies in refusing to do what is expected of them and communicate clearly to teachers the message: 'You cannot make me do what you want me to do'.

These students can be recognised by observing their behaviour. They are stubborn, apathetic, lazy; they produce endless excuses, while their work is careless and frequently late. They accept your criticism but do nothing about it. Teachers react to these students by feeling personally challenged while their reaction to the students' inadequate behaviour has the effect of escalating the problem. Conflict cannot be resolved until the real issue of the conflict is pinpointed.

3. Change your own behaviour

Deciding what others must do only fuels the conflict while attempting to make others conform to your demands makes you dependent on them. In a conflict situation, each party knows only what the other should do. It is analogous to a dialogue where only the lines of the opponent are known. When teachers complain, it is about what students are or are not doing; when students complain, it is about teachers; when principals complain it is about teachers while teachers complain about principals.

> Everybody is full of good intentions, provided the other one will change. We all try to change the other and have no luck. Stop thinking what the other one should do: the only one we can change is ourselves ... as long as you think about him and her and them, there is no possibility of a solution to the conflict, because you've overlooked the only one who can do it — yourself (Dreikurs, 1972:205).

Teachers can immediately resolve conflict if they are prepared to stop thinking about what others should do and begin thinking about what they can do. As long as teachers are concerned about what students should do, there is no possibility of a solution of the conflict because the teachers have overlooked the only individuals who can resolve the conflict, themselves. When a student wants to fight with a teacher and the teacher eliminates himself from fighting, he is no longer party to the conflict. Deciding what they will do, rather than what students should do, puts teachers in control of themselves.   ·

Accepting responsibility for one's own behaviour requires, according to Dreikurs (1972:35), a belief in one's own strength, a realisation of the tremendous influence which we have but seldom use.

> We are so concerned about what others should do that we fail to use our potential to influence by considering what we can do. It doesn't pay to be a threat to others; you can only find yourself when you stop thinking about status, power, prestige and authority; we get nowhere if we keep thinking that we are right and they are wrong.

In a conflict situation, teachers must always focus on the needs of the situation rather than on the demands of the parties concerned. What the teacher wants is irrelevant; what the student wants is irrelevant; both give way to what the situation requires. The library requires quietness; the corridor requires walking; the machine shop requires safety glasses; and the classroom discussion requires one-at-a-time. Once the needs of the situation are determined, teachers can indicate the behaviours for which they are prepared to be held accountable. Rather than argue with students concerning the need to submit science practical books by a certain time, the needs of the situation are determined and teachers then base their behaviour on those needs. 'I can only mark practical books which are in by 3 p.m. Friday' indicates the behaviour for which the teacher is prepared to be held accountable. Students now have a choice as the needs of the situation redefine the problem and avoid maintaining or increasing the conflict associated with the late submission of the science books. 'I can only teach students

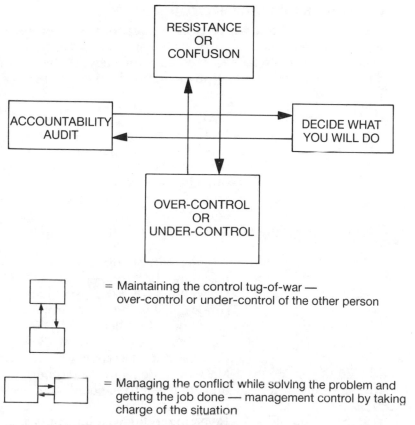

Figure 13   From power conflict to problem solving

who are wearing safety glasses' announces the teacher after determining the safety needs of the machine shop. 'I can only read stories when children are sitting quietly' decides the Grade 1 teacher after a discussion which decided that quietness was necessary during story reading. 'I can only see parents who have made an appointment through the general office.' Rather than decide what others must do, teachers determine the needs of the situation and decide on the behaviour for which they will be accountable. This process is represented diagrammatically by Kopp (1987) in Figure 13.

4. Create a listening atmosphere

In a conflict situation, words become weapons. Each party to the conflict sees only his or her own side, knows only what he or she wants and fails to recognise the views of the other party. Typical communication errors made in conflict situations are:

Avoid These	*Why*
'Why?'	Indicates blaming. A trigger word. It is better to ask: 'What do you want me/us to do now?'. This question sets new goals and separates reasons from goal setting.
'Empty picture frames'	'I don't want the class texts put there'. 'We don't want any more assignments presented like that'. Doesn't tell what is wanted.
'No'	A hook. 'I will find a way around your hook.' Conflict results. We carry our 2-year-old 'No' with us and test it in classrooms.
'Why don't you ...' 'What I want you to do ...'	Makes you dependent on others and adds fuel to the conflict.
'Yesterday, you did ...'	Referring to the past indicates a power struggle.
'Last week, you were...'	Never refer to the past but only to the future.

Conflict Resolution

◄──────────────────────────────────────►

Past	Goal	Future
Scolding		Resolving
Blaming		conflict

Effective listening is a basic skill in conflict resolution. If students know that you see their side, they are more willing to see your side. 'I know it must be difficult for you to complete your assignments when there are so few resources' rather than 'Get your assignments done. I want no excuses' helps move a potential conflict situation into one of mutual agreement based on the needs of the situation. Teachers must reach solutions to conflict situations involving students, by shared responsibility and through mutual agreement, which increase the likelihood of a successful outcome.

By withdrawing from coercing students, leaving them free to decide what they will do, teachers diffuse the conflict, focus on the students' responsibility for their behaviour, and hold them accountable for their actions. Leaving others free to decide what they will do does not mean that they can do as they please without consequences. Consequences will always result when behaviour occurs which defies the needs of the situation.

5. Act: Firm but friendly

Teachers who are democratic leaders will be firm but friendly in their dealing with students. You can only be firm once you know what you intend to do. You cannot be firm about what others should do. It is only possible to be firm when the needs of the situation have been determined. Teachers who are firm but fight with students will maintain the conflict. Yet friendliness while giving in will also maintain the conflict. Only when teachers are firm while being friendly, can they decrease the conflict and reinterpret the relationship. Holding firm to what you will do based on the needs of the situation is the key to resolving conflict.

While teachers declare their action leaving students to decide their own, the implementation of consequences are used for establishing student accountability. As discussed in Chapter 6, a consequence is a corrective action which follows each future occurrence of problem behaviour. While punishment maintains or increases the conflict, consequences meet the needs of the situation with firmness but without hostility or coercion. To be effective, consequences must be immediate not delayed, specific rather than general and easily implemented as opposed to requiring complex administration. A child who throws a stone in the playground is immediately removed and deprived of playing time until the following recess.

Basically, conflict resolution suggests the need for democratic leaders who are skilled in group dynamics but who recognise the need to reach agreement by shared respon-sibility. As Dreikurs (1972:9) observed, 'We have no national leaders; we have no leaders in our homes and our school, we have no leaders who can inspire, who can win without fighting, who can integrate'. Effective leaders bring people together to listen to each other, to realise that all problems are common problems, to share the responsibility for con-flict resolution, and to gain victory over the problem instead of seeking victory over each other.

Try these (Adapted from Symmonds, 1990)

(1) In any conflict situation, which are present?
    a. co-operation
    b. communication
    c. agreement
    d. none of the above
    e. all of the above.

(2) The majority of all conflicts deal with:
    a. the consequences of what is wrong, e.g., student lateness
    b. the cause of what is wrong, e.g., lack of a clear disciplinary policy
    c. the need for the parties involved to improve their relative positions
    d. faulty interpersonal relationships.

(3) Conflict is:
    a. a power struggle
    b. a form of competition
    c. functional, i.e., constructive
    d. dysfunctional, i.e., destructive
    e. unavoidable.

(4) When involved with a conflict with a parent, the best tactic is to:
    a. recognise the validity of the parents' argument
    b. persuade the parents to modify their demands
    c. indicate to the parents what you will do
    d. indicate to the parents what they should do.

(5) Leadership in resolving conflict requires:
   a. empathy and equality
   b. empathy and neutrality
   c. neutrality and equality
   d. empathy, equality and neutrality
   e. none of the above.

(6) When government and unions clash, the most common issue is:
   a. salaries
   b. working conditions, e.g., support services
   c. who will win, e.g., government/union
   d. unjust procedures, e.g., dismissals
   e. other (please specify) ....

(7) In a conflict with a colleague, you must avoid:
   a. giving in to the demands of the colleague
   b. telling the colleague what he or she should accept
   c. continuing to fight with the colleague
   d. modifying your own position
   e. all of the above
   f. none of the above.

(8) Conflict resolution is best approached by:
   a. reformulating the conflict in a way that permits new orientations to a solution to emerge
   b. emphasising areas of agreement and de-emphasising areas of difference
   c. searching for solutions that bring a degree of satisfaction to each party
   d. addressing the conflict in a problem-solving mode
   e. exerting your own impartial viewpoint.

(9) The threat of punitive measures in a dispute:
   a. is often an effective means of achieving objectives
   b. hinders the perception of the situation by the other party
   c. occurs naturally in a situation
   d. elicits resistance and the use of counter-threats.

(10) The most effective way of influencing people is to:
   a. decide what course of action you will take
   b. suggest an acceptable course of action for them to follow
   c. point out the weaknesses in their argument
   d. persuade them to see the other party's point of view
   e. argue from a position of power.

Answers

(1) e; (2) d; (3) e; (4) c; (5) d; (6) c; (7) e; (8) a; (9) d; (10) a

12

Concluding Remarks

Teachers are a vital influence in the development of children. Not only can teachers correct much of the damage that children have suffered in their homes and in their community, but they can empower children to develop more adequate views of themselves, of others and of society.

The widespread concern with the increasing number of difficult and disruptive students reflects on the ability of teachers to correct the current concern. Dreikurs, Grunwald, and Pepper (1982: vii) have referred to the need to

> encourage teachers, who in these troubled times, are beginning to doubt their own ability to motivate children in school, and who are either accepting defeat and are leaving the teaching profession, or who are resigned to a fate of failure and misery until such time as they can retire.

We are witnessing a dilemma in our schools as teachers vacillate between autocratic methods, democratic methods and permissiveness. The more teachers attempt to impose their will on students, the more students rebel, openly and defiantly. When permissive strategies are employed, anarchy results. Uncertainty prevails and much of the advice which teachers receive only worsens the situation.

The source of much of the uncertainty in education today can be attributed to the great social changes which have radically altered the traditional relationship between teachers and students. It may be argued that all difficulties in the teaching of children are mistakes in human relationships, mistakes which originate from the accelerating social changes of our time.

The traditional superiority of the teacher over students has been the basis upon which the majority of classroom practices have been based. Rewards and punishments, domination, competition, sole responsibility, criticism, pressure, and fault finding are appropriate to and supported by a society which reflects that relationship.

Confronted with the far-reaching social changes which have occurred in the past two decades, teachers are in a state of confusion concerning their appropriate function. Social equality, the right of each individual to be treated with respect, to be involved in decisions, and to decide one's own values, is generally accepted today and is the root cause of the major revolution which must occur in our schools as it has in society.

Many teachers are aware of their precarious position. They are faced daily with the increasing independence of a student body which rejects authoritarian control while they are urged by those who are threatened by the growing democratic society to exercise control and to maintain their traditional superiority. It is a predicament which they share with both parents and managers, groups which are also caught between the two social systems.

This book has approached teaching as a task which requires a new set of principles which are more attuned to concepts of social equality, shared responsibility, self-discipline, mutual respect, and co-operation. To stimulate children, the teacher needs to be aware of the dynamics of behaviour and of the methods of motivating students. Many of the approaches suggested require a reorientation within classrooms by teachers who must see their role today and their means of influencing students within a classroom as being radically different from those of their predecessors. The basic premises on which schools operate must be adjusted to the model of humanity which is implied by democratisation. Until this is done, the deficiency of teachers in coping with the problems of young people will become more obvious while the public criticism of schools will become more vocal and insistent. The principles outlined in this book are designed to provide teachers with the means of promoting co-operation, responsibility, and learning in children. Based upon the psychology of that remarkable person, Alfred Adler, the book shares this belief with him: 'The hope of preparing the children of tomorrow rests primarily on converting the schools and teachers'.

References

Adler, A. (1927). *The practice and theory of individual psychology*. New York: Harcourt, Brace & Co.

Adler, A. (1930). *The education of children*. Chicago: Gateway.

Adler, A. (1931). *What life should mean to you*. Boston: Little, Brown & Co.

Adler, A. (1956). Individuum and Gemeinschaft. In H.L. Ansbacher & R.R. Ansbacher, *The individual psychology of Alfred Adler*. New York: Harper & Row.

Adler, A. (1957). *Understanding human nature*. New York: Fawcett.

Allport, G. (1950). *The nature of personality*. Reading, Mass.: Addison-Wesley.

Ansbacher, H.L. & Ansbacher, R.R. (1956). *The individual psychology of Alfred Adler*. New York: Harper & Row.

Applied Psychology Research Group. (1989). *Teacher stress in Victoria*. Department of Psychology, Melbourne.

Baruth, L.F. & Eckstein, D.G. (1976). *The ABCs of classroom discipline*. Dubuque, Iowa: Kendall, Hunt.

Block, J. (1979, February). Individualized instruction: A mastery learning perspective. *Educational Leadership*, pp. 337-41.

Block, J. & Anderson, R. (1975). *Mastery learning in classroom instruction*. New York: Macmillan Publishing Co.

Block, J.H., Efthim, H.E. & Burns, R.B. (1989). *Building effective mastery learning schools*. New York: Longman.

Bloom, B.S. (1968). Learning for mastery. *Evaluation Comment*, **1**, No.2.

Bloom, B.S. (1972). Innocence in education. *School Review*, **80**, pp. 332-52.

Bloom, B.S. (1976). *Human characteristics and school learning*. New York: McGraw-Hill.

Bloom, B.S. (1978). New views of the learner: Implications for instruction and curriculum. *Educational Leadership*, **35**, pp. 563-76.

Bloom, B.S. (1979, July). A summary of human characteristics and school learning. *Modern Teaching*, **47**, pp. 1-7.

Bloom, B.S. (1980). The new direction in educational research: Alterable variables. *Phi Delta Kappan*, **61**, pp. 382-5.

Bloom, B.S. (1984). The search for methods of group instruction as effective as one-to-one tutoring. *Educational Leadership*, **41**, (8), pp. 4-16.

Bullard, M.L. (1963). *The use of stories for self understanding.* Corvallis: Oregon Society of Individual Psychology.

Canter, L. & Canter, M. (1976). *Assertive discipline: A take-charge approach for today's education.* California: Canter and Associates.

Catholic Education Commission of Victoria. (1988). *Pastoral care in Catholic schools.* Melbourne: Catholic Education Office of Victoria.

Committee of Inquiry into Pupil Behaviour and Discipline in Schools (1980). *Self-discipline and pastoral care.* Sydney: Government Printer.

Corsini, R. (1977). Individual education theme issue. *Journal of Individual Psychology*, **33** (2a), pp. 292-410.

Dewe, P. J. (1986). An investigation into the causes and consequences of teacher stress. *N.Z. Journal of Educational Studies*, **21**, pp. 145-187.

Dewey, E.A. (1978). *Basic applications of Adlerian psychology.* Coral Springs, Florida: Communication and Motivational Training Institute.

Dinkmeyer, D. & Dreikurs, R. (1963). *Encouraging children to learn: The encouragement process.* Englewood Cliffs, N.J.: Prentice-Hall.

Dinkmeyer, D. & McKay, G.D. (1976). *Systematic training for effective parenting.* Circle Pines, Minn.: American Guidance Service.

Dinkmeyer, D. & McKay, G.D. (1983). *STEP/Teen: The parent's guide.* Circle Pines, Minn.: American Guidance Service.

Dinkmeyer, D., McKay, G.D. & Dinkmeyer, D. Jr, (1980). *Systematic training for effective teaching: Teacher's handbook.* Circle Pines, Minn.: American Guidance Service.

Dreikurs, R. (1953). *Fundamentals of Adlerian psychology.* Chicago: Alfred Adler Institute.

Dreikurs, R. (1954). The psychological interview in medicine. *Journal of Individual Psychology*, **10**, pp. 99-122.

Dreikurs, R. (1955, April). The psychological approach in the classroom. *American Teachers Magazine*, **39**, pp. 9-12.

Dreikurs, R. (1959). Do teachers understand children? *School and Society*, **87**, pp. 88-90.

Dreikurs, R. (1960). The role of the group in education. Unpublished paper.

Dreikurs, R. (1964). *Children : the challenge.* New York: Duell, Sloan and Pearce.

Dreikurs, R. (1968). *Psychology in the classroom*. New York: Harper & Row.

Dreikurs, R. (1971). *Social equality*. Chicago: Henry Regnery.

Dreikurs, R. (1972). Technology of conflict resolution, *American Journal of Individual Psychology*, **28**, pp. 203-6.

Dreikurs, R. (1977). Holistic medicine and the function of neuroses. *Journal of Individual Psychology*, **55**, pp. 171-92.

Dreikurs, R. & Cassel, P. (1972). *Discipline without tears*. Ontario: Alfred Adler Institute.

Dreikurs, R., & Grey, L. (1968). *Logical consequences: A new approach to discipline*. New York: Meredith.

Dreikurs, R., Grunwald, B.B. & Pepper, F.C. (1971). *Maintaining sanity in the classroom*. New York: Harper & Row.

Dreikurs, R., Grunwald, B.B. & Pepper, F.C. (1982). *Maintaining sanity in the classroom*. 2nd edn. New York: Harper and Row.

Education Department of South Australia. (1989). *Draft guidelines for practice in student behaviour management*. Adelaide: Government Printer.

Education Department of South Australia. (1989). *The student behaviour draft management policy*. Millswood, SA: Education Department of South Australia.

Ellis, A. (1970). Humanism, values, rationality. *Journal of Individual Psychology*, **26**, pp. 37-8.

Ferguson, E.D. (1984). *Adlerian theory: An introduction*. Vancouver: Adlerian Psychology Association of British Columbia.

Ferguson, E.D. (1984). *Adlerian theory: An introduction*. Vancouver: Adlerian Psychology Association of British Columbia.

Friesen, D. and Williams, M.J. (1985). Organisational stress amongst teachers. *Canadian Journal of Education*, 10, 1, pp. 13-34.

Gerstein, A. & Reagan, J. (1986). *Win-win approaches to conflict resolution*. Layton, Utah: Gibbs M. and Smith, Inc.

Glasser, R. (1969). *Schools without failure*. New York: Harper & Row.

Good, T.L. & Brophy, J.E. (1977). *Educational psychology: A realistic approach*. New York: Holt, Rinehart & Winston.

Greene, D. & Lepper, M.R. (1974). Intrinsic motivation: How to turn play into work. *Psychology Today*, **8** (4), pp. 49-59.

Gronlund, N.E. (1959). *Sociometry in the classroom*. New York: Harper.

Hill, S. and Hill, T. (1990). *The collaborative classroom*. South Yarra: Eleanor Curtain.

House, M. (1991). A study to ascertain the level of agreement of parents and teachers at a Melbourne Catholic, independent boys school. Unpublished thesis, Monash University, Clayton.

Janhom, S. (1983). Educating parents to educate their children. Unpublished doctoral dissertation, University of Chicago.

Jennings, H.H. (1959). *Sociometry in group relations*. New York: Harper.

Justice, B.J. (1988). *Who gets sick?* Houston: Peak Press.

Kefir & Kefir. (1971). Life Style. Unpublished ms. ICASSI.

Kern, R.M. (1982). *Lifestyle Scale*. Coral Springs, Florida: CMTI Press.

Kern, R.M. and White, J. (1989). Brief therapy using the life-style scale. *Journal of Individual Psychology*, **45**, pp. 186-190.

Kindsvatter, R. (1978). A new view of the dynamics of discipline. *Phi Delta Kappan*, Jan., pp. 322-324.

Kopp, R.R. (1986). Styles of striving for significance without social interest: an Adlerian typology. *Journal of Individual Psychology*, Vol. 42, pp. 17-25.

Kopp, R. (1987). Resolving power conflicts: helpful questions and answers. Lecture handout, International Committee of Adlerian Summer Schools and Institutes.

Kopp, R. and Kivel, C. (1990). Traps and escapes: an Adlerian approach to understanding resistance and resolving impasses in psychotherapy. *Journal of Individual Psychology*, **46**, 139-147.

Lewin, K. (1948). *Resolving social conflicts*. New York: Harper & Row.

Leyton, F.S. (1983). The extent to which group instruction supplemented by mastery of the initial cognitive prerequisites approximate the learning effectiveness of one-to-one tutorial methods. Unpublished doctoral dissertation, University of Chicago.

Lindgren, H.C. (1956). *Educational psychology in the classroom*. New York: Wiley.

Louden, L.W. (1985). *Disruptive behaviour in schools*. Perth: Department of Education.

Manaster, G. & Corsini, R. (1982). *Individual psychology*. Itasca, Illinois: Peacock.

Matheny, K. & Kern, R. M. (1989). *Personality and Illness*. In *Lifestyle, Stress and Wellness*. Interlaken: ICASSI.

Moreno, J.L. (1953). *Who shall survive?* New York: Beacon House.

Mosak, H. (1977). Lifestyle in Mosak, H. *On purpose*. Chicago: Alfred Adler Institute.

Neill, A.S. (1960). *Summerhill: A radical approach to child rearing*. New York: Hart Publishing.

Nickelly, A. (Ed.)(1971). *Techniques for behaviour change*. Springfield, Ill.: Charles C. Thomas.

Nordin, A.B. (1979). The effects of different qualities of instruction on selected cognitive, affective, and time variables. Unpublished doctoral dissertation, University of Chicago.

Pepper, R. (n.d.). *The characteristics of the family constellation*. Chicago: Alfred Adler Institute.

Phi Delta Kappa Commission of Discipline (1982). *Handbook for developing schools with good discipline.* Bloomington, Indiana: Author.

Popkin, M.H. (1983). *Active parenting handbook.* Atlanta: Active Parenting Inc.

Reimer, C. (1967). Some words of encouragement. In V. Soltz, *Study group leader's manual.* Chicago: Alfred Adler Institute.

Rosenthal, R., & Jacobson, L.F. (1966). Teacher expectancies: Determinants of pupils' I.Q. gains. *Psychological Reports,* **19**, pp. 115-18.

Soltz, V. (1967). *Study group leader's manual.* Chicago: Alfred Adler Institute.

Spady, W.G. (1985). *Essential operational components of outcome-based education.* San Francisco: Far West Regional Educational Laboratory.

Stagner, R. & Rosen, H. (1965). *Psychology of union-management relations.* Belmont, California: Brooks-Cole Publishing.

Symmonds, H. (1990). Conflict resolution in industry: An Adlerian perspective. Unpublished Master's thesis, Monash University, Clayton, Victoria.

Sweeney, T.J. (1975). *Adlerian counseling.* Boston: Houghton Mifflin.

Victorian Ministry of Education (1985). Ministerial Paper No.4. *School councils.* Victoria: Publishing Services, Statewide School Support and Production Centre.

Victorian Ministry of Education (1989). *The personal development framework: P-10.* Melbourne: Office of Schools Administration.

Walberg, H.J. (1984). Improving the productivity of America's schools. *Educational Leadership,* **41** (9), pp. 19-27.

Walton, F.X. (1974). *Winning children over.* Illinois: Practical Psychology Associates.

Working Party on the Abolition of Corporal Punishment (1983). Melbourne: Education Department.